JAMES V. SCHALL, S.J.

THE DISTINCTIVENESS
OF CHRISTIANITY

JAMES V. SCHALL, S.J.

THE DISTINCTIVENESS
OF CHRISTIANITY

IGNATIUS PRESS   SAN FRANCISCO

CONTENTS

INTRODUCTION   9

PART I
FROM A DISTINCTIVE TRADITION

Chapter I: On Leaving Rome   13
Chapter II: The Condition of Catholic Intelligence   34

PART II
WITH A DISTINCTIVE OPPOSITION

Chapter III: On the Removal of Christianity   53
Chapter IV: The Anti-Catholic Bias in the United
                States   67

PART III
FOR DISTINCTIVE DOCTRINES

Chapter V: The Distinctiveness of Christianity   79
Chapter VI: The Christian and the Human Lot   98
Chapter VII: Trinitarian Transcendence in Ignatian
                Spirituality   114
Chapter VIII: On the Rediscovery of Charity   126
Chapter IX: Technology and Spirituality   141

PART IV
BY DISTINCTIVE INSTITUTIONS

Chapter X: An Elite Church?   161
Chapter XI: The Future of the Christian Clergy   173
Chapter XII: Christian Guardians   185
Chapter XIII: Monastery and Home   200
Chapter XIV: The Christian University   218

CONTENTS

PART V
TOWARD A DISTINCTIVE SPIRITUALITY

Chapter XV:	Dryness	235
Chapter XVI:	On Things That Cannot Be Forgiven	247
Chapter XVII:	On Spiritual and Physical Exercises	256
Chapter XVIII:	Letters and the Spiritual Life	271
Chapter XIX:	Paths That Lead to Rome	286
CONCLUSION		295

ACKNOWLEDGMENTS

Parts of this book were previously published; the author wishes to acknowledge their source and thank the respective journals for permission to reprint them here. Modifications by the author have been made to fit the present context.

Chapter I: *Commonweal*, 232 Madison Avenue, New York, N.Y., 10016 (25 November 1977) 744–50.

Chapter II: *New Oxford Review*, Oakland, California, copyright 1979 (September 1979).

Chapter III: *Social Survey*, Melbourne (March, 1979) 37–41.

Chapter IV: *Clergy Review*, London (March 1979) 96–98.

Chapter V: *New Oxford Review* (September 1978) 4–6.

Chapter VI: Proceedings of the Fellowship of Catholic Scholars, Kansas City (1978) 6–12.

Chapter VII: French translation published in *Cahiers de Spiritualité ignatienne*, Quebec (July–September 1978) 183–90.

Chapter VIII: *Spiritual Life*, Washington (1979).

Chapter IX: *Communio* (Summer 1978) 122–34.

Chapter X: *Homiletic and Pastoral Review* (March 1978) 8–14.

Chapter XI: *Vital Speeches* (February 1977); reprinted also in *Military Chaplains' Review* (Winter 1978) 97–104.

Chapter XII: *Downside Review* (January 1979) 1–9.

ACKNOWLEDGMENTS

Chapter XIII: *American Benedictine Review*, vol. 29 (December 1978) 307–19.

Chapter XIV: *Homiletic and Pastoral Review* (March 1979) 17–24.

Chapter XV: *The Way*, the Jesuit Quarterly Review of Spirituality, London (1979–80).

Chapter XVI: *The Way*, London (1979–80).

Chapter XVII: Part I, in *The Hoya*, Georgetown University (7 April 1978); reprinted in *Catholic Mind* (February 1979) 8–10. Part II, in *U.S. Catholic* published by Claretians Publications 221 West Madison Street, Chicago, Illinois, 60606 (June 1979) 18–22.

Chapter XVIII: *The Way*, London, Supplement (Autumn 1978) 133–48.

Chapter XIX: *Social Survey*, Melbourne (May 1981) 121–25.

INTRODUCTION

The great danger of the current age is that of the disappearance of Christianity. That will sound, perhaps, overly dramatic, since Christianity has been disappearing and reappearing almost since it was founded. Furthermore, the agonizing possibility exists that Christianity could disappear and no one would even notice, because its chief advocates had busied themselves in informing us that this faith was really just like every other religion and science. One side of Christianity, certainly, has been its openness to "reason". Indeed, historically, it could even be argued that the validity of reason itself has something to do with the validity of Christianity. Nonetheless, Christianity does not profess to be merely a supplement to what otherwise could be known by the careful human mind.

The great modern movements—ecumenism in the Church and development in the Third World—have tended, perhaps contrary to their own best interests, to emphasize either how all Christian sects are like each other or how Christianity is like the most powerful of the modern ideologies—liberalism, socialism, and Marxism. Further, the idea that modern science judges Christianity is still about with a considerable following, so that the mission many Christians mistakenly set for themselves is that of adjusting the tenets and practices of the faith so that they "agree" with the varying trends and fads prevalent in the physical, social, or biological sciences.

In this context, however, there is a case to be made for the reasons and causes why Christianity is *not* like anything else. Moreover, this distinctness is quite the best thing about it. This is not, of course, to be an arrogance or even an apologetic, but merely a fact. From its very beginning, Christianity has considered itself obligated to pass on from generation to generation what it has received and heard. It had peculiar traditions and institutions of its own by which it could do this, by which it could continue to identify itself to itself and to the world. We must be loyal to the past as well as to the present and future if we are not to conceive the human race as divided into different chronological groupings, which would make some men different kinds of beings from the others.

There is some urgency, then, in recalling the distinct traditions, oppositions, doctrines, institutions, and spiritualities of Christianity. And to "re-call" something means something very active, very creative. Faith is meant to be a challenge to our reason. It should incite us to think in ways we could not otherwise have realized. It is not an exaggeration to say that much of the modern intellect can accept everything about Christianity *except* its essential doctrines, Incarnation and Trinity. What is unfortunate is that these exceptions are precisely what makes Christianity worthwhile and believable to men in the world. To have some sense of the uniqueness and fertility of what is different and distinct about Christianity, then, is what is proposed here. The only real objection against Christianity was, as I believe Chesterton said, that it is too good to be true. The modern world has forgiven Christianity everything except its claim to be true. And this is the only thing about it that cannot be forgiven.

PART I

FROM A DISTINCTIVE TRADITION

I

ON LEAVING ROME

Rome, according to its most sentimental song, is a place to which we fondly sing "Good-bye—Arrivederci", on leaving it. Not everyone who has ever left this "Eternal City", of course, has preserved a sense of nostalgia about it. Martin Luther, for instance, who stayed at the Augustinian Convent on the Piazza del Popolo, had this to say in 1520 in his *Appeal to the Ruling Class*: "The Romanists themselves have coined the saying, 'The nearer Rome, the worse the Christians. . . .' Another saying runs, 'The first time one goes to Rome, one has to look for a rogue; the second time, one finds him; the third time, one brings him back. . . .' Indeed, in Rome they have coined for us this catch-phrase, 'It would be better not to have seen or known Rome.' "

And the great Horace, who escaped the Mighty City to his nearby Sabine Farm, wrote in ancient times to his villa foreman:

> Once, a laborer, you prayed heaven for the country,
> and now, a foreman, you long for the city,
> the baths, the circus.
> You know I am consistent. I always leave with a sigh
> whenever loathsome business drags me back to Rome.
> Our ideals differ then. . . .   (*Ep.* I, 14)

And Rome is still a place whose value, on going and coming, depends on our ideals.

Yet, dreams are often much less wonderful than reality, while reality itself is something of a dream, something that

13

might not have been. When I was a boy back at Knoxville High, I might have heard something of Rome. Certainly, it was not a pressing topic of conversation in Marion County, Iowa. We had, nevertheless, for some now unaccountable reason, two years of Latin from Miss Cooper. But I never understood a word of it. True, I was one of the few Roman Catholics in town, so I must have had some conception of the then far-off place. I even recall once a heated debate with some local Jehovah's Witnesses, who had claimed ominously that the "Black Flag of the Roman Catholic Church" was flying on some invading fleet or other. At the time, I somehow knew that the papal flag was yellow and white—and triumphantly told them so—but, alas, I had not a clue as to why there might even be a papal flag in the first place. The idea that I might actually live in Rome for over a decade never crossed my midwestern mind, which at that time had never been beyond East Dubuque, Illinois.

Yet, as I said to myself on leaving Rome, *here I stand*—rather unlike the way Martin Luther once used that same phrase—graduate of the class of '45 from KHS, in the summer of '77, ending a seemingly short but also long period of twelve years at the Gregorian University in the heart of classical Rome, just up from the Trevi Fountains, a few blocks from the Forum and the Campidoglio, down the hill from the Palazzo Quirinale, Renaissance and Enlightenment home of popes, present home of the Italian head of state. The Biblical Institute was just across the Piazza, as was the lovely Church of the Twelve Apostles, where Clement XIV, the man who suppressed the Jesuits, still lies, along with the great composer Frescobaldi, and I do not know who else, as its crypt is full of the bones of martyrs. The expelled Stuarts of England lived in the

Palace at the far corner by the Dodici Apostoli, while Napoleon's mother had her residence one block over on the Corso.

Eventually, I was to return to the Government faculty at Georgetown University in Washington, where I did my doctoral studies during Mr. Eisenhower's second administration. I had been obliquely reminded of this before leaving when, down by the Trevi, I ran into a large number of slightly tipsy German soccer fans from Moenchen-Gladbach, in Rome for the European Cup of Champions against Liverpool. Moenchen-Gladbach was the home of the famous Catholic Social Center from which Professor Heinrich Rommen, who directed my thesis, finally came to Georgetown after escaping Hitler's growing power. *Urbi et Orbi*.

Of course, during many of these same years, I had also spent the fall semester at the University of San Francisco, so I may not have been totally "Romanized", the ultimate clerical sin. In any case, whatever the attractions of Washington by contrast—Professor William O'Brien at Georgetown had his doubts if there were any—I did not doubt that Rome and San Francisco were the loveliest dwelling places our kind has fashioned in its wisdom—and its folly. Both are worldly and spiritual, simultaneously provincial to a fault and international—cosmic, even. A drink at the Top of the Mark on a clear late afternoon with the Bay or the Golden Gate Bridge below on the horizon leaves no doubt that few other places are even worth bothering with.

And yet, when I read in Stendhal's *Roman Journal*, a book I love, what he wrote on Christmas, 1827, I can still agree with him without hesitation: "I have never seen anything so imposing as this ceremony; St. Peter's was sublime in magnificence and beauty. The effect of the dome especially seemed to me wonderful [in his day, it was lighted with many flickering oil lamps]; I was almost as much a believer as a Roman." The last spring I was in Rome, I attended the Easter Vigil Service in St. Peter's. What Stendhal forgot to mention was that the place was sublime *and* chaotic at the same time, the true sign, I have come to suspect, both of humanity and of Catholicism. Thus, that year, at that precise magnificent moment when the huge basilica should still have been in complete darkness at the last "Lumen Christi", so that the whole vast interior would glow and dance in the light of the thousands of candles held by the faithful, someone prematurely turned on the bright-as-day overhead flood lights to destroy the whole effect. Beauty betrays its most divine origins, I thought after the manner of Augustine, at the precise moment it is most fragile, most likely to be ruined.

Rome, it strikes me, is the only "real" city in the world. Though I enjoy the countryside as much as Horace, I must say I am more touched by this vital "Babylon", as Peter called it in his epistle, this place that was not, as Chesterton said, first loved because it was great, but became great because men first loved it. This, of course, is the exact symbolic status we Christians have in Christian theology. We are not loved because we are first lovable but rather we are lovable because we are first loved. And so, compared with Rome, San Francisco and Washington, Paris and Berlin, are but of yesterday. Rome is the only city that has been constantly lived in and constantly important for most of its more than twenty-seven hundred years. There are cities older than Rome perhaps, Chinese and Indian ones, cities once more famous—Athens, for instance, and even

Jerusalem—but none has its constant world-historic significance in almost every age and generation, for almost every people. Thus, in Rome, no one can walk around the corner without being conscious of a good part of mankind's history. Rome, consequently, is an infinite place. No man can comprehend it. This was one of the reasons, I think, why I most appreciated it. The Eternal City seemed to me justly symbolic of my own finiteness, a place where I could live out all my allotted years and days and still barely begin to comprehend it all. This was a place of the most annoying pettinesses and of equally extraordinary vistas. Here, it was easy to be a romantic and a cynic in order finally to glimpse the wisdom beyond both romanticism and cynicism. Gregorovius, who did not at all like Pius IX, told of being in St. Peter's on Palm Sunday, 1860, for the procession which had to pass through two notices of excommunication posted on the main gate pillars. He continued:

> By chance above these notices, there were two others, earlier ones, in which we were encouraged not to blaspheme. Immediately above the Pope's excommunication (for those at war against the fast-declining Papal States), we read: "Blasphemers! Do Penance! Think well on it! In the very moment of your blasphemy you will be tossed down into hell!"

If I had thought for a moment that such a marvelous sign were still up, I should have hustled over to St. Peter's to find it before I left, even though I did not consider blasphemy to be one of my major vices.

So if Rome was sublime and mysterious, it was also small and narrow-minded too. Stendhal noted in his *Journal* on June 26, 1828, in words still largely true: "It should be observed that Rome is more of a small town than Dijon or Amiens; not everything is told, but everything is found out." And Gregorovius quipped of a great French bishop: "Dupanloup d'Orleans preaches every day in the Church of the Gesù—they say he is a '*chiacchierone*', a chatterbox, a yakker." And even more maliciously, on July 3, 1861, when it seemed the Papal States would finally be lost, he remarked: "Today is the Vigil of the Feast of St. Peter. On this day it is customary to distribute a medal: the one today bears on one side the portrait of the Pope [Pius IX] and on the other, the significant effigy of Daniel in the Lion's Den." And yet, when Gregorovius himself arrived back in Rome from Germany in the fall of 1863, the great historian also was moved by the spell of the city: "I arrived in Rome yesterday at 12:30. Now I have already reordered everything. My manuscripts which were deposited in the Archives of the Embassy and which were humid, I have exposed to dry out so tomorrow I will begin again my eternal work in the Eternal City." And yet, when I read Gregorovius, I cannot help being reminded of these classical lines of Horace in which, in a Roman scene, he depicted forever the nature of a bore:

> Walking along the Sacred Road, as is my habit,
> I was reflecting on some trifle, quite engrossed
> When up comes somebody known to me only by name,
> And grabs my hand. . . .

Perhaps that is part of Rome's grandeur; even bores are wondrous figures along the Via Sacra, while distinguished bishops are chatterboxes in the Gesù.

But life goes on in Rome. Before he ceased drawing, Al Capp showed the old postman on the U. S. Mule riding up to Dogpatch to shout to L'il Abner, "Special Delivery from the Govamint". And Abner, in return, wept, "O, Bless the Govamint! They is so prompt wif their mail." In Rome, too, I had often wept over the mail, but *never* because it was prompt! Undoubtedly, one of the mysteries not resolved this side of paradise is how much of my correspondence did not get through. Peter Nichols, in an article in that phenomenal *Famiglia Cristiana*—by far the largest-circulating magazine in Italy—told, in an analysis of the Italian postal service, of an Englishman in frustration going up to an Italian postal clerk and chiding him for his inefficiency and lackadaisical attitude. "Don't you know you are a public servant?" the Englishman asked, with what he thought was the ultimate logic. The clerk was insulted. The last thing he conceived himself to be was a public servant.

One of the sobering things about living in Italy over the years was the brutal realization that the ordinary citizen is too often at the mercy of the bureaucrat. The "public servant" owes his job to the party and to union power. Public service has nothing to do with it. And when something finally is done for someone, he goes away with the feeling that he received a "favor", not his due as a citizen. Service is thus a function of clout, not of practical politics based on effective popular sovereignty. The old Roman notion of the client—"I'll take care of you"—is one of the most abiding facts of life in those parts. No ideology is immune from it, least of all Marxism.

When I ask myself now what was the most striking change in Italy during the years I was there, I think I would have to say that it was a distinct change in manners, especially among the young. There seemed less joy and vitality, more fear. There is an unaccustomed harshness in contemporary Italian culture. The Italians, of course, have always reserved their real selves for their families and intimate friends. The "bella figura" of the Italian in public is not always his best self. The state has always been "the enemy", even the Italian version of the democratic polity. No one has ever dared to trust anyone beyond his own narrow circle. What seems new is the attention given, especially by the Marxists in the tradition of Gramsci, to culture. The "social" has come to be seen as a vital area of struggle and change. Politics and economics are left aside in this revisionism which gives Italian Marxism its claim to be the real wave of the future. The older Christian customs and ideals are being replaced by confrontation, mass indoctrination, ideological slogans, a brutality that is contrary to the classical Italian character.

After years of watching university students in Italy—"the sons of the rich in the left universities battling the sons of the poor in the police", a former Minister of the Interior bluntly put it—march down the Corso or the Via Nazionale or into the Piazza Navona, all in red, with signs of "Death to This", "Struggle against That", "Away with the Other Thing", it was hard to escape the impression that the bloody rhetoric had its somber effect on the sign-bearers. There was something, I thought, to the old spiritual principle that what comes out of the mouth is more important than what goes in.

Recent months and years have been filled with university riots, shootings of police and independent journalists. This violence comes directly from a generation healthier and better taken care of than any previously in Italian history. So much for an economic view of history! Salvatore Scarpino has graphically described a situation not sufficiently appreciated outside Italy:

In the great majority of cases, then, the youth do not suffer any real need. They are ignorant of what malnutrition and unhealthy environment mean, the very elements that have conditioned the youth of millions of Italians of earlier decades. Filled with vitamins, free, socially respectable, emancipated, many students of the schools only succeed, in these confused days, in expressing a desperate desire for violence and death, stylized in their paramilitary uniforms, in their light knapsacks of books, a military-syndical language of struggle, attack, strategy, and swelling with funereal and scatological images. . . . And words become deeds. . . .

No, the economic crisis cannot explain by itself their attitudes, nor can anxiety and the desire of change, attitudes proper to all youth. This cannot render comprehensible a cult so crude, irrational, and distinctive as the revolution understood as violence without end.

We must look elsewhere to comprehend such a widely diffused refusal of life and history. We must look to that no-man's land which the Italian school system has become in recent years. In this elephantine apparatus in which a million public employees work, there has been effected a systematic action of cultural disintegration that has no precedent. The school has become an autonomous social body, cut off from the rest of the country, something which has developed its own ethic and culture. . . .

In an Italy institutionally liberal and pluralistic . . . , we have allowed to grow and settle a plagiarist, class-conscious, sectarian school in which there is no longer a place for dissent or debate. For research is substituted indoctrination, naturally revolutionary and progressivist; for teaching, is substituted idle talk on themes imposed by minority factions.[1]

There is no doubt that this violent, antidemocratic attitude dominated Italian scholastic and cultural life. It is prevalent not just in the schools but also in the media, publishing houses, and unions.

There has always been a certain civil violence in Italy, to be sure, though far less in terms of, say, murder, than the average American can possibly imagine. Almost any two major American cities have more murders per year than all of Italy combined. Italian vices, for the most part, when they are not ideological-political, are the petty ones— pickpocketing, cheating a bit. The Italian always likes to appear well. And there is something pleasing about this quality which insists that we should always look our best with whatever nature, grace, and style might have bestowed on us. Vanity is not the worst of vices. And if any American city after six p.m. were as orderly as the most "violent" Italian one, the local police would feel they had already entered into the peaceable kingdom.

Yet, as I have just indicated, universities and high schools are caught up in a kind of programmed political violence that has radically changed the intrinsic outlook of the younger generation. Even the Communists are worried about it, as well they may be, since they are its major cause and hope to be its major beneficiary. Angelo Sterrazza, commenting on the total decline of the democratic, European-oriented youth organizations founded optimis-

[1] *Il Giornale* (28 May 1977).

tically after World War II, wrote in the issue of *Il Popolo* on the twentieth anniversary of the Common Market (25 March 1977): "The idea of the unity of Europe has lost any sort of attraction among the youth during the past ten years. . . ." This is true, I think, of Italian youth in particular. The remarkably gracious style that once characterized the Italians is clearly eroding. The slogans of the university scholars were as intellectual as the blood, death, and hatred they repeated *ad nauseam*.

The roots of the culture, I fear, have yielded up the very Christian and Roman presuppositions that historically grounded Italian culture and made Italy such a pleasant place to live. This should not be overstated, to be sure, but the distinct tendency is there. Europe, as a Christendom, found few followers recently—until the arrival of John Paul II, who has made that one of his main themes. And even Europe as a series of truly "democratic" societies seems a declining idea. The apparent gains in Spain and Portugal are offset by the growing power of the French and Italian left. And the reason for this is ultimately spiritual. When the kind of ideas and practices classically defined as non-Christian become the *modus procedendi* of the universities, no amount of warning will suffice. It is no accident that the Russian exiles have the greatest difficulty in speaking in Italy. Perhaps Solzhenitsyn is not wrong in claiming that many must suffer an evil to know it.

Yet, in many ways, Christendom and what it meant are being rediscovered. There is a thesis in Italy that sees the family being rediscovered in the light of the radical decline of male and female religious orders, which have historically supplied much of the religious context of Italian life. Too, when Italy was formed at the time of Pius IX, it was believed by the liberals and progressives of the era that science, democracy of an indifferentist hue, evolution, and secularism would solve all. Pius IX has been roundly condemned for a century for daring to say that the Church could not be reconciled with "modern civilization" as understood in such philosophies. Almost exactly one hundred years after the death of Pius IX, it is not the pope but the whole modern culture that is shouting that modern civilization is failing. Ben Wattenberg's long collection of contemporary condemnations of modern civilization in the first chapter of *The Real America* deserves reading in this light. And if we take the trouble to read with attention E. F. Schumacher's list in *Small Is Beautiful* of nineteenth-century ideas that even today tragically dominate the minds of educated people, ideas more current among the chic than among the slum dwellers, they will sound like nothing so much as the *Syllabus of Errors* of Pius IX.

Over twenty years ago, I wrote a short essay in *Commonweal* on "The Future of Distributism" (6 May 1955). Today, ideas of distribution, small and medium technology, nature, and person-oriented economics are reappearing everywhere. These are the heritage of certain strands of medieval economics and the central line of modern papal social thought. The paradox is that we Catholics in social and political fields have in the meantime mostly abandoned our central tradition in favor of a kind of stylish keeping-up with the radical left ideologies of the past decade, only to find the ideas we abandoned to be proposed more and more as the key to the Third World poverty problem—the ostensible reason why we abandoned specifically Catholic social thought in the first place. "Pluralism" for which we argued and fought for years has come largely to mean a single option. I suspect the *Outline of Sanity* of Chesterton is still more radically pertinent than all of our modernization and liberation theories which "opt" for socialist mobilization theories and ideological conformity. *The Servile State*, recently reissued, may be much more to the point today than when it was written at the beginning of this century.

But there is more. Schumacher's central point was not social, but ontological and religious. Our first problem is not social action, but speculative metaphysics, which can establish our being as both real and finite, given and structured, and permanent in its passing. The metaphysics of "making ourselves to be men", the metaphysics of atheism, is ultimately the force behind so many of our development and ecological movements. If I have anything sharply negative to say about the trends in the Church in recent years, it has to do with a kind of practical giving up of Christian metaphysics as the basis of the intellectual program taught in the universities and seminaries ostensibly controlled by Catholics. This has been voluntary on our part. No one has taken our mind from us.

Malcolm Muggeridge was probably right, then, when he chided that just about the time the world gets around to wanting the essence of classical Christian thought, it will discover that Christian intellectuals no longer know their origins. The opening out onto the world—the theme of John XXIII and the Council—has too often in the meantime come to mean a rejection of an independent, valid Christian tradition and thought that is not "the world". There are remarkably few centers of specifically Christian learning left and these are under tremendous pressure to teach development ideology or ecological reform as *the*

Christian orthodoxy. The valid side of this effort to relate
Christianity to all knowledge is obvious enough. Indeed, I
would hold that, more and more, a valid, independent
Christian metaphysics is the only thing that can justify and
save modern "science", once thought to be the enemy of
faith. Now it may well be that the only thing that can save
science from ideology is classical faith. But Christianity is
itself, with its own sources, methods, and moods. Grace
does build on nature, and this means it is not nature.

   I would judge that the most important theological movement during the years I was in Rome was the increasingly
successful effort to convert Christianity into a kind of social
action, phrased generally in terms of Marxist categories.[2]
Existentialism, logical positivism, structuralism, evolution-
ism, language analysis, and Protestantism have largely seen
their intellectual forces dissipated. When I first came to
Rome, still the most difficult persons to convert to Marxism were young army officers and Roman Catholic seminarians. Today, I suspect, they are often the easiest. This
comes at a time when the best and most widespread testimony from within actual Marxist states, especially Russia
and Eastern Europe, indicates that few, if any, believe in
this ideology. Perhaps the best test of my thesis, in any case
in Europe, America, and the Third World, is to look at
book publishers and reviews published under apparently
"Catholic" auspices. The number with clearly Marxist
presuppositions grows each year.

   Too, after living in Rome for a time, the automatic and, I
suppose, logical question was "Where does the papacy fit
into it all?" Rome, in spite of Garabaldi and Cavour, is still

   [2] Cf. the author's "Political Theory and Political Theology", *Laval
Théologique et Philosophique* (February 1975).

in many ways the papacy, even when it is not. The Italian state has yet to build in Rome anything that comes close to the grandeur and style of the buildings of papal Rome. One hundred years may not be enough for a fair comparison, of course, but the real reason is that modern liberal and Marxist Italy does not believe in beauty or its civil causes as the papacy did. And it remains true that Italy's greatest single "natural" resource is the artistic heritage of the popes. Destroy this—by strikes, inconvenience, inefficiency, or neglect—and Italy becomes just another Mediterranean country. Classical Rome, no doubt, also remains in remains, whereas a pope still lives in St. Peter's. A Gibbon sitting on the steps of the Ara Coeli, one-sidedly judging that the decline of Rome was due to the faith, would receive a shock to his thesis were he to look not south to the Forum, but north to the Monumento Vittorio Emmanuele. Even though this much-abused shrine is not all that decrepit, Gibbon today would be much more hesitant in deciding what was falling and what rising.

My years in Rome were the years of Giovanni Battista Montini. The most vivid memory of how ecclesiastical Rome worked was during my first year at the Gregorian. Paul VI's Lenten address that year touched on wearing clerical garb. According to L'Osservatore Romano, as I understood it, Paul reaffirmed that the "traditional" garb of the cleric in Rome was the cassock, which I wore as little as possible. The day after this seemingly somber talk, I walked into my class, before usually filled with cassock- and habit-wearing priests and seminarians. Much to my astonishment, practically everyone was in natty suits and ties or if American, in sport clothing. To my univocal mind, this seemed either defiant or amusing.

As it turned out, of course, it was neither. These suddenly civilian clad clerics informed me that the Pope had said that the *traditional* garb was to be maintained on clerical occasions. That meant that in any *non*clerical situation, it was optional. And certainly going to class at the Gregorian was a nonclerical function! From that day forward, I had a new respect for the legal mind. The so-called Roman collar, in any case, is not Roman. To the Italians, it is Protestant. I have had many delightful discussions with ordinary Italians trying to convince them that, even in a Roman collar, I was a Roman Catholic like themselves.

During my first year in Rome too (1965), I clearly recall the scene in St. Peter's Square on the last day of Vatican II. The *Document on Religious Liberty* and *Gaudium et Spes* had just been signed. Pope Paul greeted numerous people from various nations and walks of life during the Offertory of the Mass. Perhaps the most touching moment for me was the introduction of Jacques Maritain. At that time, Maritain was still considered the model of Christian intelligence, the spirit of the liberalizing movement that incorporated humanism into Christianity, religious liberty into Catholic thought. By the time I left, Maritain was looked upon by too many as reactionary, while the cause of religious liberty was mostly a dead letter, a fetish of Russian and Eastern European Christians. Catholics as a group in the West have done practically nothing for fellow Catholics suffering precisely from lack of religious liberty. There has never been less religious liberty in the world, in many ways. Indeed, the great two-century battle to establish the civil principle of religious freedom has been largely set aside by current ideological movements which claim to work for "this-worldly" development. Ironically, almost the very day that "development" became the catch-word of modern political thought, religious freedom began to fall on hard days—and it has never had very easy ones.

Paul VI had been judged severely by his contemporaries. According to varying ideologies and presuppositions, there were several clashing views about him. Probably the first was that he was too liberal and lenient. *Populorum Progressio* (1963) was seen to be merely a baptism of Père Lebret's rabid anti-Americanism. Paul rapped the knuckles of an insignificant Archbishop Lefèbvre but did nothing about the Marxists within the fold. A second view, then, was that Paul had not gone to the left far enough. *Octogesima Adveniens* (1971) pulled in his horns. But the cure of the world's ills lies supposedly in socialism and Marxism. Paul had not seen the wave of the future. There is no Catholic social doctrine, the radicals held, so why not opt for the method that was taking over anyhow? Thirdly, there was the anti-*Humanae Vitae* school, which judged the validity of the papacy on this one issue. And in this case, with much superficial analysis, the pope was seen to have been wrong. Yet, what was frightening about *Humanae Vitae* was not how wrong it was, but how right. We have seen in these past years laws and mores evolve pretty much as Paul had predicted. When the period began, the doctor who induced abortion was acting illegally. When the period ended, the one who did not was more and more held to be violating a woman's "rights".

Finally, from an opposite angle, Paul had been increasingly held to be too weak. He had not disciplined his own house, so that the faithful no longer knew which theologians, doctrines, and practices were right and which wrong. Paul had been too kind, too easy, especially on free-thinking intellectuals, ever to exercise the necessary kind of public authority that would serve to keep the basic content of the faith clear and authentic.

My own feeling about Paul VI was rather that he was the most intelligent pope in modern times in terms of analytic penetration and awareness of precisely the intellectual aspect of the faith, something John Paul II, I think, has recognized in him. Coming as he did immediately after John XXIII and, more especially, during the myth of John, Paul tried to exercise papal authority in primarily an intellectual way. No one who reads carefully the vast and remarkable work he produced—and all said he did most of his own writing—could doubt that here we had one of the most underestimated men of our time. We really did not expect to have such an "intellectual" as pope. On almost any theological or cultural issue on which he was criticized, Paul revealed much more insight than his critics. Many doubted if it was desirable to have had such an intelligent pope precisely because the intellectual tends to rely too much upon persuasion and the appeal of truth by its own force.

The number of times Paul returned to this notion that truth should be believed for its own sake is remarkable. This is the key, I think, to why he did not "exercise" authority. In this he was more Thomist and rational than Augustinian. He was reluctant to believe that men, especially Christians, more especially academics, clerics, and religious, would not be convinced by clear argument. I could not help but admire such a quality, and I am not at all sure Paul was not correct. I still suspect that, as the years pass in the context of newer popes, we will come to wonder how we had such a perceptive pope and why it was that a good part of the Catholic world wasted its energies disagreeing with him, when history was proving him basically right.

But Rome, even religious Rome, is more than the papacy. This city is ever full of men and women who do seek to do God's will. The condition of man's spirit is part of this city. Reporting on Rome by the secular media often tends to reduce what went on there to questions of pure power, ambition, and personality. And there are these questions. In another sense, however, there is something truly mysterious about the humanity of the Church, something that seems to touch the Eternal City in a special way. There is a dogged instinct about the sane and sensible in our lot as well as about our openness to God. Rome ever looks wrong or distorted to anyone who deviates in the slightest from the wholeness of Christian truth and practice. And our relation to truth always remains more than intellectual. Indeed, if Christianity means anything at all, it means that our relation to goodness and truth is something of a gift. The Epistle to the Romans of Paul of Tarsus remains at the very roots of our civilization. "In these is no distinction. Since all have sinned and fall short of the glory of God, they are justified by his grace as a gift, through the redemption which is in Christ Jesus, whom God has put forward as an expiation by his blood, to be received by faith" (3:14–15).

Thus, to leave Rome was to leave a place that has seen the world grow and go by. Rome gives us one of the great freedoms known to man, the freedom to escape the pressure of the present, to rediscover the past of almost any period of man, the joy of knowing a real privacy, without which, as Hannah Arendt once remarked, there is no public. There are things that are truly our own business—ways and friendships and prayers and ideas we do not have to share with the world. Anyone who has spent a leisurely *pranzo* in an Italian *ristorante* or a quiet *cena* in the evening will appreciate not only the freshness and goodness of Italian pasta, fruits, vegetables, and wines, but also the sense of friendly atmosphere that makes the Roman *trattoria* one of the world's great cultural events, and this mostly because it is private, even when there is conversation, laughter, song, and a sense of belonging.

During my last days in Rome, I was fortunate enough to have a surprise visitor. Showing Rome to someone who has never been there was itself one of the pleasures of being in Rome. We went up the Michaelangelo steps to the Campidoglio to see Marcus Aurelius on Horseback, then into the Museum to see the Dying Gaul, the heads of Cicero and Homer and Tiberius, to the other side to see the Boy with the Thorn. We went into the Ara Coeli where a German Mass was just beginning, to see Pinturecchio's magnificent Death of Bernadine of Siena. We saw the Gesù, Santa Prassede, Santa Maria Maggiore, Santa Maria in Trastevere, the great Arches of Septimius Severus and Titus, St. Peter's, and Santa Maria degli Angeli. We heard *La Traviata* at the Opera and went to the papal audience on Wednesday. I wondered if I was seeing it all for the last time. I knew that I was just beginning to comprehend even a little of it.

Later, on a clear Sunday in June, after a heavy rain, I walked unsuspectingly into the Piazza Venezia for a cup of coffee. In the distance I could hear a band. Presently marched into the Piazza some two hundred mounted *Carabinieri* in full dress on their brown and white matching horses. Then gradually into the Venezia marched some thirty-eight hundred troops from the various units of the

Italian military, myriads of colorful uniforms and quick steps. Finally, the tall Quirinale Guard lined the steps leading up to the Tomb of the Unknown Soldier. The commander called the massed troops to order: *"Brigate, presenta armi in honore del Capo dello Stato."* The massed bands played the stirring Italian national anthem while Giovanni Leone, then the president of the republic, climbed to place a wreath on the tomb. The scene was glorious, except that during the whole ceremony, the loudspeaker system broadcast so much heavy static that not much could be heard, not even the bands. As I left Rome, it was such a scene that would most probably remain with me, this almost perfectly beautiful scene, marred, as in St. Peter's at the Easter Vigil, by some foible to remind me that I was still *in via*.

And so we have even here no lasting city, as Scripture tells us. Even Rome must be added to this truth. And yet, Rome will last. Luther was wrong. It would not have been better not to have seen Rome. I did not throw a coin into the Trevi Fountain, and yet, I hoped that I would come back. On leaving Rome, I knew I should be gone from an infinite city, the Eternal one symbolic of our lot and our condition. I somehow did not doubt that the political and intellectual fate of Rome during the remaining years of this century will largely determine the next century. For the ability of Catholicism to remain itself is the drama of Rome, and, as I suspect, of the world itself.

Meanwhile, the sentiments about the hearts left in San Francisco and the good-byes spoken in Rome are mostly true. Happiness and beauty are ever much harder to bear than sadness and pain: this is the mystery that these cities teach us.

II

THE CONDITION OF
CATHOLIC INTELLIGENCE

Rome is then a City and a Faith. Christianity forbids us to think of faith as if it did not have roots in this world, just as it forbids us to think of it as only a worldly movement. It is essential to think of what is bothering religion today, what kinds of opposition it encounters, its own capacity to perceive the validity of its own mind. To these questions I will turn first. Perhaps the best way of doing this is to begin by citing three statements from the past hundred years about Catholic intelligence and the context in which it must see itself.

Whoso turns his attention to the bitter strifes of these days and seeks a reason for the troubles that vex public and private life, must come to the conclusion that a fruitful cause of the evils which now afflict . . . us, lies in this: that false conclusions concerning divine and human things, which originated in the schools of philosophy, have crept into all the orders of the state, and have been accepted by the common consent of the masses.

—*Leo XIII*, Aeterni Patris, *August 4, 1879.*

As for reason, [the Catholic] monopoly is practically admitted in the modern world. Except for one or two dingy old atheists in Fleet Street (for whom I have the greatest sympathy), nothing except Rome now defends the reliability of reason.

—*G. K. Chesterton*, The Well and the Shallows, *London, 1935.*

The currently established academic religion has as its first principle that no proposition may be held with such certitude as to exclude its contradictory.

—*John Senior, The Death of Christian Culture, 1978.*

What each of these citations from a century has in common, of course, surely is the stress they place on the function of reason and intelligence in the faith, not merely reason's place, but the claim to reliability made for it by Christianity.

The severest and least attended-to crisis in the Christian Church in general and in the Roman Church in particular is *not* service to the poor, nor the quality of spiritual life, liturgy, scriptural or historical studies, nor is it the loss of vocations or the capacity of episcopal and papal leadership. Neither is it the virtual self-destruction of many female religious orders, nor even less any weakening of faith. Such are indeed problems of particular import, but behind each of these lies something deeper, the erosion of Christian intelligence itself.

About two decades ago, John Tracy Ellis argued that Catholic scholarship was not as rigorous or as insightful as comparable secular intelligence. What has happened in the meantime is not so much an updating or increasing of the quality of Catholic performance in the various secular fields —though this has also happened—but rather a massive loss of identifiable Catholic intelligence together with the institutions that support it—journals, publishing houses, universities, seminaries—such that it is largely impossible to discover and identify a Catholic intelligence distinct from corresponding secular values and views. Professor

J. M. Cameron recently remarked on this point in his *On the Idea of a University*:

> I was much struck by a passage in Jencks's and Riesman's *The Academic Revolution* (1968). They wrote, after noting the general tendency of Catholic universities and colleges to emulate the secular universities and colleges, with the possibility that they will in the end be indistinguishable from them: "The important question . . . is not whether a few Catholic universities prove capable of competing with Harvard and Berkeley on the latter's terms, but whether Catholicism can provide an ideology or personnel for developing alternatives to the Harvard-Berkeley model of excellence."
> This is not to be evaded or avoided. . . . Is there within the tradition of Catholicism a richness capable of offering something that is to others recognizably a contribution to university education and at the same time so distinctive that it is more than simply such a contribution but is as different from what is to be found elsewhere as apples are from oranges?[1]

The argument is not over the things that secular and religious faith may have in common—the Thomist tradition—but over the things they do not share. Indeed, a century after the publication of Leo XIII's encyclical on the importance of intellect in matters of faith, the very existence of an independent and unique Catholic mind is questioned by those observing Christianity from the outside.

Put in terms that combine faith and reason from a classic Christian view, however, there is a Creed, and the Creed is true. Conformity to it is the criterion of order for the mind, a point Dorothy Sayers made so well in her *Whimsical Christian*. The contemporary non-Christian intelligence al-

---

[1] J. M. Cameron, *On the Idea of a University* (Toronto: University of Toronto Press, 1978) 81–82.

most instinctively recognizes Christians deviating from their own traditions. The Creed, of course, is precisely a credo, an "I believe", such that it seems distinctively odd to argue the case for a failure in intelligence in terms of deviation from a norm that includes an element of faith.

Yet, we are dealing here precisely with Christianity, so that it is extremely important in this era of ideology, Eastern religions, and tragic cults to recognize that the precise frontier wherein Christianity separates itself from all other religions and mind-oriented systems is that of intelligence itself.

The question, moreover, is not merely about the capacity of the intellect to know and judge truth and error, right and wrong—the Christian tradition includes quite clearly affirmation of this capacity, yet *with* the consequences of original sin—but about the positive exercise of the will actually to let the mind operate and accept its own conclusions. "The Gospel invites us today to intelligence," P.-J. Labarrière wrote. But he further reflected, it is impossible "to hide a resurgence in our time that is perennial: I mean *a certain refusal to perform the act of intelligence*, taken in all its rigor and vitality, and that even when this refusal conceals itself in a phraseology of great intellectual complexity."[2] Not only has the vast wealth of modern scientific and cultural knowledge tended to paralyze our capacity to distinguish and judge vital issues in terms of truth and error, right and wrong—the purpose for which the faculty of intellect seems to exist in the first place—but we have often allowed ourselves to be overwhelmed by the claim that truth itself is tyrannical because of its very insistence

[2] P.-J. Labarrière, S.J., "Plaidoyer pour l'intelligence", *Études*, (Paris: February 1978) 244, (January 1978) 86.

that some positions and opinions are wrong, no matter how widespread they may be lived or held. To understand all is *not* to forgive all. Forgiveness is a function of truth, not a process of approving whatever in fact happens, whatever men do. This is why it is revolutionary in both conservative and radical regimes, why truth cannot rely on our formulations, why it is ultimately a discovery.

Hannah Arendt, in spite of her rather heavy Kantian presuppositions, had an unerring instinct in her last book, *The Life of the Mind*, when she traced the relation of the internal acts of the mind—perception, thinking, willing, and judging—to any sound grasp of the public and historical order. It seems ironical, in a way, that something taken for granted in the older Christian intellectual traditions should now need rediscovering as the key to any proper understanding of the world. The relationship which the practices and movements of our time have had to Christianity has been obscured for us because we have not seen them in contradistinction to the Creed and the kind of intellect it demands and presupposes. Chesterton wrote in *The Well and the Shallows*:

> We have done far less than we should have done to explain all the balance of subtlety and sanity which is meant by Christian civilization. Our thanks are due to those who have so generously helped us by giving a glimpse of what is meant by a pagan civilization. And what is lost in that society is not so much religion as reason. . . . We did not believe that the rationalists were so utterly mad until they made it quite clear to us. We did not ourselves think that the mere denial of our dogma could end in such dehumanized and demented anarchy.[3]

[3] G. K. Chesterton, "The Return of Religion", *The Well and the Shallows* (New York: Sheed, 1935) 79.

The function of Christian intelligence is first that it remain identifiably itself, and this precisely so that it can remain capable of judging what is not of its spirit. Perhaps one of the most remarkable signs of the need of this sort of approach can be found in Professor A. H. Armstrong's address to the Plotinus symposium at Catholic University. Armstrong's thesis concerned, ostensibly, the value of the "negative" theology tradition as a tool to unmask all absolutisms. In the process, however, Armstrong broached a topic too long unattended to, namely the relation of Greek intelligence to Christian faith. Surveying current Christology, Armstrong held that the alliance between intelligence and faith is now coming apart, especially because of the kind of biblical criticism that seeks to find the primitive Church or the original Jesus. Armstrong's option was itself a basic challenge to a Christianity neglectful of the stake it has in intellect:

> The Biblical and the Hellenic elements are, apparently, coming apart. And, if they come apart, it is not as certain as Christian theologians and preachers seem to suppose that most of those who remain at all interested in the matter will choose the Biblical and reject the Hellenic. . . .
>
> I really do not think that I have much reason for allegiance to "authentic", truly "Biblical" Christianity, whether radical or conservative. And, now that because of the breakup of the Conglomerate, I have to choose between the Biblical and the Hellenic, I shall choose the Hellenic, though I can only choose it as a "myth".[4]

The instinct of Professor Armstrong in preferring intelligence to faith or myth, as he called it, is one that has

<hr>

[4] A. H. Armstrong, Address delivered during the symposium on Plotinus at Catholic University of America, Washington, D.C. (October 1978).

much broader implications than the historic one about the way early and medieval Christianity assimilated the Greek mind. Any attentive reading of missionary theology today, for example, reveals this same effort to relativize or eliminate the heritage of Greek intelligence from Christianity.[5]

Yet, the central line of Catholicism, a line that was reaffirmed precisely in the great Reformation controversies over Aristotle in particular, did recognize the stake it had in intelligence. This is why any weakening or inattention to this aspect of faith can only result, for the central Catholic tradition in any case, in the reduction of faith to myth alone, however exalted this latter function might be. For the "myth" of Christianity, like that of Plato, was understood to be precisely "true", which is why Professor Armstrong's effort to exalt negative theology as a tool against absolute truth must remain fundamentally unchristian in tendency.

Thus, what I want to suggest is that there are no longer many, if any, centers wherein precisely the uniqueness of "Catholic" intellect is known and reflected upon. The great religious orders that have been particularly responsible for this vocation to intelligence—the Dominicans and Jesuits especially—are, as their current critics keep reminding them, busy about many other things. In a certain sense, Chesterton's remark, again in *The Well and the Shallows*, applies to the way most Catholic and Christian intellectuals have orchestrated their educational and cultural enterprises during the past quarter of a century: "Those who leave the tradition of truth do not escape into something we call Freedom. They only escape into something

---

[5] See Eugene Juquet, "L'evangelisation, peut-il respecter les cultures?" *Études* (Paris: November 1978).

we call Fashion."[6] The note of religious intellectual life in recent years, particularly since the middle 1960s, has not been the preservation of the truths of Greek intelligence and Christian dogma, the classical Christian enterprise, but mostly contemporary fashion, a tale followed with grim astonishment by Dale Vree in his *On Synthesizing Marxism and Christianity*, or by John Senior in his remarkable *The Death of Christian Culture*, a book that should obviously be read along with Christopher Dawson's *Religion and the Rise of Western Culture*.

So fashionable indeed have we become that we have hardly even noticed the deep and growing roots of anti-Catholicism in the West.[7] And we have not noticed this because our intellectuals have not been attuned to those central dogmas and practices of the faith against which the bigotry, with sure instinct for what is vital, is directed —against life itself, against the family, against a God-directed human order, rather than an autonomous human one. We do not lift an eyebrow when, say, the Los Angeles City Hall is ordered to turn off its Christmas lights because they form a cross.[8] Christianity, in its credal formulations, is rapidly becoming illegal, while Christians, ironically, are worrying about how to restructure the whole world. The

[6] Chesterton, 67.

[7] See Chapter 4 of the present work. See also N. Miller, "A New Anti-Catholic Bigotry?" *The Wall Street Journal* (14 December 1978); Russell Shaw, "How Pronounced Is Anti-Catholic Bigotry in Government Circles?" *Columbia* (January 1979); James Hitchcock, "The Not So New Anti-Catholicism", *Worldview* (November 1978); in addition the Letter of Senator Moynihan to the American Hierarchy on Anti-Catholicism (1978).

[8] George Nicholson, "Los Angeles City Hall Ordered to Turn Off Christmas Lights", *Contra Costa Times* (21 December 1978).

secular order is more and more determining what can be believed within its political realm.

In Paul VI, the Roman Church had one of the most intelligent men of this era, intelligent precisely for his awareness of where ideas led, but few realized this unique good fortune. By any statistical criterion, Christian intellectuals were arrayed mostly against papal intelligence during this era. I suspect the same fate will eventually greet John Paul II as he reaffirms the central line of Paul VI and the longer Christian tradition, as he seems clearly intent on doing. In any case, the remarkable analysis of Leopold Tyrmand argued that the almost unique success of the Polish Church must be attributed to that most neglected of disciplines—the discipline of Catholic intelligence:

> The Church responded to the Communist political, cultural, social, and administrative onslaught by resorting to its neglected, almost forgotten weapon: intellectual riches. . . .
> Now, when the totalitarian ideas and social concepts deem themselves scientific, Aquinas' arguments seem to many more valid than ever. Simply put, Thomism leads to a theory of human liberty that is entitled to distinguish between the absolute and the dogmatic in matters of faith, and firmly rejects determinist philosophy such as Marxism.
> Pope John Paul II knows that the Christian weapon—faith— is useless today without a philosophical dimension and that Catholic personalism, the belief that humans transcend social-political conditioning, is the center of the global struggle.[9]

Needless to say, the study of Christian intellect, as of Christian personalism—their metaphysical and theological foundations—has not been prevalent in recent years in

[9] Leopold Tyrmand, "Poland, Marxism, and John Paul II", *Wall Street Journal* (8 December 1978).

Catholic intellectual circles. If anything, the fashion of Catholic intellectual life has been one of reacting against the central ideas of its own academic tradition. The cast of recent Catholic thought has largely been accommodation to absolutism in the social field, seen as a tool of modernization, and ethical relativism in the moral field, both exactly the opposite of classic Catholic intelligence.

Thus, it would be enough to ask who reads Maritain or Gilson, were we not afraid to ask, Who reads Aquinas? Indeed, some writers, like Professor Senior on Maritain and Professor John East on Aquinas, think we must ask, Who reads Augustine?, a theme Garry Wills also takes up in his *Confessions of a Conservative*.[10] And there are still others, such as Professor George Kuykendall, who fail to grasp the central importance of precisely human intelligence in the structure of Christian thought as it faces the world.[11] And these are not just idle questions for anyone who teaches today in universities in which little of the classic tradition of Christian intellect is taught or even presented.[12] But what is surprising about contemporary students is that they are ready to read the Christian intellectual tradition if given a chance—this in a world in which, as my colleague John Ryan at Georgetown put it, *The Idea of a University* no longer has inexpensive editions in print.

[10] John East, "The Political Relevance of St. Augustine", *Modern Age* (Spring, 1972). See Garry Wills, *Confessions of a Conservative* (New York: Doubleday, 1979).

[11] See George Kuykendall, "Thomas' Proofs as *Fides Quaerens Intellectum*: Towards a Trinitarian *Analogia*", *Scottish Journal of Theology*. no. 2 (1978).

[12] See Chapter 14 of the present work. See also James Hitchcock, *Catholicism and Modernity* (New York: Seabury, 1979); Russell Kirk, *Decadence and Renewal in the Higher Learning* (New York: Regnery-Gateway 1978).

Curiously, the low intellectual caliber and quality of various academic and media clergy and laity have become something of a cause of humor today. Malcolm Muggeridge is ready to believe in his "Seventy-Five Theses on his Seventy-Fifth Birthday" that individual Jesuits hold almost any fuzzy doctrine; something, alas, he can come pretty close to documenting so nobody challenges him. When the conservative columnist M. Stanton Evans wrote recently about a "College [which] Teaches [the] Art of Thinking", he was not talking about any religious-founded institution.[13]

And when the Englishman Christopher Derrick wrote his *Escape from Skepticism: Education as if the Truth Really Mattered*, the said truth was not something he found at Notre Dame, Fordham, or Santa Clara. Perhaps the most insightful comment, however, in this regard comes from Australia. Commenting on the future of the hundred-year-old Jesuit College in Melbourne, Gregory Denning wrote:

> Deep in [the Jesuit's] tradition is a trust in the rationality of man. Their great heroes, Peter Canisius and Robert Bellarmine, were as learned as they were saintly. . . .
>
> The Jesuits' abiding gift to the world in the last four hundred years has been the witness they have given to the freedom men of faith can have when they stand on the frontiers of knowledge. . . . Now in their expertise as the prophets of the new Church, they are still the thoroughly educated men they were before, but the language and mode of their education is narrowly theological and religious.

---

[13] See M. Stanton Evans, "College Teaches Art of Thinking", *Contra Costa Times* (22 December 1978). See also Christopher Derrick, *Escape from Skepticism* (La Salle, Ill: Sherwood Sugden, 1977).

They know their scriptures and their sacred history, their spiritual counsels and their liturgy. They have overthrown yesterday's formalism in their scholastic and ecclesiastical training. But they have put their older skills in humanities and science aside. They seek no longer to make discoveries among the stars or in the Earth, or in history, or in literature.

In the second century of the school [Xavier College], they will have this problem. While they speak for boys' souls, who will speak for boys' minds? Who is left in the whole wide world to gamble as they once did that a total commitment to secular learning and a total commitment to faith enriched soul and mind together?[14]

This is indeed well put and serves to re-center the issue of the nature of intelligence in Christianity.

In a similar manner, the French Jesuit journal *Études* recently published an analysis of the new style of Jesuit education in France, the home of such a long history of Jesuit and Christian intelligence. This was not the education the Jesuits proposed for their external students as in the Australian reflection, but the education designed for Jesuits themselves. Not only was the prescribed course of studies quite short, by traditional standards, but it seemed to be guided by little definable sense of Catholic intellect. The Australian complaint that the Jesuits knew little but theology was matched by the French program that made theology a kind of gentleman's acquaintance with the various problems of man and the world.[15]

Roger Troisfontaines, writing in *Nouvelle Revue Théologique* on the nature of decision-making processes among

[14] G. Denning, *Xavier: A Centenary Portrait* (Melbourne: 1978).

[15] P. Valadier, S.J., "Former les jesuites", *Études*, (Paris: October 1978).

contemporary Jesuits, was conscious of the criticism that the Jesuits in particular have radically changed their intellectual orientations:

> Seen from the point of view of living unity as well as cohesion in action, the changes effected by the factual situation as also the juridical changes, permit us to speak of a new image of the Society of Jesus, while retaining the permanence of the Jesuit identity. Moreover, both from without and within, some are tempted to think that it is a completely new Society in reality, more acceptable without doubt in the society and Church of today (but has the Ignatian creation ever from the 16th Century been acceptable?) better perhaps in itself, ideally or really . . . but on the other hand, less rigorously bound to its specific reason for existence, less total, a Company less adequate also, some insist, to the guidance of superior ecclesiastical authority, especially of Paul VI.[16]

Meanwhile, the Benedictine Dom Jean Leclercq, writing on contemporary monastic tendencies, did not list a consciousness of the importance of Catholic intellectual life as one of the recent tendencies.

That the problem of religion is more and more that of intelligence is becoming more clearly recognized, though often this recognition is precisely "rationalist", in the sense always rejected by Catholic instinct. Arthur Munk, for example, in *Intellect*, revealed something of this confusion:

> One clear result of our diagnosis is, of course, that religion is sick today chiefly because it is inflicted with the plague of insidious irrationalism. Furthermore, while this irrationalism is certainly evident in religious factionalism in terms of its

[16] Roger Troisfontaines, S.J., "Dynamique de la decision dans la Companie de Jesus" *Nouvelle Revue Théologique* (March-April 1978), 267.

many shapes and forms, it is likewise evident in much current theology as found not only in cults and sects, but even in the established religious bodies.[17]

I cite Munk's analysis because it serves not so much to further the argument but to warn of the dangers of both intellect and anti-intellect. And it is precisely this paradox of the value of intellect within an overarching sense of its limits that constitutes the crucial import of Christianity in the world. As *Le Monde*'s remarks on the death of Gilson intimated, there was indeed a Christian philosophy, without which Christianity could not defend itself, or even understand itself.

No one was more aware of this issue than the early Eric Voegelin (there are certain problems about the later Voegelin's loyalty to his original insights).[18] In *The New Science of Politics*, Voegelin argued against Max Weber that Weber failed to study Christian medieval civilization precisely because that civilization contained within itself a rational metaphysics which was not neutral with regard to values, because it required a rational justification for values themselves. Voegelin even intimated that intelligence is no longer intelligence once revelation is given:

> Philosophy and Christianity have endowed man with the stature that enables him, with historical effectiveness, to play the role of rational contemplator and pragmatic master of a nature which has lost its demonic terrors. With equal historical effectiveness, however, limits were placed on human grandeur; for Christianity has concentrated demonism into the

[17] Arthur Munk, "Whither Religion? A Plea for a Return to Sanity", *Intellect* (December 1977) 250.

[18] See B. Douglass, "Gospel and Order: Eric Voegelin on the Political Role of Christianity", *Journal of Politics* (February 1976).

permanent danger of a fall from the spirit—that is man's only by the grace of God—into the autonomy of his own self, from the *amor Dei* into the *amor sui*. The insight that man in his mere humanity, without the *fides caritate formata*, is demonic nothingness has been brought by Christianity to the ultimate border of clarity which by tradition is called revelation.[19]

This means that philosophy is indeed philosophy, that the mind when given revelation is still capable of thinking, but that the relation of mind to revelation is such that at the frontiers where faith and reason meet—best described in Aquinas' question about the "necessity" of divine law (I-II, q.91,a.4)—a refusal to incorporate the truths of revelation will corrupt precisely intelligence.

In conclusion, then, what I wish to suggest is that this latter consequence has largely happened to the modern mind. The decline of specifically Catholic intelligence—the view of the faith that does not set faith apart from reason—has left the world with no intellectual basis for any profound understanding of itself. Thus, in these hundred years since Leo XIII attempted to reemphasize Catholic intelligence as such, what seems most striking is the feebleness of a peculiarly Christian intelligence. Leo was not wrong to sense that the crucial, unseen struggle would be in the area of philosophy itself.

The conclusion that seems most obvious, then, is that the heart of the modern crisis lies in the condition and independence of an authentic and traditional "Catholic" intelligence, one whose attitude to the mind is that the mind is a faculty for knowing truth and that truth can

---

[19] Eric Voegelin, *The New Science of Politics* (Chicago: University of Chicago Press, 1952) 78–79.

be known.[20] And further, since revelation is given to men, it is also true that what God has given to us is also to be thought about. The speculations of Greek philosophy were not mere accidents or cultural expressions but witnesses to the meaning of mind being revealed to mind. In the end, perhaps, it would be an exaggeration to say that the refusal of monks—clerical and lay—to study the core of the Christian tradition, its historical intelligence, is the main reason for our current confusions. But if it is an exaggeration, it is only a small one.

[20] See E. F. Schumacher, *Guide for the Perplexed* (New York: 1977).

PART II

WITH A DISTINCTIVE OPPOSITION

III

ON THE REMOVAL OF CHRISTIANITY

Christians have been taught to love their enemies, no matter how difficult it seems, no matter how few are able to accomplish this goal. Many have often, however, interpreted this to mean that they had no enemies so that they were quite unprepared to envision just what an "enemy" might be. Obviously, an enemy is someone who "attacks" our lives, beliefs, or property. But perhaps even more, an enemy is someone who does not think our beliefs or way of life have a right to exist, someone who takes steps to forbid and eliminate them. The Christian doctrine of love of enemies was not meant to promote illusion. No doubt, we are to give everyone the benefit of the doubt, but real respect for an "enemy" includes the clear recognition of what he stands for and his method of action. The "forgiving" of our enemy we hope may affect him; it may stop the process of retributive justice. But if it does not, as it need not, the enemy remains someone to be reckoned with. The doctrines of "tolerance" and "peaceful co-existence" might, if agreed upon, limit what enemies would do to one another, but both of these doctrines may also be only interim truces until one side or other gains more power.[1]

The "enemies" of Christianity would, presumably, be those who want to eliminate it entirely, or at least reduce it to insignificance. Such elimination could, evidently, take

[1] See the author's chapter on "The Love of Enemies", in *The Praise of 'Sons of Bitches': On the Worship of God by Fallen Men* (Slough, England: St. Paul Publications, 1978).

several forms. Annihilation or expulsion are, historically, tried and not always unsuccessful means in certain ages. However, the classic ways to eliminate Christianity are to show that it is wrong from some scientific or cultural viewpoint or else to make it hostile to the political society in which it tries to exist. Perhaps the classic case in this latter regard was the charge that Christianity was responsible for the fall of the Roman power, a charge to which Augustine responded, one which Gibbon revived in the last century. Thus, whenever a serious political or cultural crisis exists, there will be those who argue that religion is its cause. Today, perhaps the locus of anti-Christian sentiment is most often found in population-ecology areas. Still others would argue that since religion deflects man from improving his world, it must either be destroyed or, more recently, converted into a worldly political movement with the same ethos as various ideologies.

No doubt the atmosphere, at least in the West, is full of apocalyptic fears. Governor Jerry Brown of California felt the key issue in current politics must be "the United States' headlong rush to destruction".[2] On the other hand, we remain in something of a dilemma in deciding whether this danger arises from our rapid elimination of traditional morality, laws, and values or whether our failures remain because religion has not been removed rapidly enough. Columnist James Reston, remarking on our failure to decide about aid to religious schools, wrote that there was a more basic issue involved, that we must decide precisely "whether this nation, in this secular and permissive age, is somehow threatened by helping finance the instruction and

[2] *San Francisco Chronicle* (15 July 1979) A4.

practice of religion, or whether it is in trouble for lack of religion."[3] The former position is probably predominant in practice.

A friend of mine, for instance, was recently proofreading some work he was doing on Scripture. In the last draft before printing, he suddenly noticed that, without his permission or consultation, someone had deliberately removed all the "A.D.'s" and "B.C.'s" after the dates in his text. Needless to say, not only did this make his paper unintelligible, but it was just one more sign of a very activist effort to remove any sign of Christianity from public view. "A.D." after all means *Anno Domini*, the Year of Our Lord, and that is supposed to be "prejudiced". We are to use "After the Common Era"—A.C.E.—instead, as if that is any less prejudiced. A suit, as mentioned previously, prevented the Los Angeles City Hall from displaying a traditional lighted cross during the Christmas season, again prejudice. In Virginia, Christmas plays and carols, even with voluntary attendance, were objected to in public schools. When the religious symbolism of even the Christmas Tree is discovered, it will last no longer than the Crib and the Christ Child.

Frank Getlein, in a rather fanciful column, reflected upon taking seriously a sign he had read in Congressional halls which read: "What If Jesus Christ Had Been Aborted?" He felt that, on the surface of it all, some rather positive things might have come about. The Holy Innocents would not have been massacred by Herod. The idea of a separation of spiritual and temporal would not have occurred, so that maybe the Roman Empire would not have fallen; thus it

[3] James Reston, *New York Times* (3 June 1979) E 19.

might have been able to incorporate the barbarians more easily. Finally, the old polytheism would have been the norm, no backward Puritanism for us to wrestle with.

> Beyond the several concerns of the several gods, the very idea of several gods—whose interests, as we know from Bulfinch and Edith Hamilton, are often in conflict—more readily corresponds with the conflicts most of us find within ourselves from time to time than does the desolate and awful solitary divinity. If, as the Enlightenment maintained, man created God in his own image, in many ways, Graeco-Roman polytheism did a better job of it than Christianity.[4]

Aside from overlooking the fact that the Christian God is not "solitary" but "Trinity", this still suggests that without a Jesus, without an Incarnation presumably—an aborted Jesus, technically, would have fulfilled the requirements of Incarnation—the world would have evidently struggled on, more adequately for some.

On a world scale, the efforts of the Chinese, Hindu, and Islamic governments to limit or remove Christian presence have gained considerable force in this past quarter of a century. This is an area to which John Paul II has paid considerable attention.[5] Peregrine Worsthorne, writing on "Islam: Exorcising Western Gods", remarked:

> How short memories are: for as recently as the beginning of this century the Mohammedan world was seen as an alien force which Christendom had every reason to fear. Nor was this primarily because of the military power of the Ottoman Empire, great as that still was. Much more deep-seated was an atavistic fear, based on historic experience, of an ancient religion which had for centuries proved its capacity to inspire masses of men

[4] Frank Getlein, *The Progressive* (14 April 1978) 15.

[5] John Paul II, *Redemptor Hominis* (Boston: Daughters of St. Paul, 1979) 38.

with beliefs, for which they were prepared to die, inimical to the Christian faith.[6]

Thus Hilaire Belloc, at the end of his book on *The Crusades* (1937), suspected that if Islam should ever regain power, it would also gain its political zeal. The only thing Belloc could not have anticipated was how power could be in oil.

But the effort to remove or mollify Christianity comes not only from the other historic religions and cultures. The whole encounter of Christianity with socialism has resulted, within Christianity itself, in a drastic downplaying of its central doctrines. Classical socialism has always claimed, as Ferdinand Mount has observed, that our whole system is corrupt; but socialism has now mostly given up its central concerns with the industrial workers, who are satisfied enough with the present system. Socialism is now worried about a distant problem.

> Socialism, in its origin essentially a metropolitan phenomenon, has retreated to the provinces. There is a parallel here with the Christian Church, in which modernists have withdrawn or shelved the central claim of the Incarnation while zealously pursuing the secondary intimation of the social gospel. The strategy can only have a limited run. The secondary intimations depend, after all, upon the original central claim. If all this business of turning the world up-side-down and changing men utterly is not to be taken seriously, then all those socialist tactics, treaties and factions are mere frivolous diversions.[7]

Christianity without the centrality of the Incarnation is, of course, hardly Christian, let alone being the social gospel.

[6] *Wall Street Journal* (25 January 1979).
[7] Ferdinand Mount, "The Marginal Left", *The Spectator* (London: 26 August 1978) 2.

The capacity of the various Christian churches to remain themselves before such contemporary ideology seems seriously questionable. This drift has been traced in three recent studies. Paul Seabury's analysis of the Episcopal Church in the United States was a trenchant and disturbing account of the yielding of the organization of that church to contemporary movements regarding its own religious norms.

> If God is conceived as evident in the world, then the faithful can become Christian soldiers and the symbols of an essentially transcendent religion may be employed as weapons in political conflicts. . . . The 'failure of nerve' in the churches is manifest in the conception that the world should set the agenda for the Church. The irony is that, since the world changes its agenda capriciously, the Church becomes directionless. . . .
> The collapse of transcendency, as Episcopalians now know from experience, transfers the religious community to the domain of secular politics.[8]

Stephen Chapman detailed the even stranger case of the transformation of the presumably pacifist Society of Friends, especially their American Friends Service Committee, from a charitable social organization against violence of any kind to a positive supporter of various—usually left—ideological and revolutionary movements.

> All this suggests several things about the AFSC and its involvement in foreign policy issues. First, that there is nothing distinctively Quaker or even Christian about its views. The only means it has for appraising governments is a vague

---

[8] Paul Seabury, "Trendier Than Thou: The Many Temptations of the Episcopal Church", *Harper's* (October 1978). See also Michael Smith, "Jesus, the Church and Social Justice", *New Oxford Review* (July–August 1979) 4–9.

standard of "human rights". One can read through reams of AFSC documents and talk for hours to AFSC staff people without ever hearing even a passing reference to the gospel or to God. . . . By draining the religious content out of its politics and elevating the claims of social and political ideals above the imperatives of individual morality, the AFSC had badly undermined the moral case to be made for pacifism.[9]

Finally, there is Professor Ernest Lefever's critical study of the similar transformation within the bureaucracy of the World Council of Churches.[10]

Efforts in this same direction within the Catholic Church are well known. One of the best ways to eliminate something is to make it into something else. The classic Marxist effort to overturn religion in recent years yielded rather to an effort to so translate Christianity that it means exactly the same thing as the Marxist ideals. Dogmas are interpreted in a way in which their verbal statement is the same but their meaning changed. In a curious essay entitled "Keeping the Faith", Roberta Lynch recounted changes in the Church as evidence of its supposed inability to retain its classic doctrines: "the handshake of peace helps to orient people away from a solidarity focus on the altar and toward each other."[11] There is a widespread effort "to change Roman Catholicism." Into what? Evidently into a new social environment in which social and personal ethics are united. The personalist-pentecostal revival will not work.

[9] Stephen Chapman, "Shot from Guns: the Lost Pacifism of American Quakers", *New Republic* (9 June 1979) 17.

[10] Ernest W. Lefever, *Amsterdam to Nairobi: The World Council of Churches and the Third World* (Washington: Ethics and Public Policy Center, 1979).

[11] Roberta Lynch, "Keeping the Faith", *The Progressive* (April 1978) 34.

But while these movements may offer temporary solace, they cannot offer real solutions to the empty hole many people find at the center of their lives. The old codes—whether carefully preserved or elegantly refurbished—no longer suffice. Historically, people have not merely turned to religion for communication with an eternal being or the promise of an afterlife; they look to it, as well, for answers about how and why to live. But the vision of a religious ethic completely distinct from the social ethic that governs society is daily being proven obsolete. . . .

American capitalism, despite the proclamations of trust in God on its coinage, produces an ideology that contradicts much of the basic message of the religions by which its citizens have tried to live. . . . The answer, some Christian activists argue, does not lie in religious revivals but in the efforts to forge a new morality as part of building a new social system.[12]

Such an analysis, of course, reduces Christianity to a social theory which not merely refuses to look at the empirical results of that theory whenever it is put in practice but also considers the reality of religion either irrelevant or indifferent to the ideological structures.

There are not a few, however, who consider that on the intellectual level, the situation is considerably worse than on the social level. Religion, when it does appear, becomes a kind of programmed eclecticism. Describing the make-up of the religion department at his university (the University of Northern Iowa), Professor Thomas Thompson wrote:

We have been especially fortunate in the wide range of different temperaments that characterize our faculty mix. Philosophers in the department, save one, were trained in the analytic persuasion. But their graduate school linguisticism

12 Ibid., 35.

has been all but exhausted. Only the memories linger on. One person calls himself a skeptic. Another has been labeled a Marxist. The other two are difficult to categorize. With trepidation, I might describe one as a Spinozist who retains Platonic and Hegelian resonances. The other is a Cartesian dualist with a compatible interest in humanistic psychology. On the religious side, two are Asianists and Buddhist specialists (but one hails from Taiwan and the other from Indianapolis, Indiana). One person is a systematic theologian with current interests in psychosocial theories of the transpersonal and transformational. Our religion-and-literature specialist is Chicago-bred. Biblical courses are taught by a Jew. We are different enough to present a wide range of options to students.[13]

Variety thus becomes the search for truth. From a Christian viewpoint, one cannot help but wonder whether such a "wide range of options" is not equivalent to no option at all. In any case, it is difficult to see where and whether classical Christianity is at all present in this religion-philosophy department.

The present Holy Father, in any case, is noted for his intellectual acumen, for his awareness of the importance of intelligence in contemporary ideological and religious struggles. He has insisted that there is such a thing as Christianity which does not depend upon its accommodation with current ideology. He told some American bishops:

> This then is my own deepest hope today for the pastors of the Church in America, as well as for the pastors of the universal Church: "that the sacred deposit of Christian doctrine should be more effectively guarded and taught" (John XXIII).
>
> The sacred deposit of God's word, handed on by the Church,

[13] Thomas H. Thompson, "Philosophy and Religion in Tandem", *Bulletin*, The Council on the Study of Religion (June 1979) 75.

is the joy and strength of our people's lives. It is the only pastoral solution to the many problems of our day. To present this sacred deposit of Christian doctrine in all its purity and integrity, with all its exigencies and in all its power is a holy pastoral responsibility.[14]

Inattention to and deviation from the content of the faith are, in other words, the causes of the confusion that seeks to eliminate Christianity itself as a definable and identifiable force in the world.

In his *Death of Christian Culture*, one of the most significant books to appear in the United States in recent years, Professor John Senior, of the University of Kansas, wrote:

> Now again, over a vast and increasing area, it is a crime to be a Christian, and even in the United States, the stain of antichrist is in the books and taught in the schools, deadening the vital centers of cultural life. . . .
>
> And Christians look fearfully toward a second age of martyrdom, this time without the lions, under the reign of a sophisticated terror by lobotomy and drugs to create international, nondenominational, multiracial moral and political imbecility. The Church herself is split by apostasy within, far worse than any that has ever been without. Christians who have lived in the hope that the Church would save *them* must fight to save the Church.[15]

Jacques Ellul, the French Protestant theologian, in his powerful *The Betrayal of the West*, was even more blunt:

> It is in our day that Jesus is, in the fullest and most radical sense, being rejected by everything—I mean literally every-

---

[14] John Paul II, Address of November 9, 1978, *The Pope Speaks* 24, no. 1 (1979) 41.

[15] John Senior, *The Death of Christian Culture* (New Rochelle, N.Y.: Arlington House, 1978) 143.

thing—and in the very area of man's endeavors: his thinking, his willing, his undertakings, his building of his world, his consumption. It is in our day that Jesus is being, in the fullest and most radical sense, humiliated: simply left aside as possessing no interest or significance in comparison with what man discovers for himself and bestows on himself. It is in our day that Jesus is, in the fullest sense, being put to death, since none of his words or actions or miracles has any relevance. . . .[16]

Ellul considers that Western Christians no longer know just what it is that their culture has, what is unique about it, and how this relates to the origin, progress and well-being of the faith itself and the future of the rest of the world.

Thus, in theology, the elimination of precisely Jesus means an attack on Christ in Christology, for it is unjust, to egalitarian and pluralistic social theories, that there be only one Jesus who was personally divine. In politics it means that, since Jesus preached a way and a goal that transcended politics, he is eliminated if he be merely a social activist. In education: since the case for reason and revelation is no longer known, he is eliminated if he only be human. As Christopher Derrick bluntly wrote:

But it needs to be said in all charity that in the United States today, the typical Catholic liberal arts college is in very bad shape indeed, the typical Catholic university too. This is primarily because of . . . the current weakening and distortion of faith among the Catholic intellectuals.[17]

And this brings us full circle—the public efforts to eliminate Christianity and its traditional signs are in fact

[16] Jacques Ellul, The Betrayal of the West (New York: Seabury, 1978) 78–79.

[17] Christopher Derrick, Escape from Skepticism: Education as if the Truth Really Mattered (La Salle, Ill.: Sherwood Sugden, 1977) 106.

parallel to a weakening of Catholic thought itself. This means that there is a growing incapacity of Christians to understand their opposition, especially when it arises from a very strong faith or commitment in the older religions. Ironically, in the modern world of recent years, Marxism has made most of its gains against Christianity, while at home, as Solzhenitsyn acknowledged, Marxists have lost their own faith. Islam and Judaism, on the other hand, as well as the Hindu religion, are the ones strengthening their own religious commitments.

In calling attention to the current efforts to eliminate Christianity, then, I believe it well to recall again the comment of Ferdinand Mount about the tendency of Christians to substitute social philosophy for the primacy of the Incarnation itself. George MacDonald, the man C. S. Lewis called the closest to "the spirit of Christ Himself", wrote:

> Man is not made for justice from his fellow, but for love, which is greater than justice, and by including supersedes justice. *Mere* justice is an impossibility, a fiction of analysis. . . . Justice to be justice must be much more than justice. Love is the law of our condition, without which we can no more render justice than a man can keep a straight line, walking in the dark.[18]

In other words, the central complexus of the faith, both its doctrine and its living, the latter only through the former, the former through the latter, is what needs to be recovered.

One of the unique things about Catholicism in particular has been its capacity for holding what was handed down

[18] *George MacDonald, An Anthology*, ed. C. S. Lewis (New York: Macmillan, 1974) no. 51.

from the beginning, holding it in communion, among the faithful of all kinds, as Karl Schmude so well put it.[19] Undoubtedly, if we no longer find this retention clear among the Christians themselves, we seem to open ourselves up to the deepest aberrations of the human spirit. Writing on the cultic phenomenon after Jonestown, the noted psychologist Robert Jay Lifton wrote:

> We may view the cults as a continuation of the experiments and protests of the 1960s. They are a product of historical dislocation—of the loss and frequent dishonoring of traditional symbols of family, religion, authority, government— the life-style in general. In the past, these symbols have provided means of continuity beyond the self, or what I call symbolic immortality. That is, they connected ordinary life with eternal structures and spiritual principles.[20]

The Christian, however, is not merely interested in symbolic immortality. The symbols are not intended merely to explain life on earth. Christianity has never believed that untruth or even symbolic truth was enough to account for the realism of its Creed.

In other words, then, the vocation of Christians is precisely to know, believe, and practice what is uniquely theirs. Christianity may well be eliminated for a given time or area by political power or militant religion. Yet, in addition, it seems worthwhile to notice that the elimination of Christianity can also be something like a suicide. We should not doubt that the hatred of precisely Christ is possible and real. Yet, the only answer that Christ has

---

[19] Karl Schmude, *Catholicism* (Melbourne: ACTS, 1976).

[20] Robert Jay Lifton, "The Appeal of the Death Trip", *New York Times Magazine* (7 January 1979) 27.

given to this, besides the love of enemies, is faithfulness to what he has taught. The difficulty in finding out what the Christian faith really is, especially for and from its most intelligent members, is perhaps the most striking mark of Christianity in our time.

Scripture, to conclude, never led us to doubt that all this *could* happen. But neither did it see it as a mark of the Spirit. Orthodoxy is what Vincent of Lerins in the fifth century called, *"Quod ubique, quod semper, quod ab omnibus creditum est."* That we have so much difficulty in precisely knowing what always, everywhere, and by everyone has been believed marks our culture. There are those who would remove what is left. And there are those who would delight in discovering what is being lost. More than anything else, which of these two tendencies will predominate will, undoubtedly, determine the character of the next decades.

IV

THE ANTI-CATHOLIC BIAS
IN THE UNITED STATES

Attention to the efforts to eliminate Christianity is one thing, but perhaps something further needs to be said about the belated recognition of the degree and nature of anti-Catholic bias in the United States. James Hitchcock's assessment is still among the best:

> Anti-Catholicism can be expected to continue, especially in the form of propaganda in the media and even in the educational system, a concerted attempt to deprive Catholics of moral and intellectual legitimacy in the public eye. Perhaps it is only fitting to give the last word to Paul Blanshard, who did so much to make anti-Catholicism newly respectable after World War II: "Why allow Christian salvationism to flourish side by side with scrupulously accurate science as if they were legitimate twins in our culture, when you know that the Christian doctrine of salvation is untrue?" It is not farfetched to think it just possible that the clear threat implied by Blanshard's words might someday be carried out in a thoroughly "enlightened" America.[1]

Unlike the Jews and other minorities, Catholics often enough do not even seem to know the degree to which they are discriminated against. They have been practically silent in the legal area, the arena of the widest efforts to expose bias of other sorts, when it comes to isolating and combating this bias.

[1] James Hitchcock, "The Not So New Anti-Catholicism", *Worldview* (November 1978) 48.

In 1978, a strong but unsuccessful political effort in Congress was made to get tax credits and some basic justice for Catholic parents and students suffering obvious economic discrimination for their religious beliefs, for sending their children to Catholic schools. The defeat was in part engineered by teachers' unions wanting these same Catholic children to populate state-supported schools, to guarantee their jobs. The quality of opposition to any sort of just aid to Catholics in this area can be ascertained in the comments of veteran aid-opponent, Ed Doerr:

> It is unconstitutional and violates church-state separation. It would also erode interfaith harmony by taxing all citizens to support religious institutions. It would provide tax subsidies for religious, ethnic, class, and other forms of discrimination and imbalance common in non-public schools; and it would favor larger over smaller religious bodies. Furthermore, the plan would weaken public control over the use of public funds and would jeopardize the freedom and independence of parochial schools from government controls. Aside from all that it would run counter to public opinion.[2]

Needless to say, here are all the rationalizations necessary to continue to foster a basic violation of justice. The humanist claim to control the child has seldom been stated more clearly.

After the defeat of this proposal, Senator Daniel Moynihan of New York wrote a frank letter to the American Catholic hierarchy. He pointed out that the moral opposition was due principally to a clear bigotry among southern legislators and northern liberals. More and more today, the

[2] Ed Doerr, "Federal Parochiaid Again", *The Humanist* (July/August, 1979) 61.

unpleasant truth of the aphorism—"Anti-Catholicism is the anti-Semitism of the liberal"—is cited by Catholics just beginning to wake up to the implications and methods of the powers leveled against them in the crucial areas closest to their religious interests and beliefs.

Moynihan's argument was that the so-called "institutions associated with progress in American culture" were against Catholics on the issue of any aid to schools. Leading this opposition was the Presidency itself, that power in the American system which in modern times has probably enjoyed most support from the large bloc of Catholic voters.

> The administration was adamant and, on the edge, vicious. [This in the Department of Health, Education and Welfare, rather than the White House.] The great liberal unions, churches, and political associations were equally opposed and equally energetic, in their opposition. The National Coalition to Save Public Education suggests the range of these opponents and the number of "civil rights" organizations involved. This marks a new development in the sad history of this issue. Support for non-public education has been transmuted into resistance to civil rights.[3]

This appears to be the main area wherein the old southern Protestant, conservative anti-Catholicism has joined forces with northern intellectual liberalism to oppose the basic Catholic world and moral outlooks as they appear in the public forum. Moynihan concluded that this discrimination against Catholics "is perhaps the last frontier of civil rights in this nation. We are the only English-speaking

---

[3] Letter of Mr. Moynihan. Letter's partial text provided by the Senator.

nation in the world that still lives with this legacy of those far-off Elizabethan tragedies. That we do is, not least, a scandal to Christianity. . . ."

George Will, the widely read columnist, commenting also on this anti-Catholicism, has pointed out the double standard of "progressive" sectors which welcome Catholic support, even survive by it, but never return anything to the vital issues Catholics think religiously and morally important. The difference between the nineteenth-century style of anti-Catholicism and the more recent variety ought to be stressed.

> Nineteenth-century nativism expressed itself in the fear that unwashed immigrants, infected with Old World clericalism, could never become "real" or "integral" Americans and eventually would produce a demographic revolution swamping "American principles". Today anti-Catholicism involves less lurid, even less conscious assumptions, and rather obvious political motives. It is in part a manifestation of aggressive secularism, in part a vague contempt for old things, in part an expression of a timeless dilemma.[4]

One of the many letters to the editor of a similar article by Michael Novak, however, read: "We are founded as a Protestant nation. Despite its imperfections, the English system of government, coupled with Protestant values, assured a firm foundation for the democratic government we have today. Frankly, I would not want to live under any other system."[5]

The older blatant anti-Catholicism of the nineteenth and early twentieth centuries—my father in Iowa witnessed

[4] George F. Will, "Liberals' Very Own Bias", *Washington Post* (21 September 1978).
[5] Letter, *Washington Star* (11 October 1978).

crosses burnt on Catholic properties—seems obvious, in spite of such sentiments. Today, the bias tends more to concentrate on opposition to those Catholic views and values critical to liberal presuppositions. Catholics who appear to have no problems in the areas of abortion or medical experimentation or socialist-Marxist-type justice, are often rewarded with publicity and fame. The lead article in the *Washington Star* on the election of John Paul II, for example, the one analyzing its impact, was by Gary MacEoin who argued, without any irony or scruple, that the Polish Pope's experience with socialism would make him look on it with favor.[6] Again and again in the televised reports during the two conclaves, a "modernized" papacy was presented as one which would change the Church's doctrines on birth control. Catholicism, because of its internal divisions, thus appears most often as a house hopelessly divided. On any issue, enough Catholics can be found publicly to oppose classic Catholic doctrines, so that the wise politician concludes that Catholicism need not be taken seriously *politically*—Catholics will not vote as their public beliefs seem to suggest.

Moreover, the large foreign immigration still entering this country, the kind of immigration that caused much of the older bigotry, is made to appear as primarily ethnic, not religious. Indeed, a kind of retrospective process has been occuring in which one's race or nationality has become the chief criterion of identification. Religion, except perhaps in the case of the large Jewish immigration, has almost disappeared. All Americans today are given, on entering schools, universities, military service, government

[6] *Washington Star* (17 October 1978). Cf. the author's letter on the subject in the *Star* (28 October 1978).

employment, or other occupations, a list from which to select their ethnic classification for the state, a classification ostensibly designed to fight discrimination. These categories are: a) Caucasian, b) black, c) native American or Eskimo, d) Oriental, e) Spanish-surnamed, or f) other. The dangerous political implications of this highly dubious type of classification, let alone its scientific basis, are largely lost. But Portuguese, Italian, Asian, Indian, and other groups are beginning to understand that if jobs and benefits are apportioned according to the above list, they had better begin to have the categories expanded, or change their identity to conform to the list.

Catholics too, this time not as Irish, Italian, or Spanish, are beginning rightly to wonder if they get a proportionate share of jobs at all levels. Michael Novak wrote:

> By and large, Catholics have tried the ostrich tactic: Pretend that anti-Catholicism does not exist. Ignore the slander and the innuendo. Laugh along with the cruel jokes. Show one's own "liberalism" by joining the chorus deriding certain Catholic faults, errors and practices. Give no offense.
>
> But the double standard is still applied. Fifty percent (and more) of the population of Massachusetts is Catholic. Yet the university presidents, deans and faculties of the state universities in Massachusetts are not Catholic.[7]

Father Vergil Blum in Milwaukee has long argued that Catholics need to recognize the depth of the discrimination and its intellectual implications, to organize strictly, like the Jews and Mormons, against it. This needs to be both intellectual and political, with acquisition of information and political power.

[7] Michael Novak, *Washington Star* (23 September 1978). Cf. also D. Anderson, "Religious Bias in Jobs", *Los Angeles Times* (6 June 1979) 11.

Professor John Murray Cuddihy, in a recent book, *No Offense: Civil Religion and Protestant Taste*, has again wondered if there is not some intrinsic incompatibility between the great faiths, including Catholicism, and "modernity", something well treated by James Hitchcock in his *Catholicism and Modernity*. And this may be all quite true. A whole host of Catholic doctrines would define "modernity" in many of its presuppositions as quite wrong at one point or another. Indeed, if we grant some vague "modernity" the power to decide what is believable, then it becomes itself a kind of neo-orthodoxy, itself a norm against which religion supposedly gains its value, and not vice versa.

Professor Hitchcock patiently traced examples of anti-Catholic bias in the press, in the broadcast media, in the presidency of Mr. Carter.[8] He made the valid point that only Catholics have been required or expected to prove their "Americanism" before the electorate, to almost disavow any influence of their faith on their politics, in part the legacy of the Kennedy presidency. Furthermore, since so many decisions contrary to Catholic interests and beliefs have been coming from the courts in recent years, it would seem pertinent to remark that the one Catholic justice on the Supreme Court, William Brennan, has had perhaps the best record for decisions that go against things Catholics have believed important, a result we would never expect of Mr. Justice Thurgood Marshall on black issues for example, or any of the Jewish justices on Jewish issues. In a sense, Catholics have not been represented on the Supreme Court in recent years.

What is to be concluded from this awareness in the United States that a real, increasingly powerful streak of

[8] Hitchcock, op. cit., 43–8.

anti-Catholicism is coming to the surface? The first conclusion, perhaps, is the one that the *Wall Street Journal* saw
fit to describe regarding the lesson of the Polish Pope:

> As more people examine this [Polish success], we hope
> they'll notice a couple of things. First, the church has been able
> to maintain its voice in the face of Communist hostility only
> because the church in Poland holds its own power. Americans
> who care for the fate of human rights around the world might
> take note: It does no good to mouth pious expressions without
> taking some care to protect the power that can enforce it.
>
> Second, it might be useful to note where this church power
> comes from. It doesn't come from the ballot box, since the
> country has no free elections; and it certainly doesn't come
> from the force of arms. What it does come from is the attach-
> ment of a citizenry that has maintained its morale and its
> capacity to care for the values the church represents.[9]

There are still some who might hold that the Church is safe
insofar as there are members of it who uncritically hold
every idea and value of the surrounding society. But this, of
course, simply removes the distinctiveness of Christianity
as a means to preserve it.

Instead what seems to be the case is a growing sense
of the incompatibility between many things Catholic and
many things in the values and metaphysics of "modernity". Novak's rather frightening example is not an un-
common one: "Consider a Harvard friend of mine, with
whom I have for years been active in ecumenical work,
confiding politely over lunch at my house that, 'no personal offense intended, but the sooner the Catholic Church
disappears from the face of the Earth, the better.' She said it
as a matter of fact."[10] The major issue for Catholics, then,

[9] Editorial in the *Wall Street Journal* (18 October 1978).
[10] Novak, ibid.

remains what they will still believe and what they are willing to stand for as Catholics in the public order. St. Thomas Aquinas remarked in a famous passage that we cannot expect "heroic virtue" of the ordinary citizen, so that a public order more and more ruled against Catholic beliefs and values puts the normal Catholic in most difficult circumstances. The Polish example suggests that perhaps there are some limits to Thomas' principle, but this requires a tightly believing community.

The second thing that needs to be recognized is that anti-Catholicism is indeed a reality. The kind that is merely unfriendliness or ignorance is not so harmful, though it needs attention. But there are intellectual worldviews today that argue that the Roman Church is one of the major causes of disorder in the world and this *because* of what it holds. We do well to follow this carefully, and we need to be much better organized to meet it. On the other hand, Catholics have been taught that there would be not merely misunderstanding of their beliefs and practices in this world, but actual hatred for them. And they have been taught from Scripture that there are evils that ought to be hated.[11]

I believe that one of the great lessons of Catholicism in particular in the modern world has been that Catholics have in fact *suffered* real, objective, often virulent discrimination. They have not organized and reacted as other groups have done. And there are valid religious reasons for this.[12] Their weakness is their strength insofar as its lesson is perhaps the ultimate one of religion itself, that complete justice and

[11] See the author's chapter, "On Hatred", in *The Praise of 'Sons of Bitches': On the Worship of God by Fallen Men* (Slough, England: St. Paul, 1978).

[12] See Chapter 8 of the present work.

order and humanity are not the lot or even immediate hope of most men who actually live on this earth. Whatever the current enthusiasm in religious circles for promoting a better, even perfect, worldly order, Catholicism, if it means anything, must mean a religious body which suffers injustice differently. This, I believe, is both its record and its future. In this sense, the rising anti-Catholic bias in the United States challenges both the content of the faith *and* how it is lived in practice. Somehow, the drama of the world seems often to remain principally locked up in the hearts of believers, something I believe Augustine taught us better than others.

PART III

FOR DISTINCTIVE DOCTRINES

V

THE DISTINCTIVENESS OF CHRISTIANITY

"When the word 'orthodoxy' is used here," Chesterton wrote in 1908, in *Orthodoxy*, "it means the Apostles' Creed, as understood by everybody calling himself Christian until a very short time ago and the general historic conduct of those who held such a view." Dorothy Sayers wrote something quite similar:

> At this point, before he has time to sidetrack the argument and entangle us in irrelevancies, we shall do well to reply boldly that a faith is not primarily a "comfort", but a truth about ourselves. What we in fact believe is not necessarily the theory we most desire or admire. It is the thing which, consciously or unconsciously, we take for granted and act on. . . . Only when we know what we truly believe can we decide whether it is "comforting". If we are comforted by something we do not really believe, then we had better think again.
>
> Now, there does exist an official statement of Christian belief, and if we examine it with a genuine determination to discover what the words mean, we shall find that it is a very strange one. And whether, as Christians declare, man was made in the image of God or, as the cynic said, man has made God in the image of man, the conclusion is the same—namely, that this strange creed purports to tell us the essential facts, not only about God, but also about the true nature of man.[1]

Christianity, for all of the studies of comparative religion, is really not like anything else. How it is unlike, and why, are perhaps only dimly realized by most people,

[1] Dorothy Sayers, "What Do We Believe?" *Christian Letters to a Post-Christian World* (Grand Rapids, Michigan: Eerdmans, 1969) 27–28.

even Christians, today. But I suspect that this distinctiveness of Christianity is the most important thing we can know. The Creed is not a comfort but a truth, and the strange creed purports indeed to tell us the most significant things about God and ourselves.

Heresy—what is against something of the Creed or faith at a specific point—may well be one of the most neglected yet intellectually fascinating and stimulating areas of cultural study, the arena wherein the meaning and dignity of man are ultimately maintained or abolished. In recent times, heresy has been rapidly passing from social action, where it has largely been lodged during the past half-century or more, to Christology and the Trinity, the two areas that really distinguish the Christian faith.[2] Even *Time* magazine is beginning to be concerned about this.[3] No one conversant with the history of Christianity should be in the least surprised at this, except perhaps at its cultural tardiness. Monsignor Ronald Knox, in his *Enthusiasm*, had told us it would be mostly this way. Who is God? Who and what is Christ? These are now at the center of our concerns in a way they never have been in modern times. Undoubtedly the growing question of the meaning of Israel in secular and religious terms has something to do with the increased kind of attention the uniqueness of Christ is receiving. "The destiny of the Jewish people is the most mysterious of God's designs," Jean Daniélou wrote in his *The Salvation of the Nations*.[4] Our very politics are forcing the question in a new and unique way.

    [2] Cf. the intitial address of John Paul II to the Latin American Bishops (28 January 1979) *The Pope Speaks* 24, no. 1 (1979).

    [3] *Time* (27 February 1978).

    [4] Jean Daniélou, *The Salvation of the Nations* (Notre Dame, Ind.: University of Notre Dame Press, 1962) 87. See also Jacques Maritain,

Furthermore, such is the climate of opinion today that even such infallible secular sources as *Time* would like to know who is identifiably a Christian and who is not. Moreover, this is not a question of practice. "Sinners" in the history of the Church have usually been fundamentally orthodox. Indeed, sometimes they are the most orthodox. It is a perverse doctrine that would make a faith based on repentance exclude those who deviated from its norms. Our present problem is not whether or not we are sinners. This we admittedly are, for the most part, even so *de fide*. Rather the difficulty is that such things traditionally and clearly rejected as fundamentally at odds with the faith —homosexuality, for instance—are now either approved or considered potentially acceptable by ostensibly Christian thinkers. This serves to confuse and alienate those who chose to join or stay in the Church because of the stable truth it stood for in these matters. It was no wonder that even George Gallup found that Catholics, particularly the youth, "want the Church through its press to 'teach, guide and counsel them' and to reaffirm the Church's rich spiritual tradition."[5]

Thus, it seems, the witticism of Voltaire about the difference between the English and the French deserves considerable reflection in this connection. The French, the great skeptic mused, have one religion and three hundred and twenty different kinds of sauces for their food, while the English have only one kind of sauce but three hundred and twenty different kinds of religion. Yet, I suspect, the

---

"The Mystery of Israel", *The Social and Political Philosophy of Jacques Maritain* (London, 1956) 220–41. For an analysis of the meaning of Islam, cf. Charles Journet, "L'Islam", *Nova et Vetera* (April-June, 1967) 137–55.

[5] *Catholic Herald*, Arlington, Va. (9 March 1978).

real issue today lies deeper—the possibility that Christianity may not stand for anything unique at all, something, as we have seen in previous chapters, that modern socialist theories in particular seem to assume. This is what is at issue. This is the suspicion that makes current heresies of more than momentary interest.

The older method of distinguishing what is Christianity, the one wherein there was a central authority, one of whose basic tasks was to identify and, yes, to "condemn", to anathematize errors of faith, has apparently been paralyzed, some would say by self-doubt, others by ecumenism, still others by fear of the broadcast media. But I rather think it has been inoperative because of genuine good will. Thus, far from appearing as a rigid dogmatism, as the critics have charged, in my lifetime, at least, the Church has listened rather carefully to its critics and, to a surprisingly generous degree, refrained from any interference with sensitive issues, even when refraining resulted in confusion among the faithful. The argument has been well and, I think, justly made that if there has been any fault on the part of the authorities in the Church, it has been in allowing serious doctrinal confusions to plague the normal Christian because of hesitation to decide firmly about critical issues and truths. Noted Swiss theologians, to take a not wholly impossible example, have been far more dogmatic than what is left of the Roman curia. However, the presence of John Paul II probably indicates a considerable change in this atmosphere, for he seems a man capable of making clear decisions in precisely this area of doctrinal orthodoxy.

Nonetheless, here I am not especially interested in "heresy" in the strict dogmatic sense, but rather in that broader sense of an implied, well-articulated opinion moving in the public forum, one clearly contrary in spirit to the positions and values that make Christianity a distinctive creed in the cultural universe. There is perhaps some danger in using this broader manner of speaking. The formal, narrow, negative, legal system of defining heresy, often so uncritically chastized, was a method of liberty in historical practice. Yet, there are among us Pelagians and Manicheans, Gnostics and especially chiliasts who need to be identified and separated out if only to clear the air. I am not competent to conduct, nor at all desirous of conducting, an old-fashioned inquisition. That method's historical faults need not be justified. That is not the point. On the other hand, we do ourselves less than a favor if we simply accept the premise that ideas have no consequences and that there exist no ideas harmful to the faith and through it, to mankind.

The fact remains, however, that we should indeed be concerned about the broad confusion caused by the kinds of ideas in circulation claiming to represent what the faith is "really" about, when these popular presentations of the faith finally show themselves actually to be about some position the Christian tradition long ago felt contrary to the truth it stood for. In a sense, I want to be free enough to continue to believe in Christianity. This means that, whatever "the development of dogma" might mean, Christianity is not just anything. It cannot define itself into its opposite. There is an intellectual and historical continuity to its truth, if indeed it be true, as it claims. There is a valid sense to "freedom" in the Church, of course: the freedom to be itself. Frequently, in recent years, freedom has gained a kind of primacy over truth, particularly when cast in academic terms, such that freedom means the right to hold the opposite of what Christianity has believed and held. To be a Christian, however, means that there are some things that ought to be rejected whether they be freely held or not. Chesterton was perfectly right in his instinct: "He who wills to reject nothing, wills the destruction of will; for will is not only the choice of something, but the rejection of almost everything." To be a Christian and reject nothing is simply not to be a Christian.

In recent, widely publicized cases concerning Hans Küng, who always appealed to what he insisted to be the Christian truth, one is reminded a little of modernism, that little-loved aberration. For here we have a widely followed theologian who apparently felt that he was saving the Church from itself in the name of scholarship by not allowing himself to be condemned or by not publicly identifying himself with those sects which profess substantially what he actually holds. And there seems a large dose of the Jansenist problem in Küng: the question of whether the Church can understand what a theologian in fact maintains, even though the said theologian officially denies he has said or meant the essence of what is condemned or found problematic. All of this is connected with the effort to create a kind of second orthodoxy, defined mainly by the academic theologians, whose authority is conceived to be independent of and superior to the actual episcopacy because of a higher kind of reason or theological wisdom.

What I want to do here, however, is to ask another kind of question. Is there still a place within orthodox Christianity for those of us who still believe in the Creed as it has been classically understood? Is there only a kind of "social action in this world" Christianity left?[6] Thus, when I read a Küng or a Schoonenberg or a Sobrino, the subjects of *Time*'s wonderments, I am not particularly disposed to "argue" with them or confute them. I do have a kind of curiosity about why they would even want to stay in the orthodox Church or convert it to their views. Just what purpose it serves them to maintain that certain essential truths of Christianity have been misunderstood or wrong all along leaves me in some perplexity. In my more cynical moments, I am inclined to wonder if it is because they realize that if they admitted to all of us that they did not agree with the faith as taught, they would lose their main claim to public attention. A professed Catholic who pronounces, say, Buddhism as the "real" truth of Christianity, surfaces as an interesting oddity. One who holds the Nicene Creed is not, evidently. Yet, it is the latter who is orthodox.

Nevertheless, Ignatius of Loyola, even while giving us rules "for thinking with the Church", asked us to presume the best in others. This good advice reduces us to holding that such men, insofar as they differ with the tenets of the faith, do not really grasp its uniqueness and integrity, especially not its intrinsic freedom. But Ignatius was also the first to be concerned about the primacy of orthodoxy. "A man was meant to be doubtful about himself, but undoubting about the truth. . . ." These words, again of Chesterton, are clearly the right ones that ought also to govern the public discussions today. For the world wants to know if we Christians hold these newer doctrines or

[6] Cf. T. Fleming, "Divided Shepherds of a Restive Flock", *New York Times Magazine* (16 January 1977).

retain our connection to the classic creeds. Even Rudolf Augstein, editor of Germany's prestigious, *Time*-like *Der Spiegel*, complained that the Church does not teach what its theologians teach. And once we admit that we choose the newer views, I suspect the world will quietly walk away in the sure comfort of knowing that Christianity really did not teach anything radically "new", as it claimed historically. As a result, someone will again have to set out on the great project of Chesterton to try to discover sanity, only to find it is already there, in the Creed.[7]

My feelings about Jon Sobrino and the other Marxist-oriented theologians in shifting and shading and altering classic Christian dogmas and practices is fairly straightforward. Since they are such bad economists and refuse to see what really "develops", they presume that they must at all costs accept Marxism, almost for the same kind of reasons that other theologians think they must accept modern science. And to do this, certain basic Christian ideas must be altered. In his *On Synthesizing Marxism and Christianity*, Dale Vree has grasped that behind social philosophy today is found the prior and more important questions of heresy and orthodoxy. Unfortunately, what George Will said of the World Council of Churches' record in this area would apply to many Catholic proponents:

> This has been a bloody century not only because, as Yeats said, "the worst are full of passionate intensity," but also because some of the well-intentioned have been so useful to the worst. The record of the WCC is only in part a record of some people who are well-intentioned but breath-takingly silly. Some of the people involved are more sinister than silly,

[7] Cf. the author's "Catholicism and Intelligence", *Clergy Review* (London, July 1977).

and even those who are "only" silly are culpable. Always, but especially in the high-stakes business of politics, there is a moral obligation to be intelligent.[8]

Thus, the whole liberation movement, in spite of its growing dominance, betrays intellectually little more at times than a one-sided effort to convert Christianity into Marxist categories. Any two paragraphs from Solzhenitsyn, I suspect, are worth more in Christian terms than the whole corpus of liberation literature. In this sense, then, powerful as it is in many influential circles—so much so that we deal mainly with power and not intellect in dealing with it—liberation theology is of less interest theologically than other contemporary heresies, which do not have so many historical incarnations of their doctrines, according to which, as John XXIII once said, we must judge their actual performance. The contribution of many Christian theologians to furthering various Marxist forms of totalitarianism, often with the best of will, is not insignificant. That so many contemporary Christians can apparently no longer distinguish such practical heresy when they see it is itself one of the major causes of despair in the world today. In their search for God, men are being given the world, and this by Christians in the name of Christianity.

So, again, are we still permitted to believe in the Creed? Undoubtedly, it is very nice for a Hans Küng to insist with us that he is orthodox, while refusing clearly to tell us who this Jesus is, or at least, insisting that his Jesus is the one "really" revealed in Scripture. But let us suppose that

[8] George F. Will, "Foreword" to Ernest W. Lefever, *Amsterdam to Nairobi: The World Council of Churches and the Third World* (Washington, D.C.: Ethics and Public Policy Center, 1979) ix. See also the author's *Liberation Theology* (San Francisco: Ignatius Press, 1982).

Chalcedon is in truth "heretical" or irrelevant in its Christology. Then, do those of us who continue to follow the early Council need to form our own church, one adhering to the Creed as written and understood in Christian tradition? If this is what it takes to disassociate ourselves from Küng's Christ, then so be it, I suppose.

Yet, Küng's own persistence has had the effect of forcing some clarification. *Time* quoted Küng in this fashion—and I cite this source because I think the real damage and issue lie in precisely that kind of publicity:

> [Hans] Küng's own paraphrase of the dogmas: "God was present, at work, speaking, acting and definitely revealing himself" in Jesus. The ancient statements that the Son "preexisted" with the Father from eternity were meant merely to substantiate God's unique "call, offer, and claim made known in and with Jesus."[9]

On reading this, and here I am not much concerned with Küng but with the distinctiveness of historic Christianity, I had occasion to reread Pius XII's first encyclical, *Summi Pontificatus*, of 1939, along with the response of the German bishops to Küng. In a way, it was astonishing to come across these sources dealing with the same general subject from the viewpoint of Christian orthodoxy.

"The denial of the fundamentals of morality had its origin, in Europe, in the abandonment of that Christian teaching of which the Chair of Peter is the depository and exponent," Pius XII wrote in a manner in which even popes do not speak any more.

> That teaching had once given spiritual cohesion to a Europe which, educated, ennobled, and civilized by the Cross, had

[9] *Time*, ibid.

reached such a degree of civil progress as to become the teacher of other peoples, of other continents. But cut off from the infallible teachings of the Church, not a few separated brethren have gone so far as to overthrow the essential dogma of Christianity, the Divinity of the Savior, and have hastened thereby the progress of spiritual decay.[10]

When the German bishops came finally to speak of Küng, there was none of Pope Pacelli's bluntness. Yet, I think, they strikingly made the same point:

But he [Küng] does not present to the reader the complete Christ, nor his action in salvation in all its fullness. It is not enough to affirm generically one's faithfulness to the indispensable contents of the faith. The latter must be clearly expressed and explained in their content. . . .

But Jesus of Nazareth, if he is real man, is also real God. The two affirmations cannot be subjected to abbreviation, one cannot be reduced to the other, they are both necessary. Jesus, in fact, could not do what he does if he were not what he is: the eternal and uncreated Son of God, God like the Father, one substance with the Father, bound in the incarnation in personal unity with the man, Jesus.[11]

I have cited these statements from Küng, Pius XII, and the German bishops in succession both to argue that the latter two are the tradition and, likewise, represent the more romantic, exhilarating reality. The efforts to reduce the man Jesus to man only—classical Arianism—makes a dull world, more so than the one orthodox Christianity presents to us.

[10] Pius XII, *Summi Pontificatus*, no. 29.

[11] *L'Osservatore Romano*, English Edition (16 February 1978). See also Eric Mascall, *Theology and the Gospel of Christ* (London: SPRC, 1977).

One of the particular things behind the efforts to make Jesus only a man, of course, is that it enables us to absolutize each individual or collectivity in a way contrary to the classical Christian understanding of man. If any man—or woman—"could" have been chosen the Christ, could substantiate God's "call, offer, or claim", then we have the groundwork for a self-redemptive concept of the human race, something political philosophy has been desperately searching for in the modern era. Likewise, if some "collectivity" is what bears the redemptive suffering, some proletariat, some nation, then Jesus's unique suffering becomes irrelevant, a position argued in exactly these terms by Michael Harrington in his *The Vast Majority*. And not a few interpretations of the Jewish "holocaust" of the Nazi regime have such overtones. The distinctiveness of Christianity, however, is precisely that Jesus is true God and true man, that redemption is in obedience to him and to what he has revealed.

If the distinctiveness of Christianity is based upon the credal affirmation about Christ, it is also based upon the distinctiveness of the trinitarian God. The intellectual world today is more and more dominated by theories of justice. At first sight, this strikes us as welcome and unrelated to the Trinity. Utility and self-interest are out, justice in the fashion of John Rawls is in. Yet this is by no means a neutral question nor an abstract academic discussion. Indeed, partly as a result of the debates in Christology, justice has come to be a judgment on the kind of real world that does exist, the one in which redemption has taken place.[12] Dorothy Sayers put it in a marvelous fashion:

[12] Cf. the author's "Political Theory and the Death of Christ", *Worldview* (March 1978) 18–22.

Nevertheless, the law must be rightly understood or it is not possible to make the world understand the meaning of grace. There is only one real law—the law of the universe; it may be fulfilled either by way of judgment or by the way of grace, but it must be fulfilled one way or the other. If men will not understand the meaning of judgment, they will never come to understand the meaning of grace.[13]

The reduction of Christ to mere man theoretically enables us to propose another kind of world, while justice enables us to picture another kind of internal life of God, one that would not have made the kind of world that is.

There has been in Christian tradition an underground that was ill at ease with the Cross as a mode of redemption.[14] Ever since Augustine, however, Christians have believed that ultimate beatitude is not to be found in this world, but through Christ's redemptive death and Resurrection. Beginning at least with Joachim of Flora, it has been hoped by many that another way could be found, a salvation that rejected the actualities of this world and the manner of divine redemption. This has resulted in our time in proposals to reform the world in the explicit name of justice, a justice quite different from Christian speculations on the subject, a tradition that Rawls in his *Theory of Justice* completely—and logically, for his presuppositions—ignores.

In this connection, then, let me cite a striking passage from R. B. Fowler and J. R. Orenstein's *Contemporary Issues in Political Theory*, as a typical example of academic confusion:

Another difficulty exists in a key assumption of many who look to God and right reason for their standard of justice, a

[13] Dorothy Sayers, "Creed or Chaos?" *Christian Letters*, ibid., 45.
[14] Cf. F. Heer, *The Intellectual History of Europe* (London, 1953).

problem that is the most basic of all. They take it for granted that determining the proper norm and applying it in a contrary world are the greatest roadblocks they face, but in fact they must also justify their belief that God will inform us about justice. In fact, we may easily believe in God without being sure he provides us with a ready standard of justice. Because God is in his heaven does not at all mean that justice is there as well.[15]

This last sentence, I think, in a surprising way, is actually the case. Without denying its import, Christianity—and Judaism—has never held that "justice" is the governing virtue of God. His ways were not our ways. Justice was the virtue of the polis, perhaps, but for that very reason, God's law and activity were at a different, more penetrating level. The other side of the Cross, over against the insistence that man has his own self-redemptive burden, is that "because God is in his heaven [it] does not at all mean that 'justice' is there as well." The efforts to replace the classical characteristic of God as revealed, that characteristic which is beyond justice—what Christian theology has called the divine life, charity—with rationally analyzed justice, is precisely the central issue of our intellectual climate at its origins.[16] Christianity has distinctively held that God's will for our creation and redemption is based on a higher order which can only be grasped in faith and revelation. The Thomist tradition has held that this proper life of God, the spirit of which is revealed to us, is not contrary to reason, that is, to

[15] R. Fowler and J. Orenstein, *Contemporary Issues in Political Theory* (New York: John Wiley, 1977) 98.

[16] Cf. X. Dijon, "L'Eglise, peut-elle imposer sa morale à la société?" *Nouvelle Revue Théologique*, v. 99 (1977) 722–38.

the structure of creation,[17] itself originating in the same inner life of God. But to replace the norms of the world with mere justice is to deny the kind of world in fact given to us and the kind of redemption by the Cross that gives us our hope, if we have any hope.

One further element in the distinctiveness of Christianity in this connection should be stressed. Again, its urgency can generally be gathered from almost any casual reading of a typical modern intellectual. This brief excerpt from Lewis Lapham, editor of *Harper's*, concerning the churches, might serve:

> When man's mind functions as man's mind, that man comes into man's estate. He acquires the courage and freedom to paint pictures and work equations. Churches prevent this from taking place and say, in effect, Fear not, my son, man cannot help but behave like an ape.[18]

Again, this is a view attributed to Christianity that has been rejected by the credal faith. Lapham seemed unaware that this parody of Luther or perhaps Augustine is not orthodox. Nor did he seem aware of any problem connected with "man's estate", a problem thought about by Christians under the notion of original sin, and by rationalists, by believers in man's estate, under the rubric of utopia, some project to rid us of all our ills. One wonders, further, regarding painting pictures and working equations, just what Mr. Lapham did with Fra Angelico, Albertus Magnus, or Pascal, only to begin a list.

[17] The issue raised here is part of the contribution of Leo Strauss; cf. especially *The City and Man* (Chicago: University of Chicago Press, 1964).

[18] Lewis Lapham, "La Comédie Humaine", *Harper's* (March 1978) 9.

"Rational optimism leads to stagnation;" Chesterton said, "it is irrational optimism that leads to reform." It is still orthodox to believe that the only foundation for limiting the state is the doctrine that all men, including the rational elite, are sinners. Edmund Burke, I believe, has still made the best commentary on what results when men believe in the innate goodness of man's pure, abstract reason. Somehow, Mr. Lapham's "man's mind functioning as man's mind coming into man's estate" to me has hints of the Terror, as it did to Burke.

The effort to grant man's reason its due is as old as Aristotle and Aquinas. But our "estate" is not to be saved fundamentally by ourselves. This is the distinctive characteristic of Christianity, still more credible than any of the alternatives so far conceived by our kind. What is orthodox historically is not to oppose the churches to reason but to recognize them both. The unsolved, even maddening, challenge that Christianity gives to mankind is that our race cannot know or gain its ultimate beatitude—the possibility of which Christianity holds to be real for each of us—unless it be received as a gift, from a God whose relation to the world and to ourselves is one of his own freedom and inner life, made ours by his steadfast love, by his grace upon grace. All "heresy", if it might be put that way, is the lessening of the kind of God that is and the relation we have to him that the Creeds assign to us. Self-redemption by a law we give to ourselves, a reason that has nothing higher than itself, this is the liberalizing project that ends up by lessening even our humanity.

To conclude, one last thought from Chesterton is worth attention:

If the Church had not renounced the Manicheans it might have become merely Manichean. If it had not renounced the Gnostics it might have become Gnostic. But by the very fact that it did renounce them it proved it was neither Gnostic nor Manichean. . . . [A]nd what could it be that condemned them if not the original good news of the rumours from Bethlehem and the trumpets of the Resurrection?[19]

Ever since Paul of Tarsus told us our faith would be in vain if Christ be not risen, the doctrine of the Resurrection of Jesus has stood as a pledge for all men, the paradox that there is hope when there is no hope.[20]

Not too long ago, the *Los Angeles Times* published a lengthy article under the headline: "Vast Gap in Doctrine: 'Did Jesus Rise Bodily?' Most Scholars Say No." Writer John Dart went on to recount:

For instance, at the nine-school Catholic and Protestant Graduate Theological Union in Berkeley, New Testament Professor Edward Hobbes said he didn't know of one school there in which a significant part of the faculty would accept statements that Jesus rose physically from the dead or that Jesus was a divine being.[21]

Taking this as some sign of the trend of too much theological teaching and not so much of the accuracy of the particular instance described, clearly the issue of the distinctiveness of Christianity lies here. If it is "liberalizing" to deny Jesus' divinity or his Resurrection, as it seems to be

[19] G. K. Chesterton, *The Everlasting Man* (New York: Dodd, Mead, 1946) 277.

[20] See the discussion on the Resurrection in the author's *Redeeming the Time* (New York: Sheed, 1968).

[21] John Dart, *Los Angeles Times* (5 September 1977).

considered, we should also recognize how despairing the result of this denial is to the men and women who do exist, persons who are now told by Christian scholars that evidently their ultimate, personal beatitude in life with the trinitarian God is not possible, that Scripture has meant something else. The faith of the Creed, of the Church, still denies such despair.

The distinctiveness of Christianity lies in the fact that what we believe about it cannot properly be "believed". There is no "justice" in the heavens; the political philosophers were unwittingly correct. There is so much more. Our efforts to defy God by creating a merely just world, as our academics are zealously projecting, can only end up by giving us justice alone. This cuts us off from the real adventure. And if we read the Creed again, we shall not doubt that Christianity, while not disdaining justice, is about something other, the rumours of Bethlehem and the trumpet of the Resurrection.

"When man's mind functions as man's mind, that man comes into man's estate." To this, Christianity still recalls to us, simply, in the words of Bach's lovely Chorale near the end of his *Passion according to St. John*, these prayerful truths:

> Mein teurer Heiland, lass dich fragen:
> > Jesu, der du warest tod,
> da du nunmehr an's Kreuz geschlagen
> > lebst nun ohn' Ende,
> und selbst gesaget: es ist vollbracht!
> bin ich vom Sterben frei gemacht?
> > in der letzten Todesnot
> > nirgend mich hinwende. . . .

Dear Savior, tell me,
  Jesus, since you died once,
since you are on the Cross
  and now live forever,
and yourself have said: it is
  fulfilled!
am I made free from death?
  in my last anguish
  turn not from me.

I heard this Chorale on Passion Sunday at the National Presbyterian Center in Washington. And ultimately, as I listened, what was distinctive about Christianity again became clear, for we are to pass from dogma to prayer and through prayer to the Son on the Cross, the Son who is from all eternity. This alone is where our estate finally is.

When the word *orthodoxy* is used, then, it still means the Apostles' Creed.

VI

THE CHRISTIAN AND THE HUMAN LOT

The distinctiveness of Christianity includes not only a unique God but also, as it were, a unique earth. The uniqueness of the latter, of course, depends on the former. This means, in essence, that there is a reality present in history, in our lives, that cannot be contained by merely scientific categories. Perhaps something of this notion can be better understood by recalling something from *Don Quixote*, that inexhaustible Christian source:

> Happy times and fortunate ages were those which our ancestors called *Golden*, not because gold, so prized in this our Iron Age, was gotten in that happy time without any labour, but because those who lived then knew not those two words, *Thine* and *Mine*. . . . Justice was then contained within her proper bounds; she was untroubled and unbiased by favour and self-interest, which today so belittle, disturb and persecute her. . . .
>
> But now, in this *detestable* age of ours, no damsel is safe, even though she were hidden and shut up in some new labyrinth like that of Crete. . . . Therefore, as time went on and wickedness increased, the order of knight-errancy was instituted to defend maidens, to protect widows, and to rescue orphans and distressed persons. I belong to this order, Brother Goatherds. . . .[1]

This was written in 1605, when it was still known that there was no authentic Christian intelligence without a touch of humor.

[1] Miguel de Cervantes, *Don Quixote*, Part I, Ch. 8.

One cold February day, just after I had first arrived in Washington from San Francisco, I was walking through Dupont Circle, said to contain the highest concentration of traffic lights in creation, down Connecticut Avenue towards 18th Street. At one of those impossible seven-angled intersections which only this nation's capital, French and Deist influenced as it is, could possibly call "rational", a sign high up on a flat-iron shaped building facing the White House, was unaccountably flashing numbers. On second glance, I realized the numbers purported to be representing the ever-changing world population. The automatically increasing sum, which I did not have a pencil to copy down exactly, was well over four billion, the title of a book I had at the time just written.[2] Something like one hundred seventy-two people were said to be added every minute or every second, I forget which. Besides this, nothing else appeared on the sign.

As I reflected on this not-so-delicate propaganda, sponsored evidently by no one at all, I tried to filter out in my mind just what the message was intended to convey. Obviously, this was not, though it might have been, a joyous announcement of delight that we have on this planet vigorous new members every second whom we gladly welcome, that we are "progressing", as the nineteenth century piously thought, towards a more glorious, superstition-free future, that we are gaining new riches through new brains and talents, the only real source of wealth in the physical universe anyhow. Yet there are few optimists alive and well among us any more. Rather, here was clearly a Doomsday Plaque, a dire warning that we

---

[2] James V. Schall, *Welcome Number 4,000,000,000* (New York: Alba Books, 1977).

are our own greatest threats, that this green earth is tiny, fragile, whereas the rapidly clicking figures are unyielding, ineluctable.

And so, behind the sign was an implicit philosophical conception of man and his relation to this planet, a philosophy, as it has rapidly and unnecessarily evolved, mostly at direct odds with the classic Christian views about man's personal dignity and how he is to conduct himself in confronting the problems he does have. The computerlike increment, based on scheduled, not actual, statistics, insisted subtly that man must radically change in his structure before this on-going, ever-pressing fate that is himself. Indeed, I sometimes rather think that, ultimately, this population-based pessimism was itself invented precisely to avoid the truth of Christianity, the truth that the world does have a higher law and vision not made by man, the observation of which is alone what can save and develop him.

In the last retrospective essay he wrote in the *Rambler*, on Saturday, March 14, 1752, Samuel Johnson wrote: "The essays professedly serious, if I have been able to execute my own intentions, will be found exactly conformable to the precepts of Christianity. . . ." Johnson simply presupposed that there were such precepts, that they were knowable, that they were true. Here the question of the Christian view of man needs to be addressed. And here the intention, if it can be well executed, will likewise be to remain exactly conformable to the precepts of Christianity. To state it that way, however, sounds distinctly odd, I think. In part, the reason for this is that modern public opinion has an instinct for publicizing mostly those versions of Christianity and its thought that do not substantially conform to what Christianity has professedly held —or as Malcolm Muggeridge once quaintly put it, "There is no element of the Creed that has not been recently denied by some bishop." In part, it is also because anything clearly conformable to the precepts of Christianity appears stodgy and even dull, the ultimate contemporary sin. I put it this way because my own rather chaotic experience seems to contrast so much with what enthuses others. The only thing that I have never found dull is orthodox Christianity, whereas the slightly unorthodox versions of the faith that catch the public eye seem deliberately designed to scale down Christianity to the dimensions of what everyone else believes. And this is a kind of conformity, dullness, even hopelessness.[3]

Yet, when I think of the Christian view of man, I feel that the issue is doubly prejudiced somehow against what Christianity has to say about our lot, our condition.[4] I am somewhat in the predicament of Chesterton in *The Everlasting Man*, when he humorously remarked of a certain Grant Allen, who published a book on his views of God, that he would much prefer to hear God's views on Grant Allen. We have become, as George Rutler recently

[3] "Official Christianity, of late years, has been having what is known as 'a bad press'. We are constantly assured that the churches are empty because preachers insist too much upon doctrine—'dull dogma', as people put it. The fact is the precise opposite. It is the neglect of dogma that makes for dullness. The Christian faith is the most exciting drama that ever staggered the imagination of man—and the dogma *is* the drama." Dorothy Sayers, "The Greatest Drama Ever Staged" in *Christian Letters to a Post-Christian World* (Grand Rapids, Michigan: Eerdmans, 1969) 13.

[4] Eric Mascall, *The Christian Universe* (New York: Morehouse-Barlow, 1966.)

noted, "frighteningly patronizing to the divine Pater."
And as an example, the Anglican theologian cannily re-
membered that ". . . in his Jubilee Sermon before the
Queen, Dr. Coggan [the then Archbishop of Canterbury]
felt moved to remark, 'How right he was!' after quoting
God."[5] What individual Christians might think of man and
God is significant, to be sure. And ours is an incarnational
faith. But my impression is that Christians today have
largely confused themselves, and more especially the observing world, by constantly concentrating on man, touching on God only when he meets the approval of their social
or political outlooks.

Subtly, unwittingly, then, I fear our contemporaries are
beginning to hear from Christians themselves that their
religion is primarily a theory about man, a theory that
makes considerable effort to sound just like other fashionable theories about man. Classical Thomism, to be sure,
itself made great efforts to accept what reason proved.
Nevertheless, it did not judge faith by reason but reason by
faith. The principle of contradiction was not designed to
eliminate anything distinctive in Christianity, but rather to
show the unity of faith and reason, creation and redemption.

The Italian Marxist philosopher Antonio Gramsci is said
to have remarked that when the Church makes social life
(what it thinks about man, in other words) its most important interest, it will lose the intellectuals, for they will then
go Marxist or some other more effective way to get things
done. Gramsci's only mistake was in thinking Marxism
was an effective way of getting something done, especially
world improvement. He was right, however, in thinking

[5] George Rutler, *New Oxford Review* (17 February 1978).

that Christianity cannot present itself as primarily a social philosophy.

Thus, contrary to much current theological fashion, I doubt if the problem of God is first one of man, that "theology is anthropology". Though academically I come from a social science tradition, which I think has a legitimate though limited place in Christian thought, I believe that the recent conversion of many segments of theology and Church life to what is called "faith and justice", to social and political activism, has itself become for many the major reason for doubt and atheism. And further, I suspect, the particular form of this conversion, one no longer based on the traditional Christian neutrality to the forms of government, will prove largely responsible for the Christian's incapacity to meet the real human problems that do exist, those wherein we might reasonably expect some amelioration. The next Rolf Hochhuth is undoubtedly at work charting in obscure publications how Christians are failing to do what they can do because of an ideological enthusiasm that presumes, as R. H. Tawney once remarked, "it can establish the kingdom of God on earth."

A recent in-house Jesuit series of accounts on the causes of atheism seemed to accept almost as self-evident that modern disbelief is caused mainly, if not exclusively, by "injustice". Faith becomes a kind of reward for good works. Aquinas and Leo XIII, following him, no doubt did accept the idea that man's physical well-being was necessary for a healthy faith for most people. But, I assume, it never occurred to them that their doctrine, based on the unity of nature and grace, would come to be used as a justification for the ideologies of this world. God will not be reached primarily through justice, I think. In fact, it is my considered opinion that the current theoretical interest in justice is a judgment on the kind of God who made a world in which justice is not the primary feature. And this is precisely why such theories, refreshing on the surface, are so potentially disruptive to any civil order that is composed of actual men and women.

Consequently, when we set out to discover God, only to find contemporary theology, liturgy, and spirituality mainly speaking about man under this-worldly forms and structures, we are in fact betraying religion itself. Today, I think I would turn Aquinas' doctrine around to argue that atheism, in the sense of disbelief in the Christian trinitarian God, is caused primarily by identifying religion with what is to be done for man. The Scripture priority of seeking first the kingdom of God, and its relation to the other things we might need, still strikes me as fundamental. And this makes it doubly ironic to find the kingdom of God more and more identified as a worldly enterprise.

We should do much for man, of course, and there are Christian motivations so to do. Yet, I for one find myself tending more and more to atheism to the degree that Christianity presents itself to the world as a project of faith and justice in this world. I have meditated too long on Augustine ever to believe that such is the place wherein our hearts can rest. "It is very important," Jean Daniélou wrote in *The Salvation of the Nations*,

> that our missionary spirituality should be centered, first of all, in God. In our time, spirituality is often too anthropocentric, oriented too much toward the good of humanity as such. This degrades its most essential religious content, and it ends up by being an extension of humanism.[6]

[6] Jean Daniélou, *The Salvation of the Nations* (Notre Dame, Ind.: University of Notre Dame Press, 1962) 111–12.

Very seldom any more in social questions propounded by Christians, except in things coming from the papacy, which may be why it is so criticized, do I encounter much more than humanism in the claims of what the Gospel means for the destiny of man.

Of all the men and women who have ever lived on this planet—some ninety billion they say—none has ever lived in a perfectly just society, nor, I should judge, in even a reasonably just one. When we make faith contingent on justice, even worse when we intimate on religious grounds that we shall reach it soon, I feel we also admit logically that religion has really nothing to say to the actual people who have in fact already lived on this earth. There is a kind of other-worldliness, or better, future-worldliness in our current religion that I sense to be unchristian because it confuses the promise of personal resurrection, which might give meaning to every and any human life in any age, or any society, worst or best, with some worldly, collective, messianic kingdom, tomorrow or down the ages, some future Golden Age that promises deliverance from the detestable present.

Man "seems to exist for something which he can never attain," J. M. Bochenski wrote. And to this belief, since Plato, some three answers have been posed:

> The first . . . consists in the assertion that man's longing for the infinite can be satisfied by identifying himself with something broader, particularly with society. It is irrelevant, the philosophers say, that I must suffer, must founder, and must die; mankind, the universe will go on. . . . Most contemporary thinkers hold [this] to be untenable; for, instead of solving the puzzle, this solution denies the given, namely, the fact that the individual man desires the infinite for himself, as an individual, and not for anything else. . . .

The second solution ... maintains [that] ... man has absolutely no meaning at all. He is a mistake, a creature that has turned out wrong. ...

... According to [the philosophers], there must be a solution to the puzzle of man. But what could this solution consist in? Only in the belief that man can somehow reach the infinite. He cannot, however, do it in this life. ... But how? ... Plato once said that the final answer to this question could be given to us only by God. ...[7]

Ultimately, then, human lives cannot be justified by some projected good society down the ages. And the clicking sign of human numbers I saw on the Washington wall is indeed despair for the individuals represented if they themselves be the problem. "My kingdom is not of this world," in some basic sense, must not be denied in the kind of practical faith each person must live. When it is denied, I think there are quite legitimate grounds for despair and despotism.

On these grounds, then, I would hold that there is a connection between the efforts to change men radically —the proposal lying behind the population sign—and the popularization within the churches of ideas contrary to the central tradition of orthodoxy. The despair results from a Christianity that apparently teaches mainly this world, that does not in practice allow us the daily bread that alone men live by. This permits us to experiment socially and biologically with the kind of men we theologically are, the kind we are given if the Law and the Prophets, the Ten Commandments, the natural law, and the greatest of the commandments, mean anything at all.

The first element of a Christian view of man, then, is

[7] J. M. Bochenski, *Philosophy—an Introduction* (New York: Harper Torchbooks, 1972) 81–82.

the insistence that God is God, that the first effect of the Incarnation is *not* to substitute man for the collectivity or corporateness of man in history. Rather, it is to lead us in whatever life we are given, whatever society we are in, back to him who alone is our joy and destiny. This is why, I think, the reading and rereading of the first questions of the *Prima Secundae* of Aquinas remains the basic intellectual lesson we can start or end with. Any compromising on this trinitarian destiny is, I think, fundamentally unchristian and should not be allowed to deflect us from seeing that this is the case. The first mission of intelligence that Christians owe to the rest of mankind is that of passing on, intact, who the Father is, who the Son, who the Spirit. Anything less may, indeed, be more "believable", except that, ultimately, anything less is not what we are commissioned to maintain.

We are, then, first God-people, and our talk is first God-talk. Like the ancient Hebrews, we were not chosen because we were the best and the brightest. Indeed, and this is the second aspect of Christian tradition that constantly needs to be recalled, we are a fallen race, all of us. Everyone has probably heard the statement attributed at times to Newman, at other times to Chesterton, that original sin is the one Christian doctrine that does not need faith, that all we need to do is to go out in the streets and open our eyes. Presumably, even this is not enough, or else the streets are filled with the blind and the closed-eyed. Moreover, we have the famous witticism of de Mandeville, that our vices are the causes of our prosperity, that without tipplers and boozers to demand good, plentiful wine and gourmands to order delicate pastries, our world would be a sorry place—and broke.

The feeling that there is something wildly wrong with

our lot is, in a way, a commonplace today. This is what connects the notion that our meaning is to build a perfect worldly society with the attack on Christianity. Indeed, we have in practice gone a long way in identifying intrinsic evil with the physical destruction of humanity, something that traditional Christian sources never did. The notion of original sin has appeared in several secular forms recently, over and beyond its Marxist formulation in the capitalist classes. Most obviously it has appeared in the ecology field wherein human nature is pictured to be the cause of our ills and doom. In one of Woody Allen's films, *Love or Death*, I think, Allen remarked on the widespread feeling that the human race is guilty of a crime it did not commit, again a subtle attack on the kind of beings we in fact are created to be. Classical theologians, in this context, long wrestled with the idea that the original fault was not personal to us, yet that it belongs to each of us, that somehow the guilt does become personally ours, that its removal is possible, but not through our own agency.

"What causes the sudden self-hatred of modern peoples?" Michael Novak asked in one of his columns.

> Why do so many who stand on the shoulders of giants and who benefit at every moment from the slow and incomplete domestication of nature, look in the mirror with loathing?
>
> The human animal is far from being angelic, saintly, Franciscan, even wholly rational. Our sins are many. But perhaps it is especially in the ranks of those who were taught the proprieties of human perfectibility . . . that the recent spasms of self-hatred occur. This may be a contemporary version of sinfulness. . . .

Some years ago in his *Church and Liberal Society*, Emmet John Hughes, recalling the Enlightenment origins of per-

fectibility, also elaborated the consequences of denying
original sin. "Having effectively denied the Christian conception of original sin and the concomitant doctrine of
man's corruption and fallibility," he wrote,

> the Liberal could defend representative government only by
> his assertion of the virtual infallibility of the individual. It was
> in virtue of exactly the opposite doctrine that Christian social
> thought measured and denounced political tyranny—the falli-
> bility of all men, and, consequently, the necessity of circum-
> scribing the political authority of society's leaders.[8]

The net effect of such reflections is, I think, simply this: If
we do not have an orthodox view of original sin and what it
implies about the human condition, we will live with an
unorthodox one. And if we have an unorthodox view of
original sin, we will no longer be able to admit to ourselves
how, at the same time, there can be the Christian God and
our own perilous state, a state of fallenness that we can deny
only at our peril.

Samuel Johnson, again, put it all at its Christian best, in
the *Advocate*, on June 26, 1753: "Happiness is enjoyed only
in proportion as it is known: and such is the state of
our folly, that it is known only by the experience of
its contrary. . . ." And so we are to acknowledge both
Golden and Detestable Ages. And if we choose to avoid
congratulating God for being God because we blame him
for our fallen state, still the notion of original sin in Christianity allows us to accept that something is really quite
wrong even while denying that this disturbance in our
being, on that account at least, prevents us from acknowl-

---

[8] Emmet John Hughes, *The Church and Liberal Society* (Notre Dame,
Ind.: University of Notre Dame Press, 1944) 245.

edging a real salvation directed to and embracing ourselves as we are.

Nevertheless, in spite of sin and disorder, there is inescapably some feeling in the human race that we can reform the world to some extent. In a little known encyclical he wrote in 1932, precisely to insist on the spiritual means of social reform, the too little appreciated Pius XI wrote:

> For the unquenchable aspiration to reach a *suitable* state of happiness even on earth is planted in the heart of man by the Creator of all things, and Christianity has always recognized and ardently promoted every just effort of true culture and social progress for the perfection and development of mankind.[9]

The sign of authentic Christian thought, then, is always contained in the adjective "suitable"—the world can be improved, but this is not all we have, not our home.

In this context, then, men like Carl Sagan and John Hick have been asking what is the meaning of the cosmos itself in relation to our kind, a question whose roots go back to C. S. Lewis, if not to Galileo and Genesis itself. The recent spate of space films should not be taken overly seriously, to be sure. Yet, *Star Wars* and *Close Encounters of the Third Kind* and *Alien* do bring up the question of our relation beyond the planet, of whether a hostile or benign principle exists beyond us, assuming, of course, that we are not alone in the universe, which latter seems quite likely.

The English graphic artist, Roger Dean, produces space scenes that are marvelously modified by some intelligent sign or purpose. Much of his work appears on record

[9] Pius XI, *Caritate Christi* (13 May 1932).

album covers, symbolic of the relation of space and music, something in a way found in Plato. In a book devoted to him, his particular vision is defined in this fashion:

> For Roger Dean, the meandering yet purposeful courses traced by pathways trodden by successive generations bespeak the mark of man in sympathy with his environment. Following them, we are impressed by their "rightness", apt as they are to the placing of water and earth, rock and tree, and also to our own mental processes. For Dean, they symbolize a feeling, which though we may not recognize it, we are as yet unable to sustain: *the sense that we do know how to live in the world, that we are at home here.* [10]

This, of course, is a description of the Garden of Eden, of the Golden Age. And if we recall that for Chesterton in *Orthodoxy*, the fundamental Christian experience of the actual redemptive situation we are in is a feeling of homesickness even at home, we shall see that any notion of making our home here partakes of utopianism, of a kind we do not possess or even want. It is ultimately a vision less than the one of the trinitarian God, the one actually promised to this race of men.

Yet, the world is "for" something, and we may well be alone in the universe, as some scientists are now reluctantly admitting, contrary to earlier assumptions. Professor Robert Jastrow, in his *Until the Sun Dies*, argued:

> In science, as in the Bible, the world begins with an act of creation. That view has not been always held by scientists. Only as a result of the most recent discoveries can we say with a fair degree of confidence that the world has not existed

[10] Introduction to Roger Dean's *Views* (London: Big "O" Publishers, 1977) 77.

forever; that it began abruptly, without apparent cause, in a
blinding event that defies scientific explanation.[11]

And further, the notion that life on earth can be fully
explained by chemical changes seems more and more dubious, an article of scientific faith without real proof.

Thus, in this context, I am rather of the opinion that
space is in fact the answer to most of the problems which
the energy and population pessimists think insoluble. This
premise of insoluble problems is often that which allows
the pessimists to tamper with human value and nature
itself. Space is not the solution to original sin, however. In
this space films are probably correct: The problem of moral
evil exists everywhere in the universe. But the human brain
is fully capable of handling the problems we do have,
provided it be not sidetracked into spurious channels. This
is why orthodoxy is, at bottom, absolutely necessary to
science. Indeed, it is my suspicion that orthodoxy is the
only thing that can save science from the enthusiasms and
the pessimisms, largely because this-worldly eschatologies
and apocalypses will otherwise set themselves up as arbiters
of the truth of science.[12]

To conclude, then, I should like to recall here the passage
from *Don Quixote*, the one with which I began this chapter,
about the Golden and Detestable Ages, about the order
of knight-errancy founded to defend maidens, to protect
widows, and to rescue orphans and distressed persons. This
is still the classical Christian tradition about the human lot,
one that wants to save us, not change our being as ill-

[11] Robert Jastrow, *Until the Sun Dies* (New York: W. W. Norton,
1977) 19, 52.

[12] See the author's "Apocalypse as a Secular Enterprise", *Scottish
Journal of Theology* 29, no. 4 (1976) 357–73.

created by the Deity, one that acknowledges that the best and the worst are both parts of our destiny, that what we can do, we do, remembering those who are distressed in this world.

If with Samuel Johnson, then, we, as men and women devoted in some sense to the contemplative life as part of our very Christian vocation, strive to remain conformable to the precepts of Christianity, we shall, I think, experience the only freedom that counts. That is the freedom of choosing the kind of redemption we were actually given. And this is the redemption of Christ, the redemption from both the Golden and Detestable Ages, because our first gift, and gift it metaphysically is, is not of ourselves or even of our world, but of our God, the Creator of Heaven and Earth, the trinitarian God, the one we Christians suspect, following the lead of Plato, has given us his infinity.

VII

TRINITARIAN TRANSCENDENCE
IN IGNATIAN SPIRITUALITY

The Christian God is trinitarian, not three gods, not the monolithic God of Islam. But Father, Son, and Spirit, all three are stressed in the creeds of Christianity. St. Ambrose wrote in his Treatise on the Mysteries:

> Remember what you said: I believe in the Father and the Son and the Holy Spirit. Not: I believe in a greater, a lesser and a least. You are committed by this spoken understanding of yours to believe the same of the Son as of the Father, and the same of the Holy Spirit as of the Son, with this one exception: you proclaim that you must believe in the Cross of the Lord Jesus.

Frank Sheed used to emphasize that his single most popular lecture, the one to which the varied audience on Hyde Park Corner in London always paid careful attention, was the one on the Trinity. Karl Rahner, on the other hand, noted in *Sacramentum Mundi* that "The doctrine of the Trinity, in spite of its being extolled as the fundamental mystery of Christianity, plays a very modest role, if it occurs at all, in the actual life of Christians and in the teaching which they hear."[1]

Perhaps, because of the importance of the Trinity in Christian doctrine, it is worthwhile to take a look at the way this triune reality of God has appeared in Christian. spiritual life. For this, Ignatius of Loyola might serve as the

---

[1] Karl Rahner, *Sacramentum Mundi* 6, 304.

best introduction if we wish to have some feeling for the meaning of the Trinity in the life of the Christian. If we look carefully at the Manresa experience of Ignatius, his initial mystical experience, as well as at the sense of the *Spiritual Exercises* which he put together, we cannot fail to notice, I think, the trinitarian background contained in them. The Meditation on the Incarnation and the Contemplation for Obtaining Divine Love, key parts of the *Exercises*, are trinitarian in their essence. Moreover, many of the presuppositions Ignatius made about Preludes and Compositions of Place to aid us to pray were in fact related to ideas of Word and Spirit that find their ultimate justification in the Trinity.

What I primarily wish to suggest here is that the very reality of the transcendence of God, understood in its Christian and trinitarian sense, is the main truth and life with which Ignatian spirituality in particular and all Christian spirituality in general concerns itself. It is again the Christian insistence that there is nothing other than God for which we exist, that all deviation from Christian truth consists in suggesting that some other good of our own, or some other finite making can satisfy us in a redemptive sequence that was not set forth by the program of revelation. Thus, I wish to make this point, as it were, against a dominant mood which would strive to locate as much as possible, if not exclusively, the object of contemplation and spirituality within the world, either in the world itself or in the operations of God "*ad extra*".

To approach this subject, I should like to begin with some reflections on certain specifically Jesuit traditions and myths about them in order that the basic truths for all Christians might be clearer. Historically, then, Jesuits have frequently been accused of two rather contrary, if not contradictory, tendencies. The first and least subtle is that Jesuits were too worldly, too wily. In contrast to the older religious orders like the Benedictines or the Franciscans, then, Jesuits were to be more mobile, unsettled, restless even. They seemed to stress action rather than being. They were not fixed in a particular kind of work but were to keep themselves free in regard to place, subject-matter of effort, and time. They were the first true "liberals", as their casuistic moral theories proved. That Jesuits were experts in the most esoteric disciplines and arts was, consequently, to be expected. They were not tied down by dress or culture. They were, in fact, genuinely supposed to like the things of this world, even when they gave them up. Enthusiasm for created reality was the proud mark of the order. Thus, Jesuits in Spain were among the first to realize in economics the productive value of interest. They even had something to do with the origins of the ballet. To their critics, this was mainly dilettantism; to their friends, it was marvelous vision.

On the other hand, this worldly orientation constantly surprised or disappointed because it seemed not to be "sincere".[2] The Jesuits did not seem overly interested in the world at all. They were often said to "use" any means and to justify them by their "ends", worldly or otherwise. Their very name became an adjective of opprobrium. They were subsequently identified with power, even with intrigue, as with Anthony Passavino. This meant that all things on the face of the earth, as Ignatius put it, were to be

[2] See the author's chapter on sincerity, "The Most Dangerous Virtue", in *The Praise of 'Sons of Bitches': On the Worship of God by Fallen Men* (Slough, England: St. Paul, 1978).

used "for" something. Jesuits became the great pragmatists. As it turned out, the value of anything seemed to evaporate in their hands. Worldly folk were disappointed to discover that behind the famous Jesuit concern for this world was a prior commitment to God. The Principle and Foundation of the *Exercises* had taught Jesuits somehow to relativize absolutely everything. The principle read: "Man is created to praise, reverence, and serve God, and by this means to save his soul. And the rest of the things on the face of the earth are created for man to assist him in the pursuit of his end, that for which he was created." Thus, the Jesuit was never actually content with the world, however immediately interested in it he might be. Hence, he came to be pictured by his enemies as tricky and crafty. His image was overshadowed by deceit and shady dealings.

To those who did not believe in a spiritual reality within the cosmos or over it, one operating directly on man through the things that do appear, as Paul put it, the only explanation for this "jesuitical" conduct was power or influence. Juan de Mariana came to be seen as one of the founders of the modern nation-state power theory, of national self-interest. And too, there were unworthy Jesuits, no doubt. As a group, the order never doubted original sin to be a part of the make-up of its own members. The *Spiritual Exercises* in their First Week, indeed, were quite explicit on this point. The very structure of the order, like all religious orders, was Platonic enough to be mindful of the Guardians, who denied themselves family and property to achieve greater devotion to the Good and to the Community through it.[3] The Jesuits, then, were not accused so much of being too rich or too corpulant, but of the spiritual

[3] See Chapter 12 of the present work.

vices, of ambition and power, as if they were above the ordinary run of men, which they were not, of course. Early in its career, the Society of Jesus concentrated upon education and missionary efforts. *Verbum et Spiritum*, Word and Spirit. The Society of Jesus never produced an Augustine nor an Aquinas. But it was at the heart of more than one university system and produced numerous first-rate scholars and thinkers, the most distinguished of whom was probably Suarez, whom no one reads anymore. Furthermore, members of the order were among the first in the modern era to address themselves to the relation of diverse or primitive cultures to Christianity. The Chinese experience of Ricci and Schall, the Paraguayan Reductions, are still pondered as original and highly justified initiatives, even though they both failed. Marquette and Kino and Peter Claver and John de Britto were more than explorers and adventurers. "Ever since the dispatches from China of the first Jesuits there, in the seventeenth century, had startled Europe," J. M. Cameron recently wrote,

> ever since the great Jesuit Nobili had sought to become a Brahmin and enter Hindu society, confidence in the identification of European with human civilization had been shaken. . . . It is possible to see the defeat of the Jesuits on the question of the Chinese Rites, and the defeat of those Jesuits who wanted to root Christianity in Hindu culture, as great blunders of history. Had they been avoided it seems possible, though of course not likely, that the history of the world would have taken a different turn.[4]

Jesuits were, thus, directly involved in the central issue of the universality of Christianity to all men in all conditions,

[4] J. M. Cameron, *On the Idea of a University* (Toronto: University of Toronto Press, 1978) 21–22.

even the worst. It is said, moreover, that Rousseau himself learned of the "noble savage" from reading the letters of the French Jesuits in North America, a lesson perhaps ill-learned in the light of the subsequent use of that idea in Rousseau. Descartes went to a Jesuit school, while Pascal found them to be quite ponderous and lax.

All of this history I cite to come back to a central point in Christianity, a point which Ignatian spirituality at its best is designed to reaffirm. Frequently, and rightly, it is said of any particular spirituality in Christianity that insofar as it deviates from the New Testament and dogmatic orthodoxy, in just that degree it is not Christian. And while granting the Thomist emphasis on right reason even outside of revelation, still what is important is what is distinctly Christian. Without this, Christianity is merely another philosophy. Yet the world is not simple nor is Christianity. Neither is exhausted in a sentence or two. One of the glories of man—contrary to Marx's eschatological vision—is that everyone *cannot* do everyone else's job. There are diversities in the spirit, as Paul said. The division of labor, as it were, is also spiritual, perhaps primarily spiritual, a crucial doctrine in these days of dominant ideological equality theory. Thus, the Jesuits have not been, for the most part, great hospital builders, even though they have founded not a few medical schools. The expense and complexity of such newer technologies as television, nuclear power, and space exploration have largely excluded most religious from direct entry into these fields that so much change and charge the immediate future.

In this context, what is the *Unum Necessarium*, the one thing necessary, *Ad Majorem Dei Gloriam*, for the greater glory of God, for which the order claims to stand and to which Ignatian spirituality strives to address itself? This is not, it is important to stress, an exclusively internal problem of the Jesuits themselves. Their own orthodoxy, as it were, their own obedience to the Church reaches directly beyond themselves by virtue of Ignatian spirituality itself. The classical answer to this question, of course, was the one Ignatius himself was said to have given to Francis Xavier at Paris: "What does it profit a man to gain the whole world and lose the life of his immortal soul?" The *Spiritual Exercises* in practice were "soul" oriented, if I might use that term in a positive way. Indeed, I would say that the major temptation of many Jesuits today, and not them only, is to drop this ultimate and personal priority of the *Exercises* and replace it by a kind of "social-service", even political, concept of salvation, one that approximates the utopian concept and context of so much sociology and ideology. This is doubly paradoxical since the Jesuits were often accused in the past of being too political, a charge they resolutely denied.

The issue, however, is a central one for any Ignatian spirituality whose emphasis on one's personal life before God and the world is a key one. There are here, moreover, philosophical and theological issues of the greatest moment, issues having to do with the metaphysical status of "society" and with the relation of man to God, no matter what kind of social order he might dwell in. Initially, the issue is not unrelated to the classic Christian church-state question in which Jesuits from Bellarmine and Suarez to Liberatore and John Courtney Murray were intimately involved.

The first inquiry addresses itself to the problem of who is saved. Christian personalism has held clearly, through its trinitarian orientation, that society and its ordering are not the objects of resurrection and salvation. What are to be saved are persons with names. For the Greeks, individuals were "the mortals". Society was immortal in that it continued down the ages with the new individuals who replaced the ones constantly falling into the obscurity of death.[5] The Christian revelation was, so to speak, precisely that what was promised eternal life was not the polis but the individual person. These lines from the Stanbrook Abbey text used on Thursdays of the Third Week of the *Divine Office* reflect the classic Christian spirit:

> To you who stooped to sinful man
> We render homage and all praise:
> To Father, Son and Spirit blest
> Whose gift to man is endless days.

This eternal life, these endless days, moreover, did result from personal choices and actions and beliefs in the world, but basic to it was the recognition of the Father in the Son through the Spirit, the very way God revealed himself in salvation history.

This kind of reflection brings us back to the question of what kind of reform Ignatian spirituality was designed to foster—individual, social, or both. Is making the *Exercises* to be equivalent to joining a political party or movement? Or is that the desired effect of them? Obviously, the *Exercises* are designed to affect the world in some sense. The man pictured in the *Exercises'* parable really wanted to know how best to spend the ten thousand ducats imagined to be given to him in the Meditation on the Three Classes of Men. However, there is today a widespread assumption

[5] Cf. Hannah Arendt, *The Human Condition* (1959).

that salvation for many is prevented because of the socio-economic order so that the main purpose of "spirituality" should be to effect changes in this order. This is then considered to be the greater good, changing political society. This approach creates particular problems in that Scripture and the *Exercises* themselves seem to insist upon exactly the opposite priority: "Seek ye first the Kingdom of Heaven and all these things shall be added unto you." Consequently, there is a tendency to deflect emphasis in spirituality from God and the person to social and political structures.[6]

The argument is not about the validity of the terrestrial realities, of course.[7] Modern thought has long argued that Christians neglected this world for the next, just as Christians charged moderns with neglect of the things of the next. But the question today seems to be whether Christians have an authentic spirituality that is not simply a form of social activism.[8] Perhaps this is another way of inquiring about the nature of contemplation itself, a theme close to the heart of all Christian spirituality, especially that of Ignatius.

Ignatian spirituality, then, has addressed itself to this problem in a unique manner. No one who makes the *Exercises* can long doubt that there are things to be done in this world that are religiously and ultimately significant. There is further a careful selection or distinguishing be-

[6] Cf. the address of John Paul II to Latin American Bishops (28 January 1979) *The Pope Speaks* 24, no. 1 (1979) I,2-I,4, 52–53.

[7] See Chapter 9 of the present work.

[8] "The Church has no need, therefore, of recourse to systems and ideologies in order to love, defend and collaborate in the liberation of man for at the heart of the message which has been entrusted to it and which it proclaims it finds its inspiration for acting. . . ." John Paul II, ibid., III,2, 61.

tween things that are important and things that are less
so. The Classes of Men and the Degrees of Humility and
the efforts to make a good Election, other crucial considerations of the *Exercises*, make this clear, even when
all things good are reconciled in the last Contemplation.
"Discernment" constantly plays a central role. Ignatian
spirituality, then, is truly "contemplation in action". But
just as the whole notion of a Trinity "*ad extra*", in creation
and redemption, as Karl Rahner maintained, ultimately
leads to and reveals God in himself—in his inner life wherein God is not alone—so the thrust of Ignatian concern for
the world is not finally towards the world.[9] Any spirituality that settles for the created order is not Christian,
even though any spirituality that finds the world evil is
essentially Manichean. Yet this is why Ignatian spirituality,
in a way, always leaves the world, relativizing it even,
because it is concerned first and last with the kind of
trinitarian Godhead that Christianity uniquely proclaims.

This, again, is why classic Ignatian spirituality is right to
spend so much time on God and the individual person
before Him, why the transcendence of God is the essential
thing it has to concern itself with. The consequences of this
are important to understand, particularly within any effort
to shift to a kind of activist spirituality within the *Exercises*.
Ignatian spirituality, to be sure, is quite capable of con-
templating God in his action *ad extra*, in his guidance of
realities in the world. But Christian hope does not lie
primarily upon any anticipation of worldly success, either
for itself or for the world. Indeed, I still tend to think that a
profound reflection on all the things that do *not* constitute

[9] Cf. the author's chapter, "The Trinity: God Is Not Alone", in
Redeeming the Time (New York: Sheed, 1968).

ultimate happiness, the kind of exercise Aquinas and the great spiritual thinkers performed, is still a basic "spiritual exercise" for any real worship of God. We ought to know clearly what is *not* worth worshipping.

To maintain, moreover, that most people of our time or any time fail even in the world would be exaggerated. There is something divine about success, and about happy endings also. Yet when a Christian spirituality conceives itself to be some kind of an aid to modernization or development, it risks abandoning most men who themselves fall short, most societies which are much less than perfect. But not only this, it also risks deceiving the successful into believing that their own definition of happiness is really fulfilled by something less than God, a belief resolutely denied by Aquinas, Ignatius, and every authentic Christian spirituality. In this light, then, it is no accident that modern atheism presents itself precisely as a corporate, self-created, humanistic happiness, since that is the nearest thing we can conceive to a godlike destiny without admitting the God revealed in Christ Jesus.[10]

Ignatian spirituality, then, is designed to meet the world and its values, without identifying them with the inner life of God himself to whom we ultimately pray and who is our personal beatitude by his own gift. This means essentially that its main thrust is to God, first and last. Only then can we be trusted, as it were, with the world. Christianity is a religion, as I have suggested, that denies a principle of evil co-equal to God. But it also must account for what is not God and what is, in truth, evil.[11] Christianity has ever

[10] Cf. the author's "Atheism and Politics", in *Christianity and Politics* (Boston: St. Paul Editions, 1981).

[11] See the author's essay on evil, in *Communio* (Fall 1979).

located the source of evil in will. And this is why Ignatian spirituality is not wrong to call itself an "exercise" of the will. Accounting for what is not God as well as for what is evil, then, can only safely and wisely be accomplished in the personal and intimate relation we have with God in his trinitarian life. When we know God in faith and prayer, we are safe to be enthusiastic about the world, for we are ever in danger of confusing one with the other, God with the world, God even with the lesser good, some would say even with evil itself.

Ignatius' abiding concern for precisely "discernment" and his care with "election" were rooted, I think, in these very facts. He was acutely attentive to the reality of the Word and the Spirit because he did not ever want us to settle for anything less than the Father as our ultimate destiny through the Son and the Spirit. This is, I believe, the final trinitarian orientation of Ignatius and his spirituality, both its glory and its warning. A friend of mine wrote from a convent in Salzburg: "I miss the old retreats when the Jesuit leader would come to kneel at the Altar and say—'Let us put ourselves in the Presence of God'—and one would have a quiet moment to reflect on this. Discussion groups have their place but a retreat needs quiet, mental rest. . . . I know no place to find it except in the nuns' private chapel in the Abbey." This, I suppose, is the main thing I wish to stress about Christian spirituality. It should ever put us in the presence of the trinitarian God. My friend was quite right. We do need quiet, a kind of mental rest, since without it, we cannot even begin any true action that leads to our end.

VIII

ON THE REDISCOVERY OF CHARITY

Western philosophical and religious tradition has about it a sense of the unimportance of material things which is somehow related to the idea that God did not have to create the world. At first sight, this might seem to reduce the stature of the world, but at its more profound level, it is designed to show that God is not limited by the world by being necessarily dependent on it. Some sense of the spirit of this tradition can, I think, be gained from the following passages, which flow from the fact that the trinitarian God, because of the fullness of his own inner life, relates to all of creation in some capacity other than requirement. The relation of God and intelligent creatures must be put on a level reflective of something other than dependence or necessity. A clear strand in our tradition seems to sense this:

> Why, I mean we should keep our seriousness for serious things, and not waste it on trifles, and that, while God is the real goal of all beneficent serious endeavors, man . . . has been constructed as a toy of God, and this is, in fact, the finest thing about him. . . .
>
> —*Plato, The Laws, 803*

> My friend, I am not being unjust to you; did we not agree on a denarius? Take your earnings and go. I choose to pay the last-comer as much as I pay you. Have I no right to do what I like with my own? Thus, the last will be first and the first, last.
>
> —*Matthew 120:14–16*

All service ranks the same with God—
With God, whose puppets, best and worst,
Are we: There is no last or first.

—*Robert Browning, "Pippa Passes"*

Such themes are indicative of a reality that does not conform to the natural expectations of any public or even private relationship.

When the history of this age comes to be written, I suspect scholars of religion will note the sudden, profound disappearance in the literature of that virtue which by their own testimony most characterized the reflections of earlier Christians, beginning with the New Testament itself. The virtue of charity, it will be remarked, somehow dropped out of view in the latter half of the twentieth century, and this for largely intellectual reasons. Behind the fading away of charity lies the deeper intellectual nature of the ultimate good for which we ought to live our lives. Is the City of God something we can hope to establish among us by our own means, or, as Augustine wrote, does this City of God's making come after the resurrection?

Consequent to the decline in emphasis on charity, moreover, these same critics will trace the revival of justice and human rights at the center of religious consciousness. Spiritual handbooks will be studied in which pastors are advised to tell their penitents not to "offer up their lives and sufferings to God", but rather to go out and insist on their "rights". The poor are to be "conscienticized" to hate their injustices so they can improve their world. Some writers will trace the way "charity" came to be identified with human rights and justice, while others will discover that charity is an end product, something possible only after justice and human rights are established by economic and political movements.

That there may be something wrong with the philosophical thinking that undergirds these latter views—some, no doubt, are due to simple ignorance, to failure to study the Christian tradition itself—is now being drawn to our attention by precisely the cost of "benevolence", as it is called. Various taxpayers' revolts are symptomatic in a yet unanalyzed way of the disappearance of charity. At first sight, to be sure, this will seem rather dubious. How can we argue and imply that a virtue whose presence presumably depends on a gift of faith can be accounted for in monetary terms? On the other hand, Scripture itself suggested that we will be judged in evidently material terms of visiting the sick and the prisoners, of giving cups of water. In a society wherein charity was common and even institutionalized, many things were done—and expected—that would not otherwise have happened in it. The Good Samaritan was the scriptural symbol of this effect. In societies without Beatitudes, without Good Samaritans, many vital things simply are not done, or even thought of in the first place. In the post-Christian societies, these things remain expected and demanded; thus they have to be paid for as "rights", paid for without the corresponding virtue of charity that motivated them in the first place.

Undoubtedly, there is some kind of general human friendliness of which Aristotle spoke so well, some innate sympathy for our kind in need. Yet, as Chesterton stated, the ancient world exists for us today in many ways as an example of a world precisely without Christian virtue. The pagan world did not know it. The modern world does not know what the world without it would be like. This is why a post-Christian world is so much the more dangerous one, why the loss of charity involves the faith problem of blaming God for the world. Aquinas constantly held that there were many noble and sacrificial things we could, perhaps, conceive of doing by natural reasoning, but in fact we do not. And even when we conceive them, we do not have the energy or zeal to go ahead and do them. Moreover, there are "irrationally" rational things—"foolish" even, in St. Paul's terms—that we ought to do which we could never imagine by ourselves.

The classic example of this latter is, undoubtedly, the Christian devotion to those lives the ancients thought it quite rational to terminate—the deformed, the weak, the excessive in number, examples strikingly reappearing in contemporary society. Today, then, the attack upon the Christian insights in these areas renews the pagan forms, but no longer with the pagan innocence. Thus, if the weak or deformed live and propagate, they will injure our gene pools, it is claimed. That is, such people are not good in themselves. If the poor multiply, it will affect our environment or reduce our own intelligence quotient averages. Classical reason in a kind of perverted fashion reappears to challenge the historic results of the virtue of charity, which calls for a sacrifice, a "calling" somehow beyond justice and reason.

The weak and the deformed, in some sense, then, have come to be looked upon as threats to mankind rather than as blessings, as the reformed ethics of Christianity held. And when the rights of the poor are proclaimed, most often they become tools for political messianism, not simply treated as individual persons who need help. Irving Kristol sensed some of this, I think, in a recent essay:

> Our reformers simply cannot bring themselves to think realistically about human nature. They believe it to be not only originally good, but also incorruptible (hence the liberal tolerance for pornography).
>
> When a slum population wrecks a brand-new housing project, it is the designers of the project who are blamed, never the inhabitants. Those inhabitants are promptly relocated in other housing—which they will also wreck, since there are no rewards or punishments attached to existing motivations. . . .
>
> To question this principle of the original goodness of human nature—and its corollary: the ease of improvement of human nature—would also set limits to that most profound of liberal passions, the passion of self-righteous compassion.[1]

This "passion of self-righteous compassion" is what has happened to charity upon its secularization, its divorce from the classic reality of original sin. Our costs, as Kristol suggested, may well be metaphysical ones.

Nevertheless, and paradoxically, the results of charity's influence remain powerful in our culture. This is why the philosophical heritage of the Enlightenment cannot forget it. In recent years, moreover, practically every American building, street, and rest room—very pedestrian things to be sure—has been refashioned at tremendous cost, under public law, to accommodate the handicapped. Even though the courts permit with little scruple the abortion of a potentially deformed or retarded fetus who "might" someday have use of such a marvelous facility, if that child should

[1] Irving Kristol, "Human Nature and Social Reform", *Wall Street Journal* (16 September 1978).

manage to survive the quasi battlefield that the modern hospital has often now become for him, he is the recipient of enormous amounts of public and legal protection. This could not have happened if, historically, men had learned that the deformed were not worthy in themselves. They learned this from the example of Christian charity, then made it a "right".

Furthermore, many young students looking for something "meaningful" to do with their lives, often choose professions—medical, educational, even recreational and nutritional—that concern themselves with the weak, sick, elderly, or backward. This care is often even extended to animals.[2] In any case, we discover that the existence of members of our kind who lack one or many of our "normal" capacities, limbs, or talents, contributes enormously to humanity by providing visible evidence that something worthwhile to be done does exist in the world. In this regard, the particular love affair our world has with Mother Teresa of Calcutta, for something beautiful for God, is no accident. Even those who do not do it for God, do it because such benevolent work contains a meaning, one arising out of the notion of humanity.

Yet, historically there has been a danger in society's "needing" the poor or sick or retarded as "instruments" to justify human existence or its religious or secular profession. Often in recent years, service institutions seem like excuses for employment for the workers in them rather than institutions for some objective purpose. This is true not only for health services but also for mail, transporta-

---

[2] See the author's chapter on "The Christian Love of Animals", in *The Praise of 'Sons of Bitches': On the Worship of God by Fallen Men* (Slough, England: St. Paul Publications, 1978).

tion, and other organizations which improve human life. Little scruple is shown to cripple an aspect of society in order that one's "rights" might be gained, rights often, on examination, containing incomes and privileges far in advance of the rest of the society. The traditional virtue of charity was not primarily concerned with our own good or moral well-being. Indeed, whenever such motivations appeared in charitable endeavors, classical spiritual writers were most concerned to correct them. Ironically, the greatest danger of pride, the worst of the vices, was seen lurking precisely in the most loving enterprises. Charity's purpose, as it were, was not to supply something naturally lacking in the giver but rather to bring the receiver to a higher potential, whatever that might be. Charity, moreover, was never first just a "remedial thing", something designed to reinforce what we could otherwise figure out by ourselves. Even the naturally perfect man needed it. Indeed, in an ironic way, he needed it most of all.

Many strands of ancient and modern thought would conceive mankind as a closed system into which nothing more than man himself and his mind are either needed or desired. Christianity is a peculiar religion both because it agrees and disagrees with this latter posture. Christian "humanism" is traditionally aligned with any effort to develop fully the human potential and character. "Incarnational" theology, as it is called, has striven to emphasize and develop those things of natural and human import that could be seen as good. The "goodness" of creation itself from Genesis came to be seen as a logical development to the assumption of the flesh by the Son of God, something that would not be possible were there something naturally evil about the human condition or its place in the universe.

Nonetheless, the Crucifixion, the folly of the Cross, the New Law which did not merely repeat the Old Law of loving our neighbor as ourselves but required that we love him as Christ loved us—these things have made it clear that no simple and smooth relationship between Christianity and the world is likely or possible. Irving Kristol was right in worrying about a view of human nature that found nothing wrong in it in any sense. There is, then, something about Christianity which is not of this world, something about it which, as the Apostle John warned, the world will hate. The classic doctrine of charity held that it was the peculiar kind of love that existed in God, that the purpose of revelation was precisely to invite—the word is accurate, there is no force—individual men and women in their persons, in the concrete lives they know, to share this love. Man, consequently, was a creature whose ultimate purpose was to share in the kind of love proper to the trinitarian life of God. There are some, indeed, who hold this was the reason for creation in the first place. The result of this was that each human life centered on a dramatic "choice" structure which involved in all cases the rejection or acceptance of the unique kind of life within the Godhead, a kind of love not merited, one that did not "conform" to the laws and lines of reason which politics on the surface might imply.

Historically, then, once the motion of Christianity was set loose in the world, a new set of priorities and even values became operative. Evidently, the kind of love within the Godhead when shared in the world was like a burning fire, something that consumed actions and artifacts that did not conform to its mysterious exigencies. And as even Plato hinted, when the charity of God touched men and things, somehow its result was good and beautiful. And even when it was hated, as it often was, it was because it was indeed beautiful and good. The mystery of hate is part of the mystery of love in God.[3] Consequently, "mission" theology was not historically designed so much to decide rationally what local values and practices could be used or accepted, then to add Christianity onto them; rather it was to practice and worship the revealed faith in order that all practices might be woven into the kind of love and action this unique relationship implies. A Christian culture, then, was one in which many endeavors, many spirits were present, something which would not otherwise have been possible or even conceivable. This is why Christopher Dawson's work remains abidingly important to study, why we cannot really speculate abstractly what happens in a Christian culture but must analyze it in its historical uniqueness.

The modern state in a number of ways—insofar as it is not merely a powerful laicized absolute order—is an institution that has accepted many if not most of the ideas and institutions that arose out of Christian culture. To walk down the streets of Washington or any Western political capital, passing by welfare, social security, old age, and other beneficent-sounding agencies, is to walk by the nationalization and rationalization of impulses and institutions originally Christian. The economic crisis of these agencies, their growing costs and even clientele, has arisen because the spirit of benevolence has been largely replaced by bureaucratic rights such that service is contingent on reward for the ones giving it. We either no longer believe certain people should be helped—the fetus is defined as

[3] See the author's chapter on hatred, in the work mentioned in the previous footnote.

legally nonhuman—or else we hold that the cost of institutionalized benevolence is too high. And there are things
still no one will pay for.

In a remarkable study, *"Doing Good": The Limits of
Benevolence*, Professor Ira Glasser wrote: "The state was all
too willing to allocate substantial resources to the children
if they were removed from their parents. But the state was not
willing to provide equivalent services—probably at less
cost—directly to the family in its own home."[4] The classical Christian philosophical instinct which would maintain
that intellectual order is necessary that good be done—the
family being here conceived as the natural institution—is
nowhere more evident than here. Instincts of compassion
or benevolence, however laudable in the abstract, still
require, as Kristol implied, some sense of the true human
condition itself.

Undoubtedly, one of the major issues at stake is precisely the meaning of "human" rights. Ever since former
President Carter made the term public policy and property, there has been considerable confusion about what it
means.[5] There is a proper use of the term "human rights",
of course. Yet we cannot neglect the fact that in modern
social thought, human "natural" rights have individualistic
and even atheistic overtones. This is why the Christian
tradition is strictly one of "natural law", not natural
rights, even though these terms have been interchangeable
in recent thought. The issue is important in our context
here—the replacement of charity by justice or rights—

[4] Ira Glasser, "Prisoners of Benevolence", in *"Doing Good": The
Limits of Benevolence* (New York: Seabury, 1978) 158.

[5] See the author's "Culture and Human Rights", *America* (7 January
1978).

because much of our thinking is leading to a new form of individualistic society in which no one has any relationship to anyone else—neither parents to children, man to woman, man to man—except on the basis of justice. There are many theories of justice at bottom almost diametrically the opposite of what Christianity is about, even though classic Christian thought never saw justice and charity to be opposed. The reason we do not usually recognize the individualistic premises in contemporary rights theories is that they are couched in a distributionist language that nevertheless effectively eliminates any strict relation of one person to another.

Classical Thomism had enabled us to distinguish between reason and faith, between family and state, between state and society. These distinctions, in one sense, were designed to limit justice, the terrible virtue, however needed it might be in its limited area. Within the family, among friends, in the higher reaches of culture and social life, justice was not meant to rule. While Thomism did not conceive justice in opposition to charity, still it recognized clearly the limits of justice.[6] In one sense, a society, a friendship, or a family existing only by the bonds of justice would be one with no real "bonds", one of individuals seeking, defining, demanding their "rights", a society of lawyers, the kind Plato so worried about in *The Republic* (405). Since most of the higher, more noble things of life and death are not questions of justice, a society or person reducing everything to such terms soon ceases to be anything but a grasping one in which the interest and relationship of everyone to each other is based on his defined, ever

[6] See the author's "The Limits of Law", *Communio* (Summer 1975).

more insistent "rights". Nothing is done or felt except on the *quid pro quo* basis of justice, both commutative and especially distributive.

It is with this background that Professor Willard Gaylin's remarks are of utmost importance:

> It is fashionable these days to view paternalism and benevolence as obscene terms. The reformers of the past are often ridiculed for failures to achieve their ends. Worse, their intentions are suggested to be motivated by unconscious self-serving. . . . I have little faith in the eventual success of the best intentioned of our current laborers in their efforts for equity and justice. . . .
>
> There will always be need for parental compassion; at the same time, there will always be the need for vigilance in recognizing the limitations of institutions of government as surrogate parents. Nevertheless, it is not paternalism that is the crime, it is what is passed off for paternalism. The language of rights, with its litigious and paranoid assumptions that good can only be received from others by pursuit and protection of law, must also recognize that the good that can be received from others in that way is often quite limited. . . . Certain minimal rights ought to be defended even beyond the court—in the streets if necessary; but the solution will require that we go beyond the kind of moral behavior that can be defined in terms of plantiff and litigant.[7]

Professor Gaylin, indeed, argued for a kind of natural charity (benevolence) arising out of the uniqueness of human gestation and early childhood—not without irony the precise area of greatest deviation from the good in our society.

[7] W. Gaylin, "In the Beginning: Helpless and Dependent" in *"Doing Good": The Limits of Benevolence* (New York: Seabury, 1978) 32.

Furthermore, he noted that the theologians today hold man's likeness to the rest of creation, while scientists hold his absolute difference. This he remarked with amusement is exactly the opposite of where the scientist and the theologian stood one hundred years ago in the evolution controversies.[8] The initial human experience, so contrary to the rights mentality, is the natural basis of that sacrificial, transcendent relationship we have to those experiences of life that cannot be defined by justice. In other words, the nature-grace controversy is by no means dead, while the cost of rights-benevolence again seems to force us to reconsider what we have been doing by teaching justice rather than charity to our contemporaries in the light of the intellectual tradition in which rights are by no means necessarily presupposed to charity.

In the remarkable eighteenth chapter of Ezekiel, wherein our sins are liberated from those of our fathers, the House of Israel objects: "What the Lord does is unjust" (18:28–32). And in answer, the Lord says, "Is what I do unjust? . . . Is it not what you do that is unjust?" The Lord goes on to account for his actions, promising his people a new heart and a new spirit if they repent. Christianity has always found this passage a prophecy, a foreshadowing of how the Lord acted when he came. For Christ did act "unjustly". Were he to have acted "justly", we should all have been destroyed. The cosmos is full of the joys of the Lord, not of justice. Mercy, Aquinas said, is the foundation of creation, of its very justice, not the other way around. John Paul II's encyclical *Dives in Misericordia*, on the relation of justice to mercy, reaffirms this point.

[8] Ibid., 3.

The nearer a person or a society or a family or a friendship, then, approaches authentic charity, grace, the more it will distance itself from justice, yet at the same time, make justice more real. The social action programs of our era, of the assumptions of our political thought, which insist first on justice before faith and grace, are exactly the opposite of the orientation of classical Christianity. No doubt remnants of charity (and reason even) are scattered all over the universe, and we should discover them.[9] But to insist that our faith is justice at whatever scale is to leave us in despair. The significance of Professor Gaylin's book, I suspect, is that it represents a sudden nonreligious realization that the cost of what is lacking is even on empirical terms too high.

Christianity does not set itself up "against" justice, of course, however skeptical it might be about the ability of laws and constitutions that are called just in the public order to resolve men's goals. Christianity does believe that justice will exist in a society that is more than just, as it believes that among real friends there is "justice". What is most worrisome about the religious climate of the world today is the disappearance of charity as a theoretical presence. This is why it is not surprising to see its faint outline, the sense of its loss, arising elsewhere. God does not abandon his people, though he does castigate his followers for not having mercy.

The finest thing about us is that we are not created because God was necessitated to create us. Human persons represent the abundance of a God who did not "need" to return anything to anyone; this even Plato seemed to sense.

[9] See C. Mertens, "Charité, Vérité, Justice", *Nouvelle Revue Théologique* 99 (1977) 391–405.

We are created in joy, not in justice. This is why the last and the first can be interchanged, why the Lord can do as he wills with his own, pay the same wages to those who arrive at even the eleventh hour. But when we look at what the Lord did, it was not justice, but always something much more. All service does rank the same with God because he looks for our love, our charity, the love he gave to us first—in all of our relationships. He does not look for what we, first and last, best and worst, "owe" to him, or what we "owe" to one another, what we insist is due to ourselves. The reappearance of charity is, in the end, the condition of our faith and our future.

IX

TECHNOLOGY AND SPIRITUALITY

While Christianity has insisted that it cannot be exhausted in its dealings with the world, that indeed this is not its primary concern, still it has resolutely maintained that disorder in the world is not an indifferent thing, but indeed is a sign of spiritual disorder. Furthermore, the whole of the modern era has busied itself in accusing Christianity of being opposed to science and its results, the refutation of which charge consumed a good deal of the energy of Christian intellectuals in the modern world. Christianity has been rooted in the belief that our capacity to do anything at all is itself a marvelous gift. Further, it has held that we are not obliged to do absolutely everything, that there is a diversity of talent and burden from generation to generation. Samuel Johnson, as was his wont, probably stated this tradition better than any:

> A little more than nothing is as much as can be expected from a being who with respect to the multitudes about him is himself a little more than nothing. Every man is obliged by the Supreme Master of the Universe to improve all the opportunities of Good which are afforded him, and to keep in continual activities such Abilities as are bestowed upon him.
>
> But he has no reason to repine, though his abilities are small and his opportunities few. He that has improved the virtue or advanced the Happiness of one fellow creature, he that has ascertained a single moral proposition, or added one useful Experiment to natural knowledge, may be content with his own performance.[1]

[1] Samuel Johnson, *The Idler* (22 December 1759).

Even the least of the useful things to our neighbor is indeed useful, even though the more astonishing thing is that we are and can do anything at all.

In 1938, Raymond Corrigan, the Jesuit historian at St. Louis University, published his still readable *The Church and the Nineteenth Century*. Since the late E. F. Schumacher in *Small Is Beautiful* has insisted on a clear appreciation of the damaging effects of these same nineteenth-century ideas still prevalent in our intellectual elites and milieu, perhaps it is well to recall what Corrigan wrote in his initial description of "The Bourgeois Century":

> The forerunners of modern technology were optimists. But it is safe to say that the achievements of the nineteenth century fulfilled, when they did not surpass, their foremost hopes. . . . Werner Sombart, writing a generation ago, turns from a futile attempt to enumerate the encyclopedic array of recent inventions to search for the principle which underlies them all. . . . Technique, he observes, "has become surer, more easily controllable, more exact." Through the machine, man manipulates the forces of nature to suit his every purpose. But he also observes that "in nature . . . there is no room for an artisan God. . . ." In a word, "the Creator has been separated from his work."[2]

In retrospect, in the last phases of the twentieth century, these are remarkable lines when the very optimism connected with technology is understood by many, albeit rather superficially, to be the cause of our growing "disillusionment", a theme, as Corrigan also recalled, first catalogued in modern European history by Carlton J. H. Hayes.

[2] Raymond Corrigan, *The Church in the Nineteenth Century* (Milwaukee, Wisc.: Bruce, 1938) 17.

The relationship of Christianity to science and technology is a curious one, many of whose ramifications
were traced by Herbert Butterfield in his *Origins of Modern
Science*. Fundamentally, this relationship goes back to the
very uniqueness of the Creator-God.[3] Ultimately, as I
shall endeavor to suggest, it is related to the exact kind of
trinitarian Deity given in the Christian tradition. In a sense,
the dogmas of the Council of Nicea and other early Coun-
cils may be more important to technology than Watt's
steam engine or Galileo's telescope.[4] To be sure, the very
validity of human reason was part of the abiding heritage of
the Greek Fathers, Augustine, and the Middle Ages. Yet
the main opposition to modern science appeared to have
come from Christianity, so much so that the overarching
burden of nineteenth- and twentieth-century apologetics
was to demonstrate how faith and technology were not
objectively incompatible. In the later years of the twentieth
century, however, the whole problematic of the issue has
suddenly, radically, changed.

Under the impact of environmental and ecological concerns, then, historians began to discover, contrary to their
predecessors of the past three hundred years, that science
and technology were not in opposition to religion and
particularly to Christianity, but this faith was in fact their
cause. Few today want to "reconcile and align [themselves]
with progress, Liberalism, and modern civilization," a
position Pius IX was roundly condemned for taking a

[3] Cf. Dorothy Sayer's essay, "Man: The Creating Creature", in
Christian Letters to a Post-Christian World (Grand Rapids, Mich.: Eerdmans,
1969) 69–132.

[4] Cf. P. E. Hogson, "Third World Science", *Tablet* (London, 6
January 1979) 5–7.

hundred years ago in the famous *Syllabus*. Indeed, many scientists have even begun to wonder if, without classical faith, their legitimate interests can any longer be protected against this recent antiscientific enthusiasm. The mission given in Genesis and the concept of an orderly universe open to human reason in some basic, teleological sense has come to be looked upon as the cause of doomsday by a generation that has passed remarkably rapidly from the optimism of technology to its pessimism.

Thus, through this newer antiscientific attitude—one based perhaps more on biology than on physics—the absolute moral law and human rights, the transcendent basis of human personality, all that seemed to support political, economic, and intellectual values, were called into question when the center shifted from the individual to the group, from progress to stability as the central myth of our lot. In a sense, science and technology were losing their spiritual moorings in modern thought at the precise moment the connection between the Christian view of man and the implications of an autonomous science were becoming clear. In general, it is fair to say that human personality divorced from its trinitarian roots in Western intellectual history has come to be posited on a being not received from nature, the kind we receive but do not make, as Aristotle said, but rather on one that creates itself.

In fact, it probably can be maintained that Christianity emphasized the "received" aspect of man and nature even while accepting his unique status as the being who can think and make. Unless there is a proper "spirituality" of technology, then, we shall begin to produce a man alien to himself, alien because he conceives his highest project as "making" himself and in this way of manifesting his proper being. The Christian relation to technology is initially grounded in the position that man's own being is not constituted by himself—his individual personhood is already "received", so that what he ultimately discloses in himself is not himself alone. This frees technology, moreover, from a kind of metaphysical humanism that would make the ultimate project of science and technology the formation of a "new man" totally independent of his received being. In this sense, man is properly created in God's image, not just his own.

This same point can perhaps be made in a somewhat different fashion. Today, we tend to think of, say, New York City as a hopelessly ungovernable locality, debt-ridden, unsafe, greedy, ugly, a place whose taxes and economic attitudes have driven away the very life that once fed it. Yet, in this mood, when we take another look at the paintings of the Italo-American artist, Joseph Stella, in works from the end of the First World War period, his *Brooklyn Bridge* or his *New York Interpreted*, we find an unaccustomed fascination with steel and form, with man-made technology and its realities. Of him, John I. H. Bauer wrote: "In a sense, he outdid the Futurists at their own avowed aim of glorifying the mechanistic aspects of modern life. Actually, they seldom painted such themes, whereas Stella found in New York their perfect embodiment."[5] We have here, then, almost a mystical response to the objects of technology, the powerful beauty of the bridge, the skyscraper, the apartment house. But is the Creator to be separated from His work? Is this the spiritual result of the modern intellectual revolution? Is the towering vision of

[5] John I. H. Bauer, *Joseph Stella* (New York: Praeger, 1971) 19.

the city we see one made only by ourselves? Is this the only sign, as so much of modern philosophy has taught, of authenticity, of human worth, that it is self-made, man-made? Is there no sense in which the City of Man can reflect the City of God, however much the two differ ultimately?

The relationship of Christianity to science and technology, then, has not been easy. For many, they are rivals, not cooperators. Even Pius XII and Gabriel Marcel constantly worried that technology was the chief area in which men were likely to be separated from their faith, from nature, from themselves even. The literature written all during the Industrial Revolution from Christian sources often betrayed an uneasiness about the values and institutions that in fact made it historically operative. Under the rubric of a struggle with liberalism, Christianity has recognized a danger in compromising too much with the modern world in its basic principles. Those sects of Christianity which accepted easily the philosophies and artifacts of modernity have come to pay a terrible price. Yet, at the same time, Christian sensibility has also been alert to the danger of any Manichean tendency that would make matter and hence technology evil outright. The danger of technology has not been construed to deny that the earth was for man and to be improved by him in some essential sense.

Technology has rather created special problems for Christianity because it is related to certain aspects of original sin, the causes of evil in the world and how to eradicate them or at least remedy them somewhat. What is crucial in understanding or formulating any proper spirituality for something that partakes of this world—spirituality, after all, ought properly and mainly to be something concerned with God—is to recognize frankly that for Christianity, the locus of disorder is never primarily in things, never in creation itself, except in that Pauline sense in which creation is affected by man's own disorder. There is, to be sure, a difference between finiteness and evil. The two are not the same. For what is finite, it is good to be finite. In this sense, limits are also graces. Christianity is a radical rejection of any idea that would identify matter or its conditions with evil. This is why "Baal", as a simple artifact or idol, was not evil, though the will that chose to build it was.

Charles Norris Cochrane, in his *Christianity and Classical Culture*, wrote:

> [Christianity] was thus to see in the world of natural objects not God, indeed, nor any part of God, but . . . the *vestigia* or traces of divine activity. As for the human being, the knowing subject, what they claimed for him was the unique satisfaction of access to this eternal truth through the Word and the Spirit. And, from this standpoint, the only barrier to this progress towards full perfection was that which he imposed upon himself by his blind and stubborn refusal to see it.[6]

The consequences of this analysis should not be lost because they suggest that if technology or science in fact take on an anti-God or humanly destructive hue, as they sometimes have, it is not because of themselves but because of a will that stands behind them. The question is never properly posed as: science or faith, religion or technology. The only way for any created thing to be diverted from its goodness or potential is by being caught up in a choice, a movement originating in, or at least passing through, the human will. This is why the influential analysis originating in Rousseau and seeking to locate the origin of man's chaos in property

[6] Charles Norris Cochrane, *Christianity and Classical Culture* (Oxford: 1940) 245.

arrangements, in economic or cultural institutions, almost wholly misses the point and only succeeds in deflecting any real political or structural improvement from the real origin of change.

Consequently, in evaluating technology in authentic spiritual terms, we must return to an attitude already found in Genesis: that the earth is for man, that man is to subdue it, name it. There is, to be sure, a genuine inner-worldly context for man that is, as Aristotle said, proper to him as man, as the specific kind of being he is in the universe that distinguishes him from all others. This properly human context is not man's highest destiny, even in Aristotle. But neither is it nothing. Indeed, from the criteria given for salvation in the New Testament, the inner-worldly structure is the locus of the drama of ultimate will that will finally relate man to his final end. In this sense, the freedom constitutive of man as a person manifests its direction in what is made and done in the world. The parable of the talents can thus be taken to mean that a refusal to participate in and change the world according to the mission of Genesis and the values of Matthew is likewise a rejection of the kind of dignity envisioned for man.

By rejecting the notion of the "two truths" from the Arab tradition, Christianity has insisted in seeing a continuity between questions of ultimate destiny and those of what we do with the world. But in likewise rejecting Pelagianism, Christianity does not believe that man constructs or establishes his own being or his own beatitude, both of which remain a gift, even though the latter includes man's possibility of choosing it. Thus technology, what the tool-making being achieves for his purposes, takes its form or fashion from the will that brings it into being, into the shape in which it finds itself. As any object thrown out into the world, technology remains good in the metaphysical sense. What man makes or fashions does not derive its total value from man. Even the nuclear bomb, which many persist in trying to make an intrinsic evil as an artifact, even a potential doomsday machine that could destroy the planet, neither of these must be called evil as such, except in a very qualified sense relating to will. To do so literally would be Manichean. Our knowledge of how to make such objects is itself good and, indeed, a sign of authentic progress. There is no way to think it out of existence without calling into question the whole nature of mind and intelligence. Aquinas was clear in recognizing that the knowledge of anything evil—which would have to be an immoral action, not an evil thing—is itself good. It is of the greatest importance to keep such distinctions and the metaphysic that lies behind them clear.

Yet if technology of itself is not evil, this does not prevent us from using it in an evil way, just as we can use any natural object like a stone or a tree in some evil way. This would mean using something in a manner contrary to the known human good as that is seen established by the kind of being which man is and is called to be. This seems clear enough. Nevertheless, from the viewpoint of a spiritual comprehension of technology, it raises certain fundamental problems, which can perhaps be clarified from two angles. The first is the way technology can serve to eliminate or reduce human destructiveness. Suppose, for example, the design engineering on a major roadway is so faulty in terms of the kind of traffic, drivers, and equipment regularly using it that it forces normal drivers to take chances, panic, and otherwise increase the likelihood of serious accidents. The drivers using this road are still responsible for the actual damage they do, for not being more cautious, but the engineer is also responsible, and the architect of this particular technology, as well as the politicians that permitted the faulty system to be constructed. In this case, putting in wider lanes, better markings, longer access lanes would enable the average driver to do what he wants to without endangering himself or others. Clearly in this sort of case, technology partakes of the Fifth Commandment and is a service to the neighbor when done properly, even though it might be argued, from another point of view, that automobiles are too expensive or damaging to nature or to mental health.

The second way these problems can be seen is by considering that monument of technology, space itself. In an interview with the Chief Rabbi in England, John Wilkins recounted the following remarks:

> Unlike Christians, Jews do not believe in original sin and so pride is not, for them, the supreme human fault. . . . As Chief Rabbi he gives Passover and New Year broadcasts on the BBC and in one of them he commented on a Christian sermon he had once seen published in the *Reader's Digest*.
>
> The preacher imagined the first man on the Moon thinking to himself that here was an uncontaminated celestial body, without the slightest stain of sin or evil. A Jewish preacher, the Chief Rabbi thought, would describe the same experience differently. "He would view the empty wastes of the Moon not so much as unstained by any sin or vice but rather as unsanctified by any virtue or noble deed."[7]

What is to be remarked here, undoubtedly, is that, in both cases—the condition of the roads and the condition of

[7] John Wilkins, *Tablet* (London, 14 January 1978) 31.

space—the technology of how to get to the Moon or how to live on it is not the location of "santification". A believer in original sin notes its absence when man is absent, while a nonbeliever in original sin finds sanctification in the performance of virtues and noble deeds, which is, at bottom, also the classical Greek view. Good and evil in both cases are rooted in the human will.

Needless to say, both of these views bring up the question —itself not unconnected with the classic question of the state of nature—of whether it would be better to leave the Moon or, *a pari*, this planet untouched by any technology in the first place. If the will is the locus of sanctification, as it clearly is in some basic sense, then the form of civilization is indifferent. From the point of view of sanctification, the most primitive and the most advanced societies do not differ. All are equally near to God. Stated in this way, why bother? The accusation made by the Marxists and others seems true, that believers are too concerned about the next world or their own goodness to bother changing this world. Of course, this latter charge implies that "improvement" is not primarily a moral category but a material, technological one. Thus, not without reason, Lenin once spoke of electricity not unlike the way Christians speak of grace, as something that will supply the good life with what it needs to be good. In trying to save the primacy of the will and the goodness of creation, do we merely end up making technology at best indifferent and at worst ultimately irrelevant?

Again, the strangeness of speaking about technology and spirituality together ought to be emphasized. To locate any radical disorder in human culture in man-made things is, as I have suggested, to miss the exact drama of the historical process as Christians see it. On the other hand, there is a

kind of tangible incompleteness in the world. Inanimate
and biological natures seem essentially open to the altering
capacities of human endeavor. Plants and animals that do
not exist by nature are brought into existence for human
purposes through human intervention. Plastics and com-
pounds are developed to correct or repair or improve the
kinds of materials found on this planet before man's arrival.
So powerful is the human capacity to understand and alter
that the very corpus of man himself is coming to be an
object of experimental research in the hope of "improving"
it, even of altering it. The radical incompleteness of nature
vis-à-vis man and his own purposes would suggest that
man does have a real project on the planet, in the cosmos,
one that does not define his ultimate standing, in comparison to which indeed, it is little more than nothing, to
recall Samuel Johnson's words, but which for all that, is
worthwhile doing and in fact seems to be connected with
man's real ability to do something unique and significant in
the universe.

This is where the question of human will rejoins the question of human intelligence. Abstractly, it remains quite true
that Christian personal relations are quite possible in a
society that never knew or chose to reject technology.
Moreover, it is also true, as a good deal of literature on the
subject of modern times has argued, that the employment
of technology through the guidance of a morally perverted
will can result in the worst of tyrannies. Technology can
and does make tyranny considerably more effective, ex-
tending it perhaps to the world and even the cosmos, as
certain types of recently popular films and literature seem
to anticipate.

Professor Schumacher, moreover, has popularized, by
contrast, the notion of "technology with a human face",

the idea that human purpose, human-sized social institutions of a kind expounded in the classic social encyclicals and in Chesterton's *The Outline of Sanity*, ought to determine, that is, be the criterion of choice for any proper use of technology. What is implied here, of course, is that some sizes or shapes or purposes of technology are contrary to the best interests of man, provided he be defined in the classical Christian fashion. This does not deny that our very notion of proper size has much cultural variety in it. Furthermore, many of those arguing from a viewpoint of overpopulation appear to have an extraordinarily narrow vision of the human brain and the potentialities of this planet and its surroundings. Certain technologies, certain sizes of population are used as a norm against a broader vision of the human and planetary potential. Yet this is not so much a problem of technology as of the understanding we have of man's personality and nature.

Christian philosophy has largely accepted Aristotle's idea that the proper object of the human intellect is "all being", beginning with that being found initially in material reality. Christian theology has said that the world was made through the Word. In this way, all reality is seen as communication of intelligence to intelligence; nothing stands utterly in darkness.[8] The things created by *homo faber* are related to his will and purposes teleologically. They are expressions of his word, as it were. Christianity has insisted that its God is one who needs nothing. This means, again, that the purpose of creation is not to supply what is lacking in God. When we look at the consequences of this doctrine from the creature's side, it can only mean that no work of his hands will be properly divine. It can mean, as it did in

[8] See the chapter on Christianity and the Cosmos in the author's *Redeeming the Time* (New York: Sheed, 1968).

certain forms of orthodox monasticism, that little of this world is needed or wanted compared to God. But this was an expression of the Christian effort to remind us that God alone suffices, that however glorious his creation might be, still it is of little import when compared to its source.

Yet we live in a time almost totally dominated by efforts to create a fully human city. This in part is an effort to come to terms with the dominant heresies of our age, those which are almost invariably those directed towards this world, heresies with roots clearly in the Enlightenment project of bringing heaven to earth by essentially human means. Indeed, as I have earlier argued, the most exalted "atheist" endeavor would be a perfectly functioning, technologically advanced world, wholly man-made, wholly devoted to removing those peculiar norms which Christianity historically has defended as defining the kind of human creature made by God in the first place. If radical human freedom means anything, it means such a world is possible, one which certain strands of apocalyptic thought would suggest quite probable. In this sense, we can properly speak of a "technological spirituality" which is by choice "atheist", by choice exclusive of any remnant of the divine in the human social or personal world.

What remains, then, is to suggest where a proper technological spirituality might lie. When we speak of any "spirituality", we must necessarily refer to the human agent. A spirituality is a right orientation to God first and before all else. Only secondarily can we speak of a spirituality of any of the terrestrial realities. Essential to the human condition is precisely its capacity to suffuse with its own intentions and purposes what it touches through man's intrinsic connection with matter and through it to history. In Karl Rahner's *Theological Dictionary*, historicity is defined in this fashion:

> [Historicity is] that fundamental attribute of man which sets him in time and provides him with a world that he must accept in freedom. That is to say, that he must first overtake his own nature in the very course of transforming time and the world itself with which he is provided, turning physical time into "his" time, the mere "environment" into a real world, in the now of his responsible decision; thereby coming to himself as one-who-exists. The task, which the very possession of his spirit sets him, is one indeed that he never fully accomplishes; he is frustrated by his finitude. Nonetheless, the historical, though always unique, always "event", is at the same time always transcended in a free decision reaching out towards absolute validity. Consequently, man's historicity stands in need of healing which is not to be looked for from the internal dynamism of history.[9]

These somewhat complicated remarks on historicity serve to emphasize the crucial distinctions that must be made if we are to give man a real task in the world flowing from his given being, yet one that does not pretend to be autonomous in its view of human nature or the conditions necessary to reach beatitude in the proper sense, conditions that depend first on God, as Christian orthodoxy has always insisted.

Perhaps if we use rather the term "spiritual technology", the essential point may be clearer. In discussing the purpose of creation, the medievals used the notion that what is not God is to be made like him. Reality more or less perfectly reflects the Creator; the lowest, the highest, and the whole

[9] Karl Rahner, *Theological Dictionary* (New York: Herder and Herder, 1965) 205.

all bear some basic resemblance. But more than this, there was an active agent in the universe, namely man, whose special function was to return this universe to God in the highest sense of which it was capable. This meant that neither creation nor any of its aspects could be confused with the Creator. This signified that creation really could not be "like" God unless it was freely chosen to be like him. Ultimately, this was man's unique function. The drama of history was precisely to be found in this possibility of creation being turned towards or against God through the choices of the free creature. Intrinsic to this was the idea that things and institutions contained a certain flexibility that left them open to formation by human choice. The world could thus take on a likeness to God over and beyond its original first nature, seen to be good in Genesis, because of man's effort to imitate and follow in fact the kind of actions known through his reason or revealed by God.

Buildings like Chartres or St. Peter's thus existed because of a kind of spiritual technology; they are edifices that did not *have* to exist but did so because of man's effort to shape the universe into a praise of a Creator who did not need the praise nor the universe but who was still the ultimate goal of men who chose to be like unto him. Due to this lack of need on God's part, the reshaping of the earth freely to reflect God's glory revealed the conformity of man to what he in fact received from God—his own being and the world itself. In this sense and properly nuanced for avoiding the improper use of the term in history, we can still talk about a *Respublica Christiana*. For if there is absolutely no sense, direct or indirect, in which the human world is different because of faith, then we have indeed cut off any communication between men and God. What truth there is in contemporary political theologies seems to be an effort to recognize this idea, even though more often than seems necessary, they tend to a kingdom merely of this world. And it is this latter kind that Christians were most warned against by their Scripture and their tradition.

In our time, perhaps it is fair to say that the spiritual technology we see about us mostly reveals essentially human ends, essentially human spirituality. St. Patrick's is lost on Fifth Avenue. It is not pondered as the *Brooklyn Bridge* once was by a Joseph Stella. Yet commercial enterprises are designed to care for men's needs. They are "technologies" we have learned to make and use. The much maligned modern corporation, for all its problems, may well be that instrumentality by which men may be best fed and clothed, that not-to-be-neglected goal said to measure much of our human worth before the Lord. The reason all men are not well cared for is not just bad will; we need to learn to make and use the proper technologies and corporate organizations.

Oscar Cullmann remarked that the apocalyptic tradition of the New Testament tended to look upon the state as that edifice wherein a kingdom erected against God is most likely to be established. "*Regnum Caesaris, Regnum Diaboli*", Tertullian is said to have warned, with at least some justification. The point here is not political philosophy nor how the more positive attitude towards the state evolved in Christian tradition. Rather, it is to point out that "spiritual technology", the reflection of God's reality in the cosmos and society through the free creature is both possible and precarious. When it is accomplished, as Samuel Johnson would have said, it is a little more than nothing compared to the promises. Yet what little we do to advance the happiness of our fellow creatures, to add one useful experiment to natural knowledge, is a worthwhile thing. We can exalt our works provided we recognize they do not reach to the heart of creation promised to each of us in our spiritual lives, in our hope of personal resurrection, the ultimate connection of our beatitude in this earthly life to the God of Christianity.

Technology is the great arena of the spirit which is found in our persons, since it betrays to us best what we have chosen in our earthly existence. But what we have chosen decides ultimately, as Augustine said, what we shall be. And in this, there is no more technology. Finally what we do on this earth, in this cosmos, by comparison, is indeed little more than nothing. In the end, we need not separate the Creator from his work, nor repine that our abilities be small and our opportunities few. What the Supreme Artisan of the Universe obliges every man is that in his art and his technics, he, *homo faber*, leave some room for the artisan God, some room ultimately to discover how much more than nothing he is to be given.

PART IV

BY DISTINCTIVE INSTITUTIONS

X

AN ELITE CHURCH?

Sometime within the past decade or so, I have sensed that somehow it is more and more difficult to become a Catholic or, being one, to remain identifiably one. Furthermore, there are rather large numbers of people who can call themselves "Catholics" but who hold theses or act in ways that have traditionally been considered quite un-Catholic. There has been very little exercise of ecclesiastical authority during this period, moreover, of the kind that would serve to define or identify in any public sense who a Catholic might actually be. In a very real sense to many the Church seems almost as if it were becoming, at the same time, a sect or a cult of a few or else a conglomorate hodge-podge, which would include all by accepting all. In a way, these are but two aspects of the same problem. As the difficulty of being a Catholic increases, the temptation to recoup losses by changing criteria of belief or practice also increases.

The trend to restricted ecclesial membership is the result of certain attitudes or ideas that appear at first sight to be quite defensible. In removing much traditional form from the reception of the various sacraments which everyone once normally received, we have ended up with an ill-defined but, I think, real policy which in practice grants no sacrament *except* to those who positively choose or insist that they receive it. The prevalence of divorce and "living together" have made this area practically a one-way street away from the Church, while abortion has reduced greatly the number of children among us.[1] The main exception to this, and this probably proves the rule, is Holy Communion, which is now available almost without institutional restriction so that it is now minimally related to Confession and does not necessarily exclude in practice other denominations.

Initially, to be sure, much of this will sound like an improvement. Away with those once-a-year-at-Christmas Catholics! Down with those Italian and Spanish dandies who stood outside Sunday Mass for fifty years without ever putting a foot inside! The Baptists were right all along! Only adults can be Christian. An assistant pastor recently told a woman I know to let her child whom she wanted baptized grow up first. Then, let the child choose what church she wanted to join. We cannot impose faith on children. These seem like obvious truths to many. Yet they are a denial of a traditional belief and practice whose whole foundation was different. So we must wonder about it all.

The Roman Church, in one sense, has always been considered to be a non-elite Church, a Church in fact of sinners. This has meant that the great majority, if not all, of ostensible Christians at any given moment will manifest many aberrations, such that they will be less than they might be. In addition, we have always distinguished between our private and public selves. We have been aware that we might well observe the letter of the law but rank rather low by a more spiritual criterion. The Church from the beginning has identified, moreover, certain specific beliefs and practices so obviously contrary to Christian life that anyone who held or practiced them could be con-

[1] See James Hitchcock, *Catholic Perspectives: Divorce* (Chicago: Thomas More Press, 1979) 65–120.

sidered officially outside the fold because of them. Thus, the Church was concerned with both saints and sinners, even though some things could not logically or spiritually be reconciled with Christianity without neglecting anyone in particular. The burden of the Church's ordinary apostolate, in any case, was conceived to be normal men and women. This was the crucial area even though the call to holiness in a more specific way could not be neglected.

In many areas of the world, however, Christians have been but a tiny percentage of the population. This is, indeed, true in most of the nations of the world today. Christianity, in fact, is positively excluded or discriminated against in at least half the world's major areas, probably more, as John Paul II pointed out both in Mexico and Poland. The experience of Christianity as a minority is that of a good many Christians who see the tenor of their culture definitely slanted against them; perhaps Christians in the Arab-Islamic world realize this better than any. The tradition of "many are called but few are chosen" seems often to be quite true statistically. And even in so-called Christian regions, the expected signs of Christian belief and practice are less and less visible, more often themselves under pressure.[2] The public law in many countries has provisions and controls with which a Christian must not agree.

It is undoubtedly true, on the other hand, that there is at the same time a strong presence of deeply committed Christians within the growing loss of the masses. In the general history of Christianity, there has been place for both an elite holy and the normal, ordinary Christian.[3]

[2] See Chapter 4 in the present work.
[3] See Chapter 12 in the present work.

Indeed, the Church wisely felt that such persons who devoted themselves to holiness in a special fashion ought to be set apart in a separate life-style, so to speak, since a life of this kind of exemplary perfection, the evangelical counsels, as they were called, could not be expected of everyone. This represented a deep insight into the reality and possibility of the ordinary man. It recognized that this common life was good and proper, even though something higher might be expected of a few.

The Australian writer Karl Schmüde has stated this combination of the elite and the ordinary in Christianity well:

> The Catholic Church ... has tended to assimilate movements of authentic renewal and to incorporate them into its institutional life. The phenomenon of religious orders is striking proof of this capacity, for the Church has been able to absorb the spiritual movements which they represent, and to engage them as instruments of its wider purposes of internal rejuvenation and external conversion.
>
> Throughout its history, the Catholic Church has sought to be a universal religion—a faith of mass appeal. It has exhibited the power to evoke the passionate loyalty of ordinary persons, and to retain the allegiance of the naturally irreligious. Wherever it has struck root, it has cultivated a living and sympathetic sense of the ordinary life. In each case, it has given rise to a particular social atmosphere and ethos, a distinctive style of life: in each case, it has given rise to a Catholic people.[4]

This is well said and emphasizes the sense in which the Church must retain its reality among the ordinary.

Thus, the Roman Church made place for its spiritual elite, as it were, by recognizing its necessity and even

[4] Karl Schmüde, *Catholicism: The Faith of a People* (Melbourne: Catholic Truth Society, 1976) 5.

inevitability. But the Church never conceived itself to be composed only or mainly of an elite. Christianity always had a healthy sense of the danger of belonging to a spiritual elite, so that it surrounded its "holier" members with rules, meditations, and inner self-discipline that would prevent the elite from turning into a clique or a tyranny. Furthermore, the Christian doctrine of vocation and grace left little doubt that the movement of the Spirit, even in the best, was more important than any individual or personal element, however fundamental that also might be.

In today's Church, the manifestation of elitism has not come mainly from the religious orders as such, organizations which might consider themselves as holier than the Church, though, as James Hitchcock pointed out in *Catholicism and Modernity*, much of the turmoil is due to an elite.[5] The classical male and female religious orders are themselves more often in serious trouble, though it still may be true that the ultimate spiritual battle is fought out in the hearts of those whom God has specially called. The functions once performed by the religious orders in various parts of the world and in various levels of society have declined, leaving a vacuum on the ecclesial scene. Something of a reaction to this has been a sort of "withdrawal" syndrome taking place in the Church. Faced with hostile governments or unchristian cultures, religious thinkers are seeking to define what is minimally necessary to preserve the Church.

Historically, such "minimalization" was geared to expansion. Today, it is rather designed to save what can be

[5] James Hitchcock, *Catholicism and Modernity* (New York: Seabury, 1979).

saved. The noted Italian priest journalist Piero Gheddo, in the aftermath of Vietnam, the religious consequences of which we have failed to account for, doubted if any external structure at all could be maintained.[6] The widespread social, health, and educational services performed in many parts of the world by religious orders, institutions which had historically maintained the presence of the Church on the frontiers and within the midst of the masses, have either dwindled or been taken over by the state, with a new spirit that we are yet to come to terms with.[7] There is in Italy and in the Marxist nations a renewed interest in the family as a last outpost of the faith. And in most other Western countries, the viability of the family itself is already quite problematic.[8] Indeed, some, like Solzhenitsyn argue even further that there is more faith in Marxist countries than in the West. John Paul II has certainly called attention to faith in the most oppressed Eastern European states.

In any case the Church, even as a cultural reality, is pushed out of the centers of public life, while Catholics have rarely maintained any cohesive force to preserve their position as, say, the German Catholics did under Bismarck's *Kulturkampf*, or the Polish Church of today. Indeed, under the precise aspect of culture as espoused by the Italian Marxist theories stemming from Gramsci, a major attack on Christianity is coming forth to remove precisely the religious elements from Western culture. This in itself was

[6] Piero Gheddo, *Mondo e Missione* (Milan, January, 1977).

[7] See the author's "Rethinking the Nature of Government", *Modern Age* (Spring 1979). See also Chapter 8 in the present work.

[8] The Marxist critic Christopher Lasch has also noted some of this in *The Culture of Narcissism* (New York: W.W. Norton, 1978).

proof of the wisdom of the theories of Christopher Dawson and the nature of Western culture.[9]

While other racial and ethnic groups in the modern world, moreover, have suddenly become stronger and more articulate, religious unity and intensity in the West as a large-scale phenomenon have declined, at least as acknowledged aspects of the culture. Many would argue that the former is mainly the cause of the latter. Race and nation are new absolutes, the current false gods. And both represent a shift away from the deliberative person to the nonvoluntary group. Manifestations of racism and nationalism go practically unnoticed when practiced in the Third World by Third World peoples. Consequently, it is not without interest that many of the values once sought in religion are now claimed in race or nation, or, in some areas, in sexual groupings, especially those that deviate from classical Christian orthodoxy in the matter.

What is the problem with an elite in the Church? Can we not argue that since, in practice, we have mostly abandoned any doctrine of hell which once was a factor in urging our efforts to convert peoples formally to the Church—one thinks of Francis Xavier in this context—there is no need to worry about who "belongs" to the Church on earth? If all men will be saved no matter what, should we not accept a kind of "cultural pluralism" that does not try to "change" the Chinese, Hindu, African, or American? Nothing we do can affect their ultimate status anyhow, while religious and ethical variety are as natural as biological variety. It will thus be enough for the Church to be present behind a door

[9] See also John Senior, *The Death of Christian Culture* (New Rochelle: Arlington House, 1978).

in an upper room at Jerusalem as at Pentecost. There is no need to evangelize the masses because they cannot live a full Christian life anyhow, while their natural variety is itself the primary criterion of religious reality.[10]

Thus, there is a kind of Gnosticism about that implicitly rejects the turbulent and imperfect world of the men and women who are. There is a kind of denial of rite and sacrament to everyone who believes truly, no matter how insecurely or imperfectly. Yet, a Church for "everybody" will be full of many things that cannot be wholly edifying, from gaudy statues to pastors who drink too much, to bishops who do not rule firmly, to illegitimate children, to theologians who teach some heresy, to the publicans and harlots of Scripture. Such a Church will necessarily appear quite chaotic and disorderly. That is probably the necessary consequence of a Church of men and not angels. The classic theory of grace must mean, at least, that the condition of Christians at any given time or place is both precarious and hopeful, that the worst can become the best, that the unexpected is to be expected.

Nonetheless, the Church cannot stand for just anything. The fine line between what might be called the "normal" sinfulness of humans and a formal action against the structure of belief must be maintained if Christianity is to mean anything at all. Christianity is a religion of moral forgiveness, but not of intellectual confusion. Christianity thus has insisted that some beliefs and actions must be rejected. At first sight, this will sound like a distinctly illiberal view. But when liberalism is taken to mean the justification

[10] There is a good deal of this kind of reflection in the important works of the late Professor Leo Strauss.

of anything, it itself is illiberal. There is and must be a standard of the human and the right. There is a way to be human in an elite sense, to be sure. In a way, the Greeks stood for this in our culture, the notion that we ought to know and strive for the best because there is a best without which we all would wither somewhat. The presence of the best is a judgment on the worst. And this is so because we are free to be better. Elitism, in its best sense, is based on this fact. Where it becomes dangerous is where it denies grace and even choice in those who seem to create evil and chaos in the world.[11]

My point here, however, is a brief one. We are in a period, in the Western Roman Church at least, in which a kind of perverted elitism is a temptation for our missionary policy both with regard to newly born humans and for those outside of Christianity's normal sphere. Formerly, elitism in the Church either broke off into sects or was guided into the more stable form of religious orders. There was a vivid realization that the perfection of the Law could not be expected of everyone so that the living Church was to include many who were not perfect, far from it. This meant that the sacramental system was designed to teach, and to include more than it excluded. Much was simply left "up to God", as it were. There was an admitted need and place for an elite, but this was held to be a specialized life for a relatively few, a spiritually dangerous life if it be not solidly within the structure of the Church.

Contrariwise, the Church of sinners meant also a clear and doctrinally enforced limit on what could be called

[11] See Frederick Wilhelmsen, *Christianity and Political Philosophy* (Athens, Ga.: University of Georgia Press, 1978).

Christian. There were both beliefs and practices that could not be reconciled with Christianity. And Aquinas's restatement of Aristotle's observation that a small error in the beginning could lead to an enormous error in the end was taken quite seriously and quite literally. Further, we could perhaps argue today that while whole peoples and cultures can choose beliefs and practices so contrary to Christianity that it is necessarily excluded from their framework, this is an alternative that the Church has desperately fought to avoid, even though it must admit the possibility.[12] Christianity has believed that it could accept whatever good was to be found in other cultures or religions or nations. The dark side of this belief was that it must also accept evidence of the opposite.

We would thus be naive to say that Western culture itself may perhaps be putting itself into an anti-Christian position on several basic points, most obviously on those relating to life in its coming to be and in its departing. Should the process continue, a kind of elitism or exclusiveness might well then be almost forced on those who continue to believe in traditional Catholic doctrine. This is why, undoubtedly, the major and most sensitive aspect of this cultural issue concerns precisely the changing of actual Christian doctrine to conform with current ideology so that Christians do not feel "alienated" in its presence. In fact, this may in part be what is behind the implicit changes in baptismal, marital, and death rites and practices. Many assume that Christianity in its classical orthodox form can only be lived by a few fortunate souls. For the rest, Chris-

[12] See Jean Daniélou, *The Salvation of the Nations* (Notre Dame, Ind.: University of Notre Dame Press, 1962).

tianity will be only a residue, if that, not so much the Church of sinners—for sin is one of the things left out—but a church of cults and conformities and enthusiasms, each rejecting much of the central doctrine of the faith but still claiming allegiance to one or two main practices or beliefs.

In Scripture, we are told to be perfect as our heavenly Father is perfect. Our heavenly Father is perfect so that there is no other god like unto him. This means that we are not ourselves gods. And this is God's perfection, to have an imperfect world—however vast it be—in preference to having none at all. But we are also told to have no strange gods before us. This must mean at least that we can seek to set up a world in which God's footprints, as it were, are largely removed from our midst. The Church must be "elite" in the sense that it witness to God as revealed to us no matter what men might prefer. But the Church is also the Church of sinners. They are not an elite; everyone is a candidate. Thus, it is a Church of sinners because that is the way most men are.

The New Testament at times even seems to suggest that the generality of men, as well as just an elite, can reject God's particular plan for our salvation. They can even reject what is authentically human. What I suggest is that we are becoming elite where we should be more universal, while in terms of the structure of faith, we are being vaguely universal where we should be more definite and clear. The question of an elite Church strikes me as the very cultural center of our civilization and its precarious condition. Faith, in other words, has a content, a content that includes the human but is more than that. We are Christians to the degree that we believe this, to the degree we believe that faith is, first, a gift, and, second, a gift for all. Then, on believing both of these things, we are finally Christians when we know we can accept or reject both, that this is the ultimate heart of the divine mystery in the human heart.

XI

THE FUTURE OF THE CHRISTIAN CLERGY

Depending on whether one is an optimist or a pessimist in these matters, any discussion about the future of the Christian clergy could be entitled either "The Vicarage on the Moon" or "Life Without Father" or "Just Call Me Swami". There is one more possibility, I suppose, which could be something like "The Life and Times of Archbishop Henrietta Marie", but I shall prefer not to tread any further on such rocky ground.

Not so long ago, I chanced to see a perfectly horrid Polish film called *The Pharaoh*. To my knowledge, the movie contained a record number of historical anomalies, such as maintaining that the Jews baptized and the Egyptian priests forgave sins. Since the film was contemporary Polish, of course, it intimated that the main and permanent political problem was the struggle between a rather selfish clergy and a liberal government. Probably, something can be forgiven it as it was made before John Paul II became Pope. Anyhow, there was an up-to-date air about the scenes, mostly anticlerical, which is not something very new, if the truth were known. Unfortunately—or fortunately—such a spectacular could not be taken seriously except to remind us of the long history of priesthood and religion among men and the very biased manner in which it is usually presented to modern audiences.

The ancient Egyptian concept of religion, now mostly lost to the Egyptians through Christianity itself and then Islam, had its static nobility about it. A couple of years ago, a kindly French Jesuit showed me through the great museum in Cairo and guided me through the Pyramids at Giza. He recounted how the whole Egyptian society was organized in a permanence of worship before the source of life, a witness to man's refusal to believe in his ultimate passingness. The pyramids and the mummies in them were meant, quite literally, to last forever. No doubt, one of the great similarities and differences in all religions, including Christianity, is the way they respond to this universal belief among humans.

Evidently, then, clergy have been around in great variety and for a long time. In *The Pharaoh*, every time there was need for solemn religious music and chant, the Egyptian priests were amusingly heard to intone liturgical music from the Russian Orthodox Church. Christianity, of course, has always given the clergy a special status in the Church. Most orthodox theologians would hold that an ordained clergy and even hierarchy are essential constituents of the Church from the beginning. Furthermore, there is the assurance that the gates of hell shall not prevail against the Church founded on Peter. Thus, the obvious conclusion would seem to be that Father will be in the rectory for a long time to come.

There are some doubts about this, to be sure. Roland Bainton, the distinguished Professor of Ecclesiastical History at Yale, was asked, "What is religion likely to be by the year 2975?" His answer was not reassuring:

> The real question is—will Christianity survive? There's a great interest in religion today but a great deal of it goes into mystical movements—Zen Buddhism, transcendental meditation and the like—while others are going in for ecstatic move-

ments which may be either Christian or non-Christian. The future is uncertain.[1]

Anyone who has watched, as I once did, a line of American hari-krishnas snake their way through the Piazza di Spagna in Rome before the Shrine of the Immaculate Conception and the amused gaze of the well-dressed Italian locals and equally well-dressed—western-style—Japanese tourists, will grasp Professor Bainton's point. Since the defeats of Islam in the eighth and fifteenth centuries, it has been Christianity that has been the primary missionary and moving religion in the world. Islam itself, however, as the events in Iran and the oil crisis demonstrate, is especially alive and active again, even in the West, as the names of some of our leading athletes remind us. As Christians lose faith in their Faith, their world becomes immediately subject to the older enthusiasms at a time that has forgotten what they meant in practice. The price of forgetting the price is undoubtedly dear.

In a not unrelated vein, George Kelly at St. John's University has recounted the structural crisis in the Roman Catholic Church and the probably great price society will have to pay for it. The doctrinal structure and obedience of professional theologians to the hierarchy are now so challenged and confused, in Msgr. Kelly's view, that Catholics of post-Vatican II are in danger of repeating the liberal breakdown of modern Protestantism.[2] The attempt of

[1] Roland Bainton, "I Believe", *Modern Maturity* (December-January 1976–77) 44.

[2] George Kelly, "An Uncertain Church", *The Critic* (Fall 1976). This analysis has been subsequently published as a book, *Battle for the American Church* (New York: Doubleday, 1979).

Catholic intellectuals and theologians to declare complete independence from the magisterium, with the logical result that professor poses as pope, represents the crux of the confusion in the minds of believers about the meaning of their religion in the modern world. The Church that has no defined and enforced system of belief is doomed in this view. The result of no real orthodoxy is a skepticism and usually a counter-orthodoxy.

Several years ago, in a commemorative issue of the *Saturday Review*, one devoted to the year 2024, Theodore Hesburgh, the president of the University of Notre Dame, initially responded to the question, "Will There Still Be God?" in this way:

> The easiest snap answer to the question is that if there will be no God in 2024, there isn't one now, either. Or, the other way around, if there is a God now, God will exist 50 years from now and 50 million years from now also, for that matter.[3]

Father Hesburgh went on to suggest that science and religion—the older source of religious conflict—have never been closer together.[4] Religion asks permanent questions and confronts realities that science does not. Thus, so long as men are about, there will be men of religion who will insist that these questions of our origin, destiny, of our sufferings, faults, and loves be asked. Because of them, men will be free to receive answers not exclusively based on doubt or skepticism.

Alexander Solzhenitsyn, in a famous Easter letter to Pimen, the Orthodox Primate of Russia, accused him of

[3] Theodore Hesburgh, "Will There Be God?" *The Saturday Review* (21 August 1974) 82.

[4] See Stanley Jaki, *The Road of Science and the Ways of God* (Chicago: University of Chicago Press, 1978).

betraying Christianity to the regime and cutting off the people from their traditional faith by cooperating with a regime that has no use for Christianity. Indeed, Solzhenitsyn held that Christians in the West have been culpably oblivious to the true plight of believers in his world. They have refused to suffer with others. Further, he believed the only true Christians of the future would be those who have suffered through the lies of Marxism. He saw an inability in the West, one rooted in spiritual values, to distinguish good from evil, a disease which will eventually destroy any civilization that succumbs to it. For Solzhenitsyn, the future of the faith lies with those who have returned to a simpler life, who have refused to compromise with the monstrous evils in the world, who refuse to call evil good.

On an even more somber note, perhaps, the noted Italian priest-journalist, Piero Gheddo, as mentioned in the previous chapter, wrote a very realistic essay in *Mondo e Missione* about the religious consequences of the fall of Vietnam. In the light of these experiences and subsequent events, it is well to pay attention to the precise kind of Church we must be prepared for. Basing himself on Chinese and Vietnamese experience, which he saw as a close observer, Gheddo argued that Christians must now positively prepare, whether they like it or not, to live under a victorious Marxism in which all the values and institutions of the faith will be overturned and controlled. How are Christians practically and organizationally to survive? What will they be allowed to believe?

Gheddo held that in a more completely controlled society such as the one being formed in ·Vietnam and its empire after the American defeat, there would be a complete control and reduction of ecclesiastical structure, no foreigners, no communication with Rome. Further, since internally no independent communication could be maintained, there could be no hierarchy, nor even a priesthood. Aside from Poland and Yugoslavia, the structure of the Church is presently worse in these Marxist areas than in the first centuries. Thus, a clergy in the traditional sense is no longer possible. The faith will have to go underground, but there can be no real underground so it will have to be interiorized. There will be no books, no instruction. All work and employment will be controlled by a counter-philosophy that will brook no opposition.

In advance of this event, then, it will be necessary to destroy all records of Christian organizations and lists of Christians belonging to them in order to protect believers. All organizations will be dissolved. Gheddo summarized:

> All else which is accessory, exterior, accidental falls little by little, voluntarily to destruction by itself. The essential and eternal things are invisible. . . . Thus the clergy will have to be much more numerous at the family level. Bishops and clergy as in today's western democracies are no longer possible in Asian communist countries and even in Europe we know how they limit Christian numbers, submit them to state power, and strictly control them. It cannot be doubted that in marxist countries we require a completely different type of clergy and also of religious life. The priest can no longer be a person diverse from others. . . .[5]

Even though in Poland, for reasons peculiar to its history, the clergy is experiencing something of a growth, the future of the clergy in Marxist countries seems very bleak. Indeed, to prevent such a dire alternative, John Paul II has

[5] P. Gheddo, *Mondo e Missione* (January 1976).

constantly insisted on the need of Christians to remain firm in doctrine and practice. But if the world continues to embrace more radical Marxisms, as many Christians fully expect, this more somber prospective of Gheddo may be the most likely to emerge.

Even in Italy and France, the traditional Catholic countries, the main intellectual drive among Catholics is to adapt themselves to Marxism as the wave of the future. The *New York Times* did a piece on the renewal of the famous worker-priests in France in which priests try to regain contact with the largely Marxist workers. According to James Clarity, these priests have tried:

> to show their companions on the job that a priest can be a decent human being, willing to live a worker's life without preaching or attempting to attract people back to the formal Church.
>
> The worker-priests insist that the movement is not subtle propaganda geared toward conversion. "It is just to show people that a worker can also be a believer, to open up a kind of dialogue, to make people see that religion is not the opium of the people," a priest explained.[6]

Such priests work at every sort of job from bellhop to file clerk, make about one hundred twenty-five dollars a week, do not turn over their funds to a bishop. They do consult the bishop and have pastoral duties on weekends.

So in this radical diversity of prospects, what can be said of the clerical life? Today we are familiar with women who insist that they want to be priests and theologians who tell them that there is nothing wrong with it. We recognize that other theologians do not teach what the Church holds. We

[6] James Clarity, *New York Times* (19 December 1976).

see that the state positively discriminates against many institutions considered essential to religion, such as schools and media presentations. We find doctrines, especially in the life and death fields, coming to be held and enforced against the Christian conscience. We find the stable priesthood very unstable. We often discover that sermons begin to sound like nothing so much as freshman sociology, while forgiveness and guilt are claimed to be the exclusive turf of the psychiatrist or psychologist. We have seen Ireland, the home of so many Catholic clerics, become a symbol of religious bigotry, while in Rome the vital young seminarians are no longer from Europe or North or South America, but from Africa and parts of Asia. We should not be surprised if future bishops in the San Joaquin Valley go to Lagos or Nairobi to find priests for their churches instead of to All Hallows in Dublin.

Perhaps the best way to go about approaching the question of the future of the clergy is to ask what the clergy will in fact do—a rather pragmatic question, of course, but a good place to begin. One of the answers that seemed productive for our clergy, one often outlined by Paul VI and stressed by John Paul II, is that of service to the least of our brothers. Needless to say, as Alexis de Tocqueville pointed out, most of the then incipient functions of the modern welfare state were originally pioneered by the religious and charitable impulses of the Christian Church. Men only learned to see and pay attention to the weak and innocent when they were commanded to love their actual neighbor, whoever he be, the suffering and the insignificant especially. One of the crises the modern state is undergoing, in fact, as we have suggested, is what happens when the Christian origins of these welfare and social concern functions for the least, the weakest, and the poorest have evaporated.[7] Can the monk or the sister really be replaced by the paid bureaucrat?

It can be argued that men and women will now no longer work and extend themselves for anything or anyone unless for pure justice for which they are paid according to their power position in an organized group. We are already seeing, especially in the health field, that men are beginning to question whether there ought to be any concern for the least and the little in the first place. Society ought to be only for the best, we are told, not for the least. When we lose our beliefs, we also seem to lose our motives to keep alive and to help. We have demanded our rights only to discover that rights are not nearly enough, as Christianity has always known.

Many of the Christian clergy have accepted this "concern" level for the Christian presence as the essence of the faith. No doubt, there is no Christianity without this basic care. But this is the Second Commandment, not the First. And further, the concern for the well-being of the poor today is not exclusively Christian in effectiveness or in enthusiasm. The reverse question then must be also confronted: if we are alert for the poor and weak, are we then Christian? The Lord assuredly affirmed that a cup of water to the thirsty would suffice for salvation. And yet it is paradoxical that the ideological forms of this concern for humanity are beginning to be used against actual human persons as well as against God and the Image of Man he revealed to us.

For this reason I doubt if the major meaning and test of the Christian clergy in the next century will have much to do with concern for the poor in the classical sense of that

[7] See Chapter 8 in the present work.

term. Rather from the side of the Second Commandment, it will have to do with keeping alive in the world the relation to man of the vast and consistently underestimated potential of this earth, solar system, and universe, to encourage men not in fact to limit themselves to a narrow vision of their time and their physical place in the cosmos. The poverty problem is mainly a cosmic problem, as the beginning of Genesis already implied. Our recent era has been dominated by a pessimism as profound as any ever conceived, one contrary at almost every point to the essential dogmas of the faith, a pessimism that has pitted the earth against man and caused him to doubt the riches and even existence of providence. It is ironic today that the God of creation is a much vaster God than that of many of our pessimistic scientists. And yet we really understand something of the immensity of our universe. For this reason, I suspect, one of the major functions of religion, and particularly of Christianity, which is the one religion that has confronted science and out of which science arose, will be to save science from and for itself. The need for a scientifically educated clergy has never been greater, exceeded perhaps only by the need for scientists to cease being so ignorant of religion. In this regard, Russell Kirk wrote:

> Years ago—à propos of your remarks on my writing about the education of clerics—I wrote a piece remarking that the clergy were not sufficiently schooled in the social studies. That certainly was remedied, and more than remedied, in a hurry! Nowadays I am saying that seminarians ought to be studying not sociology, but quantum mechanics: in the renewed sciences, as interpreted by Simone Weil and Arthur Koestler, lies a fresh apprehension of transcendence.[8]

[8] Correspondence with author, July 4, 1979.

We are in a situation almost the opposite of the Galileo crisis. This time it is more often science that needs religion to see the stars and the cosmos in their ultimate meaning and order.

The major task of the Christian clergy, however, will have to do with the First Commandment, not the Second. This is to recognize that the transcendent God is to be worshipped as he is revealed to us. All else is secondary.[9] Mankind has always searched for a god other than the true God. This most perfect lesser "idol" has been found in our era, the elevation of "humanity" to the highest place in our liturgies, societies, and thoughts. This is indeed the idol most like God, the one most easily confused with him. It is for this reason that it is easy to eliminate the transcendent God in favor of our immanent one that has no connection outside ourselves. If we study the theological currents and presuppositions in our seminaries and universities today, we will see that at bottom this is the issue, the love of God *versus* the love of man, in an opposition never before structured in quite that manner. If this is so, the need and meaning of the Christian clergy in the future becomes ever more crucial, for it is no less than that of keeping the connection between God and man, that connection revealed to us in the Incarnation. The clergy, as we know from the New Testament, can betray their God. That they do not remains one of the principal freedoms of men in the world.

[9] This seems to have been the principal reason for John Paul II's insistence during his Mexican visit that priests be not confused with politicians. See Speeches of January 26, 1979 (*L'Osservatore Romano*, 5 February 1979, 10) and of January 27, 1979 (*L'Osservatore Romano*, 12 February 1979, 4).

We are not wrong, I think, to see that the "orthodoxy", as it were, of the Christian clergy is a central issue of our society, a society taught by Christianity to care for the least of the brothers. But this orthodoxy has a validity and a need that does not derive from society itself but comes rather from the very finiteness of the human condition, from the human person's joy in acknowledging something beyond his own life and even his very universe. That this God has been revealed as Father, Son, and Spirit is the truth the Christian clergy is ordained to present and keep alive in the world. Thus, the clergy's future can only be measured by its ability and its wisdom in keeping this central truth before the rest of us men, the human persons we know and are. This too is why, in the end, the world has need of the clergy, of believing in what they profess. Anything less the world has already heard. And that is not enough.

XII

CHRISTIAN GUARDIANS

The wisdom and ironies of the Platonic tradition as they are filtered through Christianity must begin with this passage from *The Republic*:

> "And the only life which looks down upon the life of political ambition is that of true philosophy. Do you know any other?"
> "Indeed, I do not," he said (521).

Of the various institutions of Christianity—clergy, hierarchy, bishop, pope, laity—few have had a more turbulent and fascinating history than the monk or the nun, those who, as they saw it, did not follow the example of the rich young man in the Gospels, but instead sold what they had, gave it to the poor, and followed Jesus. Luther felt that such were not needed. The opposition of diocesan and regular clergy has been around for a long time within the Church, which for its part has held that both kinds of life were indeed proper and necessary within Christendom.

Undoubtedly, the most outlandish and oft-cited passages from Plato have to do with his proposals for the communality of wives, children, and property for his Guardians in the Fifth Book of *The Republic*. Indeed, the proposal caused considerable consternation to Socrates' friends Adeimantos and Polymarchus themselves. And when Socrates had previously suggested that his discourse about the delicate subject of "friends having all things in common" should have a limit, Glaucon replied that "the whole of life is the only limit which wise men assign to hearing of such discourses" (*Republic* 450).

Historically, as we now realize, not even many centuries of lifetimes have sufficed to resolve the implications of the proposals of Socrates with their overtones of eugenic planning, their rigid asceticism, and their hope that economic reorganization would cure human ills. Christianity, with this same rich young man, was nowhere as radical as Plato seemed to be on the same subject, though both seemed to be driving at the same point, that some ultimate sacrifice was necessary should we hope to attain the highest things.

Yet Christianity has had a love-hate relationship with Plato, even with his Guardians. Somehow, even when Plato seemed most wrong, he seemed at the same time almost right. The Christian principle that grace cures nature has nowhere worked more remarkably than with Plato, who may well have been the greatest thinker our kind has yet produced. Thus, Plato seems like a providential precursor, a kind of intellectual John the Baptist, preparing the way for the coming of the Lord. Whereas John had said, "Repent, the kingdom of God is at hand," Plato advised: "My counsel is that we hold fast ever to the heavenly way and follow after justice and virtue always, considering that the soul is immortal and able to endure every sort of good and every sort of evil. Thus shall we live dear to one another and to the gods . . ." (*Republic* 621).

Furthermore, Socrates sighs in *The Republic*, when asked of the perfect state if it might come about on earth, that except perhaps by a "divine call", no statesman could hope to achieve good in any existing society. The only time the Socratic "voice" was silent was when Socrates went to the trial resulting in his death.[1] And Plato sadly prophesied that when the truly good man does appear on earth, he will be thought unjust, then, "scourged, racked, bound—will have his eyes burned out; and, at last, after suffering every kind of evil, he will be impaled" (361). No Christian, of course, could read such lines in retrospect without a sense of awe. And surely no one was more devoted to the good, more concerned to abolish evil than this same Plato.

Yet Plato is also accused of almost corrupting Christianity by his charm. His immortality was not the doctrine of the Resurrection; his ideals were not the kind of concrete actions in which virtue existed, evidently. His body-soul dichotomy has been chastised again and again, even though it is difficult to live without it. Professor Robert Kreyche, in a recent essay, "Christianity and the Person", attributed to Plato our failure to understand what properly a person is. He wrote:

> Part of the fault for past overstress on 'souls' often to the detriment of persons, was due to Christianity's long-standing flirtation with Greek philosophy, especially that of Plato. We recall that St. Augustine leaned heavily on Platonic ideas and expressions and so gave an impetus to a one-sided view of man. For Plato, man was a 'soul using a body'. Man did not have a soul so much as he was a soul 'imprisoned in a body as an oyster in a shell.'[2]

Plato's description of that "wild beast" which is within us harboring every conceivable form of folly and vice would

---

[1] See the author's "The Death of Christ and Political Theory", *Worldview* (March 1978) 18–22.

[2] Robert Kreyche, *Christianity and the Person*, (London: Catholic Truth Society, 1975) 4.

seem to suggest that Plato had a very pessimistic view of actual human beings. He seemed to go even beyond the classic doctrine of original sin to imply that human nature itself was somehow at fault (*Republic* 571). On the other hand, Plato seemed to expect that given the right training and the right use of dialectics, we could actually arrive at a direct vision of the good. He seemed to pass from pessimism to optimism without bothering to ask about the real condition of most men. And even when he tried to account for the way most men are, he ended up in *The Laws* mostly closer to his constant ideals. Too, he seemed almost Gnostic or Pelagian in setting forth an ideal of self-achievement in the very highest things, though he did drop hints that only some kind of divine help would make this possible.

Plato, of course, must first be judged by what he really held, and this in his own context. We must begin by being loyal to him. But we should be loyal to him as he was to the poets—"loving Homer, as I do . . ."—rejecting only what is not in conformity with the truth (*Republic* 391). Plato is not responsible for parts of him taken out of his context, though it must be admitted as an historical fact than no one is more easy to borrow things from than Plato. Professor Karl Popper once accused Plato of being at the origin of fascism, a most dubious and unfair charge against that ancient philosopher whose castigations of tyranny are still perhaps the most eloquent in political philosophy (*Republic* 773 ff).[3]

Nonetheless, Plato did inaugurate many ideas the human mind evidently cannot let go of because somehow they bear a truth even when they seem to be false. The most

---

[3] Karl Popper's later remarks on Plato and philosophy are interesting. See his *The Unended Quest* (London: Open Court, 1976).

noteworthy of these ideas is undoubtedly Plato's proposal that there be philosophic guardians in the ideal state who really know the just and the good. That they might do this, Plato proposed that the Guardians have a special kind of practical life so that they might not deviate from their first devotion to the common good of others who depend upon a real vision of the good.

Quite logically and even rigidly, Plato then followed the consequences of this conclusion. This meant that there was to be no distinction of male and female. All that was normally thought to be joined to this basic distinction and relationship was removed. Eros was completely replaced by justice in an intellectual act that probably reveals best the radical difference between eros and justice. Wives and children were to be held in common. Property, the institution that enabled the life of man in the household to come to be and continue, became part of the common pool. An ideal of poverty and asceticism was put in the place of the normal erotic and familial spirit. Plato's Guardians received practically nothing, not even honor, for they were to rule because, if they did not, someone less qualified would. Plato held that uncontrolled desires, especially those of wealth and of passion, would destroy any polis. Thus, he naturally sought to remove any such temptations from his Guardians. Consequently, he became the father of a thought that has reappeared in every era subsequent to his—namely, that if we would have men and women be truly good, we must rearrange, limit, even abolish their marital and property structures. The training of the Guardians sounds, not without reason, like nothing so much as the rule of the Christian religious orders.

This is heady doctrine, to be sure, and much more

attractive than Aristotle's sane criticism of it would seem to indicate. Plato only applied this eccentric and exalted discipline to a few, and it awaited more modern times for an attempt to apply its rigors to all, as various socialist-inspired ideas tried to do. The idea that what is wrong with the public order is due to property and family structures, however, is perhaps the most abiding and attractive of the political heresies, albeit also the most dangerous. This theory gained double plausibility when joined with the Genesis description of the consequences of the Fall such that communality of material goods and natural family relationships were seen to be the pure condition of mankind. Again Plato seemed like a prophet.

This is why, no doubt, it is extremely difficult for the human mind to accept as definitive Aristotle's perceptive caveat in *The Politics* concerning this redistributionist mentality:

> Such legislation [wives/property] may have a specious appearance of benevolence; men readily listen to it, and are easily induced to believe that in some wonderful manner everybody will become everybody's friend, especially when someone is heard denouncing the evils now existing in states, suits about contracts, convictions for perjury, flatteries of rich men and the like, which are said to arise out of the possession of private property. These evils, however, are due to a very different cause—the wickedness of human nature. Indeed, we see that there is much more quarrelling among those who have all things in common . . . (1263b, 15–25).

The question that arose historically, then, was: How was Plato to be saved from this insightful perception of his great pupil? And this especially since Aristotle was no less devoted to the contemplative truth and good than was Plato.

I do not want to argue this question here primarily in terms of subsequent political philosophy. Yet, and this will be my point, the Christian version of the Platonic Guardians is currently at the heart of a social movement to impose a modernized edition of the property/wives controversy upon the whole world. In so doing, of course, we risk losing both Plato and Aristotle. Indeed, we risk losing Christianity itself. Religious and monkish controversies are perhaps at first sight insignificant. On the other hand, there is a view of Christianity which would make them the really significant ones in the world, since what happens in the heart of the monk foreshadows what will happen in the world. Plato's own fear was undoubtedly a real one—"And may we not say, Adeimantos, that the most gifted minds, when they are ill-educated, become preeminently bad?" (*Republic* 491). Thus, confusion or corruptions in the Guardians of whatever style have vast ramifications in the political and spiritual orders.

But what does it mean to speak of "Christian Guardians"? Plato, as I have suggested, was almost right in everything he said. Aristotle's corrections taught us to realize this, as did Augustine's. That we humans look for a city in which true justice and true goodness rule for our own sake, that this good is the source of all our good—such is not a wrong vision. Indeed, it is a right one. Whether such a vision is a "political" one, however, is the crucial issue Christianity, along with Aristotle, put to Plato. Perhaps it would be better and more correct to say that it is the issue that Plato put to himself in Book Ten of *The Republic*, wherein the great astonishment over the belief in immortality is brought up. Yet, be it noted, it is only brought up after we decide what justice is and whether we ought to love it for its own sake. Indeed, the question of rewards and punishments only arises when we are assured we ought to love the good no matter what rewards or punishments we may receive. The final myth of *The Republic* was designed to prove not so much that we will be punished or rewarded in the afterlife, but that we must choose "virtue" in this life or else our afterlife will be as disastrous and as disordered as this one. Plato told us, in other words, that the life we are given is the one wherein we must initially choose correctly.

The implications of this position are that the intellectual Guardians have a special obligation to the good in the first place. Anyone who reads Plato's proposals for communality of wives, children, and property, and his eugenic proposals, is quite normally shocked by their evident inhumaneness. These ideas, however, are powerful ones, as I have suggested, so that the human race has not let them go easily, least of all that part of the human race that calls itself Christian. Plato was correct in *The Laws* in insisting that ". . . sight, hearing, sensation, life itself, are superlatively evil, if one could persist for ever without dying in the enjoyment of these so-called goods unaccompanied by justice and virtue at large" (661). If the path to this vision means the sacrifice of personal happiness for the common good that Plato required, there are many who will accept it. Hence, the Christian tradition, interestingly enough, did not reject Plato out of hand, but rather discovered a way through its own light in which what he argued could be accepted. Though their origins are not, as we have seen, exclusively Platonic, the Christian Guardians did seek to transform the Platonic vision in such a way that it could be lived without the terrible implications of the community of wives, children, and property.

How was this accomplished? There were two steps, the first made possible largely by Augustine. Since the necessity for the Guardians arose because human society needed precisely some group devoted to the highest good as its proper goal—a goal no longer political in origin but contemplative—this became the main vocation of the monk, the life devoted first to God. In the division of societal labor, itself a Platonic thought, the religious was to do that exclusive task that transcended all the others, to keep the idea of and devotion to the Lord alive within society. Thus, he too needed to be free of those goods and ambitions that might interfere with his full devotion to the good, to God. All were to benefit from this, all were to have their place and charism, but the setting aside of some to this exalted end in a special fashion set them apart from both the home and the polis.[4]

Consequently, the Platonic proposal whose purpose was to prevent eros or greed from interfering with the Guardians' life of knowing the good and ruling society in accordance with it was neatly solved by the religious vows of chastity and poverty, which bore a remarkably sane similiarity to the spirit of Plato's original purpose and avoided all its obvious, indeed, inhuman, difficulties. Now it was not necessary to worry about marital and filial problems, to speculate about eugenics. Property was in common but the rule was there to guarantee that the mine and thine were regulated within the monastery. Moreover, the distinction of a proper political life from a contemplative one, and also of a proper family one, enabled the polis to have its legitimate place but yet not be absolutely the highest good. Neatly, the city, the family and the contemplative life were saved by a Christian insight that protected all three.

[4] See Chapter 13 in the present work.

The breakdown of the Christian Guardian solution has taken two steps. The first was the Reformation in which, as Max Weber pointed out, the distinction between the secular and the religious "vocation" was eliminated. Even Plato had insisted that the Guardians ought to live a different life from the one normal to most people. Furthermore, there had always been a current in Christianity that held that monkish life was either impossible or dangerous. The traditional Church, on the other hand, held that it was possible and indeed also dangerous, but it was not for all. The service to the Lord was thus to be in some sense set apart by rule.

Consequently, Catholic Christianity realized the danger to the normal life of most people of comparing them with the monk or nun who was devoted to the contemplative life. Holiness, it had to be recognized, contained a wide variety of possibilities which ought neither to be reduced to a common level nor forbidden in its diversity. The City of God, furthermore, was not the city of the world. The mystical and metaphysical aspects of Plato were indeed worthy and necessary ones, but their fulfillment was ultimately pretty much where Plato himself placed them, in the life of immortality. This end was transformed in Christianity by the doctrine of the Resurrection and sharing in the trinitarian life of God as the ultimate and permanent destiny of man.[5] Compared to this, no earthly city was at all complete—again a feeling we get from Plato.

The Christian solution is undergoing a second transformation in our own times, when the City of God as an aspect and object of contemplation has been gradually

[5] See Chapter 7 in the present work.

transformed for many monks into a worldly task such that the purpose of religion, especially of religious life, is coming more or less to be that of aiding in the transforming of the world into the perfect and best society. The intellectual tension and faith in classical Christianity have not been holding, something skeptics from the Enlightenment on never thought could happen in any case. A vast and growing intellectual effort to transform the classic Christian doctrines into functional images and goals for a worldly purpose and city, this often under the impetus of monks and religious, has now been largely completed. Currently, the basic drama within Christianity is precisely whether this new doctrinal formulation can gain the seats of ecclesiastical power; that is, whether the contemplative content will be evaporated from the older doctrines. And this is what gives the papacy of an intellectual pope from a Marxist country such dramatic importance.

To suggest that Christian monasticism has given up its historical justification of contemplative worship leading to prayer, resurrection, and eternal life for a political role in the world would, perhaps, be too much. The older Jesuit axiom of "contemplation-in-action", however, came to be used as a tool to justify largely this-worldly activities as precisely religious. Today, people are hard pressed to find preached in their churches or proclaimed in their religious media anything that is not sociological, economic, or pseudo-religio-political. When they wonder, they are then told that this is what faith is all about.

Thus, the classic Christian idea of things of Caesar and of God has come to be practically interpreted, to be reunited in an effort to produce, supposedly, a new international order or what have you, one thus that results from transformed property and institutional structures, the modern guise of the Platonic formula. Religious zeal is seen primarily in work, not prayer, work within the world, for the world. Contemplation approaches action to the degree that it disappears as a real function of monastic life. The poverty and celibacy of religious life are to witness, when they are still held, not to God, but to a worldly order. At the further extremes, to which so many ideas currently lead, the institutions supporting classic religious life become leveled. Plato's rigid feminine egalitarianism demands entrance into convent and monastery of all alike. Children themselves have become mostly obsolete, if not evil. Population, not wickedness, has become the great scourge.

When we seek to define the goal of this kind of spirit, we must, as we do so often, go back to Plato himself, in a remarkable, prophetic passage from *The Laws*.

> If there is now on earth, or ever should be, such a society—a community of women folk, in children, in all possessions whatsoever, if all means have been taken to eliminate everything we mean by the word ownership from life; if all possible means have been taken to make even what nature has made our own in some sense common property, I mean, our eyes, ears, and hands to see, hear, and act in common service; if, moreover, we all approve and condemn in perfect unison and derive pleasure and pain from the same sources—in a word, when the institutions of society make it utterly one, that is a criterion of their excellence than which no truer or better will ever be found. If there is anywhere such a city, with a number of gods, or sons of gods, for its inhabitants, they will dwell there in all joyousness of life (739).

I cite this remarkable passage at some length since it is almost certainly the ultimate source of Marx's famous passage in his *Economic and Philosophical Manuscripts* of 1844, wherein he wanted his atheist humanism, his version of the perfect earthly city to self-create even man, even what he sees and does. Marx's words are instructive in this context:

> The suppression of private property is therefore complete emancipation of all human qualities and senses. It is this emancipation because these qualities and senses have become human, from the subjective as well as the objective point of view. The eye has become a human eye when its object has become a human social object created by man and destined for him. The senses have therefore become directly theoreticians in practice.[6]

What I wish to suggest in citing these passages is that the classic Platonic object of the Guardians, the contemplative vision of the good, has by a series of ironic, historical twists come to be identified with a practical political project to conform to the ideal now seen not as an ultimate "Form", nor as a supernatural life or city given by God, but as the construction of an earthly city wherein Socrates would not have been killed. What is new recently is that this essentially Enlightenment idea and project has appeared most obviously in religious orders.

Christian guardianship is now seen not as separate from economic and political society to preserve and worship a higher good, but rather as "doers" constructing the good so that the spiritual seeing and hearing and feeling have their objects in the public order wherein property organization and removal of sinful structures—by this very reorganization and contrary to Aristotle—will produce the

[6] Karl Marx, in *Marx's Concept of Man*, Bottomore, ed. (New York: Frederick Ungar, 1961) 132.

kind of world the Lord presumably wants here below. Underneath it all, this is the intellectual spirit of our times, an era still fascinated with part of the Platonic vision, one now reaching the extreme that not even Socrates suspected would come to be.

In Book Six of *The Republic*, Socrates said that what remains is this: "The question of how the study of philosophy may be so ordered as not to be the ruin of the state: All great attempts are attended with risk . . ." (497). This remains true and nowhere is the risk greater than in pursuing the visions of Plato, especially when the pursuers are Christians. Near the end of *The City of God*, Augustine wrote: "Some Christians, who have a liking for Plato on account of his magnificent style and the truths which he now and then uttered, say that he even held an opinion similar to our own regarding the resurrection of the dead" (XXII, 28).

In conclusion, I suspect those ancient Christians who were enamoured with Plato's style were closer to his truth than our modern Christian Guardians, who are tempted to assure us, contrary to Socrates' feeling and inspiration, that the ideal kingdom is about to become an existing one.

> "In heaven," I replied, "there is laid up a pattern of it, I think, which he who desires may behold, and beholding may set his own house in order. But whether such an one exists, or ever will exist in fact, is no matter; for he will live after the manner of that city, having nothing to do with any other" (*Republic* 592).

In searching for the completion of Plato's vision in the Resurrection rather than in the transformation of this world as the Christian truth, I suspect the Christians cited by Augustine had much the better insight into the real Platonic mystery.

At a certain point in *The Republic* (505), Plato ceased to talk about justice and began to talk about the good.[7] Recently, among what I have been calling Christian Guardians, discourse about the good, especially under the form of mercy and charity, has practically ceased, rather to be subsumed into a discourse about justice. Ultimately, however, Christian Guardians exist to tell us in all existing states that we have here no lasting city. When in their actions and speech they fail to do this, they betray not only the Christianizers of Plato, but indeed Plato himself. They still must look for the only life that looks down on political ambition, a life not only of true philosophy, but also one of true gift, not made for our own eyes and ears.

[7] Cf. Josef Pieper, *Reality and the Good* (Chicago: Henry Regnery, 1949).

XIII

MONASTERY AND HOME

If there is in current Christianity a confusion between city and kingdom, between intellectual and spiritual elites, there is likewise a confusion about the difference between the monastery and the home that needs to be attended to. Perhaps, to begin some reflection on this difference, so historic in Christianity, as pointed out somewhat in the previous chapter, it is well to begin with two remarks, the first from J. R. R. Tolkien, the second from Chesterton:

> But in God's kingdom, the presence of the greatest does not depress the small. Redeemed man is still man.

> I knew now why grass had always seemed to me as queer as the green beard of the giant, and why I could feel homesick at home.

In Christianity, if it is considered romantic, noble, or sacrificial to leave home for the world or the monastery, still, it is also considered perhaps even more mystical to stay at home. The building of the home partakes of the same creative spirit as the building of the monastery walls. The diversity of spirits is real enough, the two are not the same, yet their Lord is the same.

Not too long ago, in a sort of reverie, I was thinking of my "monastery", or more properly, as I am not technically a monk, of the community and series of communities in which I have now lived much of my life. I have always enjoyed, quite literally, large communities, even though rarely, as happens once in a while, I have seen companions flare up and get angry at one another. I have liked the bewildering variety of many men together, of their age, virtue, talents, choices, personalities, faults too. Somehow, they have always symbolized that Christian reality that suggests we are to get along with whoever is given to us, whoever he be. There is something healthy about living with the old when they are old, the crotchety when they are crotchety, the wise when they are also foolish, with the young when they are solemn. I have always been quite leery of living only with those whom I choose.

Today, I realize, there is something of a trend, even a fad, among religious, one which curiously identifies an ideal monastery or a religious community with precisely a "home", wherein presumably, we can "have guests", "cook", and "entertain", as the saying goes. This, I think, in great part explains the appearance of the so-designed "small community", established against or apart from the larger one, and this not so much for motives of apostolate, as often happened in earlier religious thought, but for religious life itself, a small community situated on just any old avenue, in any old city, nestled among the people.

Logically, of course, this also means in practice the abandonment of larger historical places, grounds, and buildings with which religious life had been associated. Several winters ago, for example, some friends drove me through St. Mary's College in Kansas, the old grounds of the Missouri Province of the Society of Jesus, a place, at the time—it has subsequently been purchased by traditionalist Catholics! —bereft of any living religious presence, a place about which I had heard so much from religious companions over the years. The California Province to which I belong, moreover, no longer operates for the same purpose any of the wonderful buildings and institutions in which I was educated—neither the Novitiate, nor Mt. St. Michael's, nor Alma College. This has meant, somehow, a break in generation and common memory, the significance of which no one has really reflected on. Perhaps, for Jesuits, the eventual fate of Woodstock College in Maryland has been the most poignant of all.

In any case, I have never been much tempted, I confess, by the seemingly obvious idea that the monastery was a home. Part of the reason for this, I think, was that I have been in too many real homes, and I know that the essence of home—the idea Chesterton said was the most metaphysical of all—can never be imitated by religious communities no matter how hard they try. To be sure, I do not object to calling religious life a "family" life, and there is a certain special "homely" atmosphere to monastic institutions. But their charism, their central inspiration and grace are different.[1]

Furthermore, one of the sacrifices of religious life, as I have always existentially understood it, was precisely the giving up of a proper home. This is not something of anguish or regret, for it is a liberty in its own sphere. But to be meaningful, it remains a sacrifice. To seek to bring the home into the monastery by the back door, as it were, seemed both naive and a bit dangerous, in spite of current enthusiasms. Consequently, I have never thought a monastery or convent ought to be just like a home. Nor have I

[1] There have been interesting recent attempts to combine monastery and home in a kind of religious commune containing marrieds, children, singles, clergy, nuns. It is believed by many that neither home nor monastery can be viable today without the other. See the author's "The Monastery, the City and the University", *Commonweal* (8 April 1972).

ever felt my friends who did choose to create and love in what is really a home ever expected me to live just like they did. In a sense, because I as a religious did not have a home of my own, I was welcome in their homes. And I was not expected to "reciprocate" in kind. It was enough that I did not have what I did not have. Christian life could be found in both home and monastery or convent, but the two lives were different too, one was not just the shadow of the other. Christianity tended to diversity perhaps even more than to unity, as C. S. Lewis implied. So Paul meant what he said about there being a diversity of spirits with the same Lord.

Thus, I reflected, continuing my day-dream, if I am gone from my religious house for a day, a week, or a semester, as at times I may and even ought to be, I know that somehow in its own cycle, with its variety and size, its peculiar rhythm will be going on without me. Indeed, I rather like the idea that I leave and return without too much fuss, for I remain a part of the community even when I am not there. Monks and sisters do their duty present or absent, since their reality is not formed "for" the monastery but for the Lord, who calls us where he wills. And when I go to a new house or visit one I have not seen before, I am ever refreshed to realize that I already know this "life" I find within new walls in a new place, one I know without knowing.

When a father or a mother is gone, however, things do not just go on "as usual". Even more profoundly, in a family, members are different "by nature", even as they are created mostly by nature. We are told to love everyone because just anyone may come into the world as our particular brother or sister. Children must grow up and depart. Should they not, the family is either in a culture of widely extended families or it is a disordered family. Husbands and wives eventually end up without their natural "community", with only each other, often not even with this, for death ends the particular family as it does not end the monastery, which has even its own burial grounds. The drama of beginning and end, personal existence, growth, love, place, work, sickness, and death belongs within the family in an absolute way.

The monastery is different. The members of the monastery or convent or religious community arrive in its confines in quite a different way than they do into a family. Without denying the fundamental element of chosenness in each personal existence, there is in Christian religious theory a particular "vocation", as it has been called, to each religious life. Thérèse of Lisieux was profoundly correct, even as a matter of actual experience almost, when she wondered at the beginning of her *Autobiography*, why all souls "did not receive an equal amount of grace". And at a deeper level, she realized that God "does not call those who are worthy, but those he chooses." It is of these latter that the monastery and the convent are composed.

Thus the monastery is, in an odd way, the Christianization of the Platonic guardians, as suggested in the previous chapter, wherein the noble ends of Plato were achieved by the much simpler and astonishing device of the three vows rather than by community of wives, children, and property. Too, it is no accident that "eros" was not a constituent part of the lives of the Platonic guardians, just as it was not to be part of the monastery. And this has nothing to do with a denial of the validity and dignity of eros as such. Plato, as Josef Pieper wrote in his remarkable *Enthusiasm and the Divine Madness*, was quite aware of the depth and value of eros precisely as a symbol of the divine nature itself. And Christianity has seen from the very beginning that one of its major vocations was to preserve the very possibility of the full growth of eros among men and women. This is what the eternal struggle against the Manicheans in all ages is about, even in our own times. This, indeed, is the profound meaning of the controversies over sexuality and marriage, as we see them today.[2] It is probably not wrong to hold within this context that one of the major causes of the disruption of the monasteries today lies in the intellectual confusion of religious over the meaning of "home". Likewise, I suspect, not a little confusion about the meal nature of the Eucharist can be reduced to this origin also.[3]

The main problem that needs to be touched upon here, however, concerns the idea of rootedness, our sense of comfort in the place where we have our feet set on this earth. The shadow of Simone Weil should not go unnoticed here. Christianity has always reminded us that we are pilgrims and wayfarers, that we have here no lasting city nor our true home. In a sense, Christians have long been suspect in the world precisely because of this part of their spiritual culture, which did not allow them to be totally committed to any earthly civilization. In one sense, this is what the long, acrimonious debate over church and state was really about. Moreover, the most dramatic

[2] See the author's *Human Dignity and Human Numbers* (Staten Island, N.Y.: Alba House, 1971); *Christianity and Life* (San Francisco: Ignatius Press, 1981).

[3] See John Paul II, Address, November 18, 1978, in *The Pope Speaks* 24, no. 1 (1979) 80.

theological debate going on in the world today is, as we have suggested, whether or not Christianity can be converted into essentially a modernization theory to improve the world. The revolutionary monk has taken as his model not the image of the Medieval Order for the Redemption of Captives, but rather precisely that of a contemplative, seeking an ideological reordering of the world. A Solzhenitsyn, who was expelled from actual tyranny, has found Christians largely concerned about other things than saving real Christians in the tyranny with which he was familiar.

Some friends of mine, old friends really in whose home I have often and happily stayed, were visiting California not so long ago from Australia, where they are now living. Just before their ship left San Francisco, they gave me a copy of a *New Yorker* magazine (26 September 1977), with the wise admonition, "I think you should read the editorial on home." The not overly cynical view was, correctly, I think, that this particular editorial represented the effort of a certain kind of secular liberal mind to justify its recent record of antipatriotism against the sense of the country, to find some kind of intellectual rationale for its actions and presuppositions. This implied that some more basic entity had to embrace us, one which would allow the truth of liberal doctrines while justifying their continued viability.

The *New Yorker* editorial, in this context, proceeded to recall a British airplane pilot, middle-aged, a symbol of civilized alienation, a man locked into his profession, into a way the young could not appreciate. After seeing the whole of the world weekly, he decided to remain where he was:

> For Daniel, society was less something that supported him than a mechanism closing in on him. He had become isolated

in a situation in which he could not grow. Daniel, in other words, was a very modern man fighting for his life in the modern western world. . . .

So in this almost Spenglerian context, the pilot had to make his compromises. There was no moving on. All that was left was the discovery of his own home.

> Every time he approached England on an airplane, he was moved: England was so green; there was no green like the green of England anywhere in the world. How many times, over and over, he must have seen England materialize on the horizon, and every time he had been comforted and restored. He belonged in England. England was home.

Here we suspect another kind of confusion—not the reduction of the monastery, but of the nation, to the home.

These reflections of the return to green England, of course, must strike anyone who knows his Chesterton as a kind of parody on the great theme of *Orthodoxy*, of the sailing around the world only to discover in the end the green and great vision of that land from which we originally sailed, that same green England. And what is more noteworthy, there is nothing here of Chesterton's acute feeling of homesickness at home, none of his sense that our final contentments and loves are in their very acts but hints and shadows of what we do not yet possess. The monk leaving the monastery for a presumed home is a tragic figure, in a sense, for he seeks what cannot be given to him even in a home. And this was why the older monks of our history built monasteries in the first place, be they in countrysides or cities, to remind us of the city, the home, the country, we still seek even when we have found.

Be this as it may, this led the editorial writer to the Spanish notion of "*queréncia*"—"affection for the place one calls home and the sense of well-being that place gives one." This sense of belonging and familiarity is, of course, endemic to our kind. Aristotle and the Romans held that the household and the family, the private as opposed to the public, were necessary for us just "to be" and "to live". Our "living well" was in the polis, which necessarily included and presupposed this private life which was not proper to it.[4] Property, place, gave the family a locality, a sense of being there, the fire and the door and the wall. This attachment to a physical place made us a part of the world and so gave meaning and identity to our individual lives. So the despair with public life, its massiveness and corruptions, forces us to accept ourselves and our country mostly for the failures and disappointments we both are.

Thus, we no longer can afford the ideal, the best of which we have proved ourselves unworthy. So patriotism in the *New Yorker* became opposed to home, not unlike the similar withdrawal theories of the post-Aristotelian philosophers, who rejected the polis for the garden and the home, the direct contrary of the classical suppositions of the Greeks. The editorial continues:

> . . . The disorder is an uncertain sense of our position in the world. It's a disorder that may be inevitable in a young country but surely not in a middle-aged one that, rather like Daniel, has come up against some hard and disappointing truths of its own weaknesses and limitations—of its ordinariness, of the fact that it is neither hero nor villain but a mixture of virtues and vices, successes and failures, much like any other country. The people of such an aging nation, in order to carry on, cannot afford to deny themselves the simple, comforting sense of their

[4] See the author's "Privacy and the Public Life of Women", *Child and Family*, no. 4 (1974) 337–48.

country as a place that, despite its faults, is on the balance dear to them because it is needed by them.

It is ironic that this is also the kind of advice Solzhenitsyn gave to the Soviet leaders in his famous letter for their country, but not the advice he gave to the Americans for theirs in his remarks to American labor union leaders. And this latter sentiment of the *New Yorker*, too, reminds us of Chesterton who, as I mentioned in the first chapter, when speaking of Rome, remarked that she was not great first, before men loved her, but rather because men first loved her, she became great. I doubt that things are dear to us because we need them, even if like our homes we do need them. Indeed, Aristotle remarked that friendship for the old, not the middle-aged, tends to deteriorate to that based on utility, on need, away from the dearness of pure friendship. Psychologically, the *New Yorker* editorial was really talking of deterioration, the direct result of its own propositions.

But I wish to return to the problem of the monastery and the convent in this context since their contemporary structures have been so much determined by the kind of politics dominant during the past decade or so. Indeed, it is not without interest that monastery and polity come to speak of home at the same time. So if we try to conceptualize what has happened to religious life conceived as a permanent place or order, in which a special kind of "life" not given to all is to be lived out, we will realize that several changes are worthy of reflection. In Italy, as mentioned, there has been a renewed interest in the family by Italian Catholics. The reason for this has been precisely the decline and, to some extent, radicalization of the remaining religious orders, which historically had educated the young in

Christian culture. Italian Christians seemed to discover that they could no longer rely on religious orders to pass on the core of Christian life, and that they would have to develop new methods and theories. Granted the politicization of Italian public life in any case, such that religious life is often profoundly attracted to Marxist thought before even Christian doctrine, this has necessitated a return to the classical frontier and front-line defense for the faith, the family.

In the United States and the English-speaking countries, on the other hand, rather a different evolution has taken place. Thanks to Napoleon, Bismarck, the tug of Paris, and the vital cultural life of the major Italian, Spanish, and German cities, there was in Europe a natural alliance of city and monastery or seminary, too much so for many. American seminaries and monasteries, however, had often been deliberately placed in the countryside, apart. And even if they were physically not in some by-way in Minnesota or Pennsylvania, they had rules which, even in the heart of Old Broadway, made them seem closer to Crowford County, Indiana, than to the Great White Way, assuming, of course, the Great White Way was really someplace. Then, as a result of several movements during the late 1950's and the 1960's, from the Second Death of God to the Secular City, together with antiwar and civil rights, a great exodus of seminaries and monasteries took place from the hillsides to the slums, or to the state university campus. There resulted an almost total loss of any rooted, traditional, independent religious and intellectual centers. All were now attached or committed to or, too often, compromised by their newer environments. Christian clerics became so used to and immersed in the life of the underprivileged, the unnatural, or the unorganized, that they had difficulty themselves in any longer perceiving the normal or what it might be.

At about the height of this movement of being "where the action was reputedly at", René duBois published an article in *Audubon* on the classical Benedictine Monastery as a perfect example of how to treat technology and nature.[5] This was designed as a counter to Lynn White's then current and famous thesis that Christianity was the real cause of our so-called ecological crisis. This was an intellectual challenge in my opinion no major religious organization, except significantly the papacy, ever really fully understood in its precise theological and public nature. Suddenly, the hurried move to the city slums and the life of academe seemed irrelevant. The intellectual fashion had changed again. Perceptive critics were wondering why there was no vigorous monastic life—farming, bee-keeping, gardens, forests, solitude, nature.

The loss of the rooted institutions, the ones that had had time to be in a particular "place", to be taken out of the cycles of time, caused an even more serious problem in another way. Neither ecology nor revolutionary movements to reform the poorer parts of the world—movements themselves often profoundly opposed to each other for philosophical reasons—were doctrinally neutral. Both implied radical changes in the fundamentals of classical morality and theology. Meanwhile, no one was about to notice that the greatest opportunity Christianity has had in modern times was being lost by default. The old controversy between science and religion was quietly settled by the ecologists, in favor of religion. It was science that now

[5] René duBois, *Audubon* (September 1970).

needed justification in the name of man, as religion since Genesis and philosophy since Aristotle had said it did.

Moreover, at about this time also, the classical task American theological thought had set for itself, that of reconciling the church to the state, under the impact of ecology and revolution was causing Christians to have second thoughts. The state no longer seemed so ethically neutral. What had been common assumptions about natural law in the area of life and dignity seemed to be now denied by positive legislation on every hand. The question thus arose at a deeper level about whether Christians can retain any sort of practical and theoretical independence without their own institutions, without their own monasteries and houses that do not presume to be "like" other secular intellectual institutions. The threat was becoming more and more evident that laws of the state would determine what could be allowed even for Christians.

What had come to be needed, then, was a body of Christians on a separate, rooted place, with a particular history wherein the cultural traditions—the books, the ideas, the disciplines, the hymns, even the languages—could be fully and freely thought about and possessed. This capacity was now largely lost in practically all the universities sponsored by Christians and never even conceded to be possible in the universities sponsored by the state.[6] The monasteries and seminaries, apparently, gave up most of their own traditions voluntarily. No longer is it easily possible that a student in a Christian-sponsored university has the slightest accurate knowledge of or contact with Aquinas, Augustine, Ecclesiastes, Paul or Plato.

[6] See Chapter 14 of the present work.

The classical heresies are a mystery to most even though they are bandied about in disguised form every day in the press and the academic journals. The secular apocalypse of ecology or the revolutionary messianism of the Third World development have become the only bibles thought worth studying. Christians, in a sense, no longer know who they were intellectually because the monks and nuns had lost their own roots. The religious ideal has come to mean being an academic, a social worker, or a guru, comparable to the secular counterpart, with a private life modeled on the home, according to the economic style of the profession.

At about this time, then, it also occurred to the professedly secular mind which historically defined and justified itself in contrast or opposition to Christian ideas, that it could no longer discover precisely what Christians were about, since many, *ex professo*, acted or talked just like everyone else.[7] For every effort to state clearly traditional Christian dogma, the popular magazines and talk shows took delight in citing learned theologians and Christian leaders who held just the opposite. The great intellectual ferment among Catholics in particular seemed to be to "justify" the precise values that they had for so long opposed. Thus, to the astonishment of most, an American Jesuit became nationally famous overnight for justifying homosexuality, with what restrictions it was difficult to ascertain. Opposition to episcopacy and papacy became the sign of academic "freedom". Socialism and Marxism had risen to the status of *de fide* in several Catholic and Protestant publishing houses. Antiabortion became the

[7] See Chapter 2 of the present work.

cause of the reactionary. Human community modeled on the warmth of the home was even confused with God. Friendship replaced grace, while justice was rediscovered by a Harvard professor, and liberation theologians seemed to follow various pipers. On top of all of this, Catholics began to "speak in tongues".

Needless to say, some reaction to all these consequences began to set in. What is surprising about this reaction, however, is that it is often conceived precisely in terms of the tradition that has been neglected. Thus, Robert Heilbroner has even rediscovered original sin. And he is not alone. In other words, what was given up was precisely the intellectual element that is now required. "What is to take the place of the soul- and life-destroying metaphysics inherited from the nineteenth century? The task of our generation, I have no doubt, is one of metaphysical reconstruction," E. F. Schumacher eloquently wrote.[8] We had laughed at Pius IX and Gregory XVI for their worries about the philosophy of the nineteenth century. We even began to think Leo XIII quaint for insisting on Thomas Aquinas, whom few any longer seriously studied, especially in the monasteries. Now, we discover to our dismay that what we largely gave up, voluntarily, in our efforts to make our monasteries our homes, make them relevant, was precisely what is most in need, if we are to save the soul of Christianity for itself. But of course, Christianity cannot save itself from anything. This, too, is the meaning of justification, and why attention to the uniqueness of what is handed down is the first and only claim that Christianity can have before the world.

[8] E. F. Schumacher, *Small Is Beautiful* (New York: Harper, 1973) 101.

Dale Vree, in a remarkable study based directly on the proposition that the true heart of modern intellectual controversies lies in the loyalty of Christians to their own dogmas, has well written that Christians seeking a New Jerusalem in this world are good people, as are the Marxists seeking the same thing. But they are both Gnostics in a basic way, who sin out of good will to improve our faulty world.

> It often seems bizarre that Christians are expected to accept their creaturehood rather than flee from it. . . . But Christians are instructed that creation is good though flawed. . . .
>
> Yes, the New Jerusalem will come—but in God's good time. In the meantime, Christians are expected to keep pace with God. Those who lack the patience . . . , who want to leap out of their creaturely condition before the appointed time—they will come to call themselves, correctly, "atheists". The sin of humanistic atheism is . . . like so many sins—beautiful, honorable and very tempting!
>
> Pity the poor orthodox, for, alas, what they must defend—this present world, this frail body, this life so very full of ugliness—is, as they supremely know, a lost cause.[9]

The Christian monastery was deliberately separated from the world partly to protect the world itself from Christian enthusiasm, partly so the monks could witness to a goal, a perfection not really of this world, a place for pilgrims and wayfarers. Yet it was to be a place for men too, men who planted, built, and printed while they sang their Hours each day.

The brotherhood and the sisterhood were not formed like the family. The mother and the father, the friar and

[9] Dale Vree, *On Synthesizing Marxism and Christianity* (New York: Wiley, 1976) 80–81.

the nun could each be holy, but their ways were not the same. They were all necessary in a way, yet different. It had been Max Weber's suspicion, in a famous thesis noted earlier, that the Reformation's destruction of the monastery and the subsequent secularizing of religious vocation to a this-worldly goal were directly related to the formation of the modern industrial world. What we must now wonder is whether we are not witnessing the final destruction of the monasteries such that there is no longer a precise place for those who know of the "lost cause" to which monks witnessed. The other side of this question, undoubtedly, is the simultaneous effort to reduce and eliminate the family with its ethos, that is, the home. The monks, ironically, begin to imitate the family when the family itself can no longer be intellectually justified in the modern world because of a denial of the Christian metaphysics of the family in the first place. It is not by accident that the family is seen by many psychologists and critics as the locus of prejudice and error because the "normal" which the family stands for is seen now to be "abnormal".

In the beginning I cited again Chesterton's homesickness at home and Tolkien's marvelous notion that in God's kingdom, the greatest and the smallest can live together, that redeemed man is still man. This means, at a minimum, that the presences of homes, monasteries, and states are not contradictory to each other. That is, they are not one another. We must keep things separate if we are to stay together. Redeemed man is still man. The opposite is true also—man is redeemed. The monastery exists that we may feel homesickness at home, that we may realize that the poignance of our existence is felt most not when we lack, but when we are given the best. All human love, even in the home, in its being human, is incomplete, even at its fullest. All homes are symbols of homelessness, pilgrimage.

The green horizon of England that we can call home needs to be rediscovered, no doubt, before we can be content with what we have in fact wrought. But the rediscovery of our place, of where we are content with our sins and limits, cannot leave us only with our rooted place. When we love, beautify, and praise a piece of this world the best we can, only then do we know that it is not enough. And for this reason Christians built their monasteries—to love places to the depth of their being "not enough". And this too was what Plato saw to be the final meaning of human love itself.

The last words I wish to recall here are those of Thérèse —God does not give us all an equal amount of grace. He does not call those who are worthy, but those he chooses. In the end, this is why there are both homes and monasteries—and why they are not the same.

XIV

THE CHRISTIAN UNIVERSITY

John Henry Newman wrote in his famous *The Idea of a University* that "The temptations which ordinarily assail the young and the intellectual are two: those which are directed against their virtue, and those which are directed against their faith." That the young *and* the intellectual seem to be open to the same kind of temptation is, in a way, of no little interest in itself, but in any case the condition of the university is of as much importance as that of the home or monastery, city or state in the modern world. This is especially true from any historical Christian point of view.[1]

Whether there are or even can be any genuinely "Christian" universities has always been considered skeptically by many a state bureaucracy and teaching union monopolizing public funds. Even though universities were given birth mostly within the Church historically, with a number of quite reputable universities claiming Christian allegiance still functioning, nevertheless, the notion of a Christian university has been considered, like Newman's ill-fated project, merely to be a famous "idea", not dissimilar to Plato's ideal state, something that would be most worthy if it could only manage to survive the rigors of this cruel world. On the other hand, more Christian oriented universities do not exist because many, including many Christians, do not want them to exist.[2] They cause embarrassing problems to church and state, indeed to intellect itself.

[1] See J. M. Cameron, *On the Idea of a University* (Toronto: University of Toronto Press, 1978).

[2] See "Church and Campus", *Newsweek* (9 July 1979).

The Christian Church has always recognized that its relation to intelligence must be a carefully thought out, even defined sort of thing because both university and religion claim that allegiance to truth alone justifies their respective being, however differently they might arrive at it. Moreover, this relation to truth can only legitimize a university within a philosophical theory that does not implicitly or directly grant everything to the state. Thus, just as the most subtle danger to the Church is to politicize its eschatology, in the Enlightenment tradition, into primarily a this-worldly mission and criterion of truth, so the most clever undermining of the university is to conceive its mission as one of reforming the world in the name of some popular goal—the nation, the poor, the weak—a goal that implies that this is the highest end for which intelligence is created. Once the university officially admits that its purpose is political in this sense, it has lost its cultural roots and justification to be a certain kind of entity—neither church, nor state, nor family, nor corporation, nor party. This danger is, moreover, why intellect needs more than the university to protect the realm of wisdom, why the free press may at times be closer to achieving the ends of the university than the university itself.

At a Dean's Meeting at the Christian university wherein I teach, the administration proposed, evidently as one of the major goals of the university as such, the promotion of faith and justice, especially the latter. There seemed to be little recollection of the meaning and history of this very idea since at least Plato, nor a sense of what it implies for the nature of the university, when this kind of goal is inadvertently embraced. Fortunately, a wise Jesuit, not myself clearly, was there to suggest that this is not the purpose or function of specifically a university, Christian or otherwise. Paradoxically, it is the function of a university in precisely a totalitarian system which logically uses intelligence to bolster its own concept of "justice", as Aristotle long ago argued it would.

Rather in all it does, the university is concerned with knowledge and truth, to seek values and promote them only by methods proper to the nature of the university itself. These are not economic or political methods. Public questions can be treated by the university only under the aegis of truth and its requirements. Once the university admits political, economic, or ideological goals as its *modus agendi*, it loses its claim to autonomy and uniqueness. The state is then fully justified in dealing with the university as a rival in its own order since the claims for special status and autonomy are no longer held even by the university itself. With this consequence, the cultural and religious loss is irreparable.

The ease with which our society is beginning to force universities to accept structures quite at variance with the true requirements of intellect must begin to cause considerable worry, even though the root idea that is causing this shift usually originated in university minds unfamiliar with the very traditions of intellect. The National Labor Relations Board, for instance, has allowed itself to become a tool for the changing of the very nature of university life and autonomy. In forcing union structures upon universities, with little understanding of the difference between factories and universities, seeing them mainly as agencies of employment, we have a vivid case of misunderstanding the meaning of a university. Josef Pieper warned in *Leisure: The Basis of Culture* that when intellectuals begin to consider themselves as laborers, there is little hope of protecting the realm of spirit and intelligence.

"My great dread, one that I know many share, is that, in the future," J. M. Cameron wrote,

> proposals for reform, mine or others, would get caught up in a process of collective bargaining between the faculty and the university administration. Conditions of work are obviously pertinent matter in any collective bargaining procedures. This makes evident the pernicious character of such procedures. For the faculty to negotiate with the 'university' is to admit that the faculty is not the university, to abandon the notion of the *universitas*, to accept a proletarian status, not under protest, but as a norm. This is in effect to abandon the entire university tradition and to accept the term *university* as denoting an employing authority, like Bell Canada or Imperial Oil.[3]

The right to organize is not prior to and a condition of the right to know. To assume that it is, reverses implicitly the classic hierarchy of knowledge and action. Thus, politicization and increasing unionization of university faculties force a culture interested in precisely the tenuous nature of intelligence to begin to look elsewhere for its protection. This was why the abbey and monastery were also crucial elements in Christendom, a locus outside of realm, university, and diocese, where prayer and intelligence and work too could be preserved and fostered. As many European universities have sadly learned, the fastest route to academic intolerance and alienation of intellect is via party control of faculty unions, evidently a rather easy accomplishment. Probably the secular form of the abbey is the small, independent journal, certainly not the mass media, though the corporation too is beginning to have a place for intelligent research also within its area.

In a very true sense, moreover, intellectual life has always been a lonely one, even within the university. The

[3] Cameron, ibid., 78–79.

modern pluri-university, to be sure, stresses and finances the corporate aspect of intelligence, organized and organizational research. Nor is the commitment of a culture to knowledge an easy one. Aristotle's principle that the highest things are precisely "useless" is very difficult to accept for the working man or the politician. It is somewhat easier for the churchman. Indeed, it is the professor who, ultimately, is most likely to hesitate before the ultimate contemplative life. Aquinas's question on the necessity of a "divine" law (I-II, 91, 4) remains at the very heart of all university life, as the careers of Leo Strauss and Eric Voegelin testify precisely when they reach the limits of reason. Hannah Arendt's posthumous *The Life of the Mind* is, in many ways, little more than a plea for the restoration of true wisdom to the university milieu, and this as a presupposition and conclusion to the life of action, politics and labor.

Aristotle, nevertheless, was correct to place knowledge, which had direct effect on the polis, under the control of the same polis, to be pursued by its methods. The university could not make itself the town. Knowledge transcended the polis, but the methods and ends of the academy were not those of the polis. When something was designed to have public effect, it legitimately had to pass through the discipline of public speech and argument. This did not mean there was more "truth" in the polis, but rather that practical affairs could only contain as much "truth" as the kind of discipline that treated them could itself yield. There were many areas in which opinion and custom were proper guides, and these always could be otherwise.

The university as Christian, however, has yet another aspect. Just as the state and the university are not properly "hostile" to each other in a valid intellectual order, neither is the Church intrinsically at odds with the university.[4] Granting that both institutions can intrude on the university, as it on them, still the Christian university in its uniqueness results from a kind of social contract in which there is agreement to recognize the validity of all knowledge within its precincts, including knowledge of God in the Christian sense, as legitimate and necessary objects of study and intellectual pursuit by means proper to the university. Furthermore, this contract, unlike the German universities after Bismarck, ought not to conceive theology as merely one "faculty" apart from and independent of all others, but rather to consider that religion is pertinent to what each faculty does. Newman clearly recognized this necessity in his last lectures in *The Idea of a University*. The point can be summed up by suggesting that sincerely believing Christians should for the most part staff the Christian university. With due regard to acknowledged and legitimate differences of views and approaches, the common good of this kind of a Christian institution would expect those who genuinely do not share this faith not to remain of their own accord within its structures.

There is something more. Just as there is honor among thieves, as the saying goes, so there ought to be honor among university students, faculty, administrators, and even employees. This seems to be something more than a legally defined sort of thing. Everyone grants there is place

---

[4] See the new Statement on Universities of John Paul II, *Sapientia Christiana*, *L'Osservatore Romano*, English edition, 4 June 1979. Unfortunately, I think, too many Christian universities fail to see the important contribution such norms and guidelines can make to the problems of present day Christian universities.

for and justification of the village atheist; still he is surprised if he be hired to teach metaphysics at a Christian university. Or to put it in another way, if more and more faculty are hired with no consideration for their relation to the specific structure of beliefs and practices characterizing Christianity, or if faculty members cease to be believing Christians, then the institution loses its very justification and claim for support and students and indeed uniqueness. Thus, from an outsider's viewpoint, someone at intellectual or moral odds with Christian ideals and beliefs—Christians are also sinners, the point is one of belief and understanding—should in honor not accept a teaching position in a Christian university.

The administration would be less than candid not to make this clear, moreover, in its hiring policies and in its promotions and rewards structures.[5] Probably, it is not at all bad to have a few professional agnostics, believing Jews, or practicing Mormons in the faculty and student body of a Christian university. More than a few people will want to be there precisely because it does uphold certain standards and beliefs even though they may not accept them totally. But for someone bitterly hostile, for whatever reason, the question is not just why he would want to teach at a Christian university, but that of the public interest to have universities in which Christianity can be taught under the form of a university. The overriding value is that the interests of truth itself require Christian universities that

[5] See Gregory F. Lucey, S.J., "The Meaning and Maintenance of Catholicity as a Distinctive Characteristic of American Catholic Higher Education". (Ph.D. diss., University of Wisconsin at Madison, 1978). See also Robert Newton, "Faculty Selection", *Religious Education* (January–February 1979) 94–99.

are able to retain their internal autonomy and integrity as such.

The historical passage of so many American universities from religious purposes to secular ones is not a real growth, it seems to me, especially in the light of the state's determination and ability to build and staff and pension enormous universities at public expense, including the expense of believers; which state universities exclude, in theory and practice, the primary aims of the Christian institutions.[6] We should want the Jews, the Muslims, the Baptists, and the Mormons, moreover, to have their own academic structures. And these institutions should not be populated with teachers or administrators (or even students) hostile or indifferent to the supporting religion. Those who find themselves at odds can easily go elsewhere, and at less expense. The state, in other words, has no right to impose a secular criterion, even in the name of "rights", on religious institutions as a condition of their continued existence.

Whether intelligence and faith are compatible can, perhaps, be considered from another angle. Traditionally, in Catholic universities at least, the local bishop was a known and familiar figure. He was given to know, usually, unless he also financed the enterprise, that he was not in charge of the place, for which he undoubtedly thanked God. On the other hand, he was recognized as bishop to be responsible for the spiritual well-being of his flock, a well-being that included doctrine, truth. The tradition of the intellectual bishop is neither accidental nor dead. The room for conflict here is, no doubt, real. Many a bishop has wondered what to do about elements in local Christian universities in part

[6] See Russell Kirk's *Decadance and Renewal in the Higher Learning* (South Bend: Gateway Editions, 1978).

or wholly heretical on basic positions, or universities which simply ceased teaching anything meaningfully Christian. For the most part, I think, American bishops at least have done little or nothing in this area. Anyone, no doubt, can cite scores of instances of dull or intolerant bishops from whom academic freedom needs protection. Likewise, among minimally well informed bishops, the vast majority no doubt, will have a list of aberrations equally as long and probably more damaging to the ideals of Christianity, things taught on local campuses with no relation whatever to the faith except perhaps that of opposition.

It is not unusual any more to run into a number of good, articulate parents who, when relaxed, tell stories, chapter and verse, of how their children lost their faith in recent years at Jesuit or other religious-sponsored universities. Such accounts are to be treated skeptically up to a point. What seems different in recent complaints—there have always been students who "lose" their faith in Christian universities, just as there are those who "gain" it at Berkeley or Ohio State—is the insistence that the loss of faith or virtue, Newman's two points, was attributed to what was taught. The students were not rebelling but following. The full account of this phenomenon, even granting that children and students also have free will, is not yet written or even investigated, I suspect.[7] The point is that many people, surely still a minority, are beginning to wonder seriously if the existing Christian universities can any longer be relied upon to accomplish their classical task. In other words, must another solution to the problem of the Christian university be formulated?

[7] See James Hitchcock's *Catholicism and Modernity* (New York: Seabury, 1979).

This problem of academic indifference or "heresy" is a real one and cannot be seriously avoided by anyone interested in the existence of Christian universities, by anyone for whom the classic creeds are still normative. Some feel that the only solution is to cease supporting existing Christian universities and found smaller, more manageable ones. There are several efforts in this direction that are succeeding perhaps better than anyone might have anticipated, such as Christendom College, or Thomas Aquinas College, or Newman College. Perhaps the most controversial variant has been the St. Ignatius Institute at the University of San Francisco, which has tried not to reject existing university structures, but to work within their framework, though the union structure of that school may eventually make this impossible.

In analyzing the criticisms against this latter endeavor, Professor Michael Scrivin, himself not a Christian, provided these interesting reflections regarding such projects and their place in the university environment.

The St. Ignatius Institute (SII) has no atheists and no Protestants and no "liberal" Catholics. Does this make it unacceptably narrow?

The SII does not present itself as a theology department or a department of religious studies. And these areas are already covered on campus. Is there no room for an Asian culture department which treats Eastern religions, even advocates them, on the University of San Francisco campus? Is USF tied by charter to "liberal" Catholicism? It is obvious that the answer is negative in each case, and the position of the critics (on this point) is, as far as we could discover, far more narrow-minded than that they project on the SII.

An outsider might have wondered whether USF needed an enclave of "conservative" theology until one saw the attacks on the SII which showed more clearly than the catalogues that liberalism has become the new orthodoxy and hence that a strong foundation for presenting the alternative was desirable.[8]

This is well said, undoubtedly. The intolerance of the left, in theology or politics or economics, continues to be proverbial. The degree of closed liberal theology in Christian universities is something that is not well appreciated. And this liberalism is now being rapidly replaced, as the liberalism of American secular political science departments has been replaced since 1968, by a radicalized social philosophy for which even liberalism is much too backward. In this context, I suspect the major task of the new Polish Pontiff will be neither pastoral nor administrative, but precisely doctrinal, to decide what stance to take organizationally to this widespread academic condition.

The Christian university, of course, cannot escape from the world, nor should it want to. I would hate to think the case for the larger existing institutions is simply hopeless, however valuable the lesson of the newer smaller colleges may prove to be. On the other hand, the theological fluctuations are no longer in theory or practice merely concerned with the pursuit of truth. Truth, in fact, is rarely heard any more in Christian university circles as their indispensable operative justification. Political or pluralistic goals are rather the norm. Yet, I suspect that Professor Jeffery Hart of Dartmouth was mostly correct in holding that Catholic intellectuals are currently taking up the causes Jewish intellectuals gave up over a decade ago.

[8] Report to the President of the University of San Francisco, June 1978.

However, there does seem a strong reaction in favor of norms, self-discipline, values, and even natural law. Lord Hailsham's address to the Canon Law Society of England on the natural law is well worth attention in this connection.[9] I have found rather enthusiastic agreement in a large freshman class on reading Reo Christensen's somewhat stoic analysis:

> It is this writer's belief that the greatest threat to American democracy comes not from overpopulation or communism or executive power or legislative weakness or structural defects in the system or the maldistribution of power within society or challenges from the Left or the Right. The greatest threat is from the decline of self-discipline and erosion of confidence in our legacy of moral value.[10]

These are also the sentiments of Solzhenitsyn and George Kennan, as they were of Plato, Aristotle, and Cicero. Indeed, I would suggest, as a text, giving to any class the Third Book of Cicero's *De Officiis* ("On Duties"), perhaps the most morally straight doctrine ever conceived. My guess is that most students will largely agree with it. There is, I suspect, less interest in moral or intellectual heresy than we might anticipate. The real difficulty is the rareness of coming across much else. Chesterton's *Orthodoxy* and C. S. Lewis' *Mere Christianity* remain in the category of near-revelation today since most will never have known that there was in fact a case to be made for Christianity, an intellectual case.

[9] See *Tablet* (28 October 1979). Address available from English Canon Law Society.

[10] Reo Christensen, *Heresies: Right and Left* (New York: Harpers, 1973) 46.

We are, in other words, becoming ready for a genuinely Christian university that professes and teaches the classical and Christian moral, religious, and doctrinal values. The real problem is that the academic desolation of the past decade has left surprisingly few who any longer know the long tradition. But anything less, I think, will cause more and more wonderment about why it is worthwhile going to a university at a cost the state and inflation have made almost prohibitive for the majority of Christians who are most concerned about the issue.

What is at stake is the preservation at the university level of a place for Christian freedom and truth. Josef Pieper wrote in *Scholasticism*: " 'It is necessary for the perfection of human society,' Aquinas writes, 'that there should be men who devote their lives to contemplation'—*nota bene*, necessary not only for the good of the individual who devotes himself, but for the good of human society." This ultimately is why we need authentic Christian universities, ones which are not exactly like the others.

Where we do not have men and women who reflect, who think, contemplate for its own sake, not only are we unable to defend the legitimacy of universities, but we cannot defend the good that transcends politics. We end, as we are ending, by making politics our good. The Christian university can be justified, to be sure, but only if it is a university, only if it is Christian. The temptations that ordinarily assail the young *and* the intellectual are the two Newman suggested, those against virtue and those against faith. To preserve or understand either needs a strong dose of sheer intelligence, an even stronger dose of grace in the Christian tradition of that term.

The Christian university, then, exists that both alternatives, faith and virtue, be and remain intellectually possible. If the need and understanding of self-reliance and self-discipline be the requirements of our time, I suspect Christian universities, insofar as they have not been places wherein intelligence lives with faith and virtue, will be held doubly responsible.

PART V

TOWARD A
DISTINCTIVE SPIRITUALITY

XV

DRYNESS

If there are distinctive Christian traditions, doctrines, and institutions, it should follow that there are distinctively Christian ways of looking at the world, ways that illuminate and instruct even in the most unexpected and unlikely areas of life. In a sense, there is only one way to know a Christian life, and that is to live it. The feeling of Christianity is that God's provident care for each person leads in a dramatically different way, even though we all live in the same world and can communicate experiences which we do have in common. No one can be more than suggestive in this area, yet it is worthwhile, I think, to offer some considerations in the light of the distinctiveness of Christian traditions and truths to hint, at least, at the extraordinary fertility of Christianity. In ending these reflections on this Christian distinctiveness I am going to choose some five areas that, I hope, might illuminate some of what I have been arguing. Those will be: dryness, forgiveness, exercises, letters, and a reflection on Belloc's *Path to Rome*.

To begin, I want to consider the topic of "dryness", something not from agriculture or weather forecasting but from the classic tradition of Christian life in its living that recognizes that faith is not a constant sense of euphoria, but a fidelity to doctrine and practice that does not always produce results that are easy to account for. Perhaps it might be best to begin with a recent review of the reissuance of Evelyn Waugh's war trilogy: "I return to English Catholicism," Michael Wood wrote, "or at least Waugh's view of it, and the destruction of dry hearts. Guy's heart is as dry as ever, and we are faced with the saddest, most minimal of religious promises: You may be redeemed, but it won't make any difference that you can see."[1] No Christian can avoid, at times, a similar feeling, and something needs to be said about it.

Aristotle began his *Metaphysics* with the extraordinarily happy notion that wonder lies at the origin of our knowledge, wonder and not necessity or compulsion. And Christianity is proposed as a religion of joy. In our time, moreover, we have tried to tone down all those aspects of the faith that remind us of the darker sides of things—no more hair-shirted Thomas Mores, no more Lenten fasts; fish on Friday is not our meat, we even die in white, never hearing the haunting *Dies Irae*, those of us who still go to funerals of our kind.

I was once given a handsome volume of meditations in Latin, selections from Vatican II, a memento of an audience with Paul VI for the faculty of the Gregorian University in the spring of 1977. The third selection, from *Gaudium et Spes* (14), recalled that "by our interiority we exceed the whole universe of things." We live in an era of "human rights" in which we are actually taught to expect that we shall receive every last one of this ever-increasing list of things "owed" to us. We will receive them—or else. . . . Ironically, somber discussions about the end of man and earth are now the common fare of scientists, not theologians, as we have earlier suggested. The scientific optimists of the modern era have become the pessimists, while the

[1] Michael Wood, Review of Evelyn Waugh's war trilogy, in *New Republic* (12 May 1979) 31.

once accused theological pessimists oftentimes seem incapable of propounding anything less than continuous bliss.

Yet authentic Christianity has always recognized a danger in stressing our glory and happiness overly much, especially when we are still *in via*, in our passing. Grace is freely given and even seems not to be given equally to equal recipients, however much that seems to violate our "rights". The best of our fellows always discourage us somehow and not only because we envy their worthiness. Rather, we despair a bit at the distance. Newman put it well:

> Man is a being of genius, passion, intellect, conscience, power. He exercises these various gifts in various ways, in great deeds, in great thoughts, in heroic acts, in hateful crimes. . . .
>
> Such is man: put him aside, keep him before you; but whatever you do, do not take him for what he is not, for something more divine and sacred, for man regenerate. Nay, beware of showing God's power and its work at such disadvantage as to make the few whom it has thoroughly influenced compete in intellect with the vast multitude who either have it not or use it ill. The elect are few to choose out of, and the world is inexhaustible.[2]

This too is, in part, why Augustine remains essential to our spirituality. "I sank away from Thee, and I wandered, O my God, too much astray from Thee, my stay, in these days of my youth, and I became to myself a barren land." Thus Augustine at the end of the Second Book of *The Confessions*.

[2] John Henry Newman, "Duties of the Church Towards Knowledge", in *The Idea of a University* (New York: Doubleday Image, 1959) 232–35.

These are memorable words—the making of ourselves to be barren lands. One winter on Market Street in San Francisco, I walked into a large book store whose total stock of Christian books came to about forty compared with numerous shelves loaded with the occult, Eastern religions, and astrology. About a third of the Christian books were unaccountably devoted to C. S. Lewis. And, as if to prove there are happy surprises everywhere, one of these was Lewis's little book *George MacDonald: An Anthology*, something I had never seen previously. At that moment, not having the required five dollars, I left to return the following day to purchase it. In retrospect, it was one of my better moves.

Lewis frankly affirmed how close MacDonald seemed to be to the spirit of Christ. This little book consisted of 365 quite brief citations from MacDonald, arranged, I take it, one for every day of the year. I read the book in a couple of days and have been quoting from it to my friends ever since, *ad nauseam*, I am sure they would intimate. But what struck me most about this book, besides so many other marvelous things, was that four of the passages Lewis selected were entitled, "dryness", including the very first, which read:

> That man is perfect in faith who can come to God in the utter dearth of his feelings and desires, without a glow or an aspiration, with the weight of low thoughts, failures, neglects, and wandering forgetfulness, and say to Him: 'Thou art my refuge'.[3]

God does console us, I have no doubt, yet consolation would hardly be recognized if that were all we knew.

[3] C. S. Lewis, ed., *George MacDonald: An Anthology* (New York: Macmillan, 1974) no. 1.

Moreover, the spiritual life, with its flux of consolations and desolations, that Ignatius was perceptive enough to account for in the *Spiritual Exercises*, itself finally depends upon a proper theology. Interestingly, Lewis selected those passages of MacDonald that stressed the divine freedom as part of the very context of our dryness:

> What stupidity of perfection would that be which left no margin about God's work, no room for change of plan upon change of fact—yea, even the mighty change that . . . now at length his child is praying! I may move my arm as I please: shall God be unable to move His?[4]

And if the divine freedom is to be quite free, it follows that what is created in God's image is quite limited, quite diverse, but likewise quite free. ". . . [E]very one of us is something that the other is not, and therefore knows something—it may be without knowing that he knows it—which no one else knows; and . . . it is everyone's business . . . to give his portion to the rest."[5] And yet, the refusal to give is likewise the path to the loss of our gift of uniqueness: "All wickedness tends to destroy individuality and declining natures assimilate as they sink."[6] As we approach God, we become in a way more unlike our friends, so that our riches are precisely unique; ultimately we have more and more worth sharing.

No doubt, there is something of the *sola fides* of Luther in MacDonald's consciousness of the role and reality of spiritual dryness. Luther wrote in his *Commentary on Galatians*:

> Contrary to these vain trifles and doting dreams, we teach faith, and give a true rule of Christianity in this sort: first, that a man must be taught by the law to know himself, that so he

---

[4] Ibid., 43, no. 97.   [5] Ibid., 107, no. 255.

[6] Ibid., 110, no. 265.

may learn to say with the Prophet: 'All have sinned and have need of the glory of God'. . . . Thus, we by a contrary way do drive men from the merit of congruence and worthiness.

Now, when a man is humbled by the law, and brought to the knowledge of himself, then followeth true repentance . . . and he seeth himself to be so great a sinner that he can find no means how he may be delivered from his sin by his own strength, endeavour and works. Then he perceiveth what Paul meant. . . . Then he seeth that all the divinity of the schoolmen touching the merit of congruence and worthiness, is nothing else but mere foolishness, and that by this means the whole Papacy falleth.[7]

Faith without consolation is, undoubtedly, a grim thing, though the old papacy might have understood this quite well.

Gregory the Great, in one of those remarkable papal "foolishnesses" so recurrent in Christianity, thus preached in one of his homilies:

I assure you it is not by faith that you will come to know him, but by love; not by mere conviction, but by action. . . . He will enter into a life of faith; from faith he will go out to vision, from belief to contemplation and will graze in the good pastures of everlasting life.

So our Lord's sheep will finally reach their grazing ground where all who follow him in simplicity of heart will feed on the green pastures of eternity. Beloved brothers, let us set out for these pastures where we shall keep joyful festival with so many of our fellow citizens. . . . Nor must we allow the charm of success to seduce us, or we shall be like a foolish traveller who

[7] Martin Luther, "Commentary on Galatians", in *Martin Luther*, ed. J. Dillenberger (New York: Doubleday Anchor, 1961) 109–10.

is so distracted by the pleasant meadows through which he is passing that he forgets where he is going.[8]

The green pastures of eternity and the pleasant meadows which tempt us to forget the end of the journey we undertake, perhaps, present a better context for the kind of "dryness" that exists in Christianity. In a sense, this is not the dryness of the atheist seeking perfection in the structures of this intractable world. And Luther seemed always too dubious about the real *vestigia Dei* that are about us. Dryness, after all, is a sign of the lack of water, not the sign of nothing at all. The dryness of the mystic or the lover does not result from a disbelief in the object of their longing. This is why the divine freedom must not be conceived in any necessitarian fashion. Paul's "My grace is sufficient for thee", is not to be taken as if somehow we already are in the green pastures of eternity.

Malcolm Muggeridge often reflects on the nature of laughter. Laughter somehow is related to the differences between our aspirations and our performances, he reflected in a lecture. Laughter is the great divine correction to remind us that it is all right to be the kind of fallible being we are. And, of course, our aspirations are both those of God's promises and those we formulate exclusively for ourselves. Christian joy, ultimately, is rooted in the News Too Good To Be True, in the fact that we are promised something so utterly grand and worthy that we really cannot believe it is true, something that relativizes the most solemn things of this world and makes religion seem to the

[8] Gregory the Great, *Homily*, 14, 3–6, in Office of Readings, 4th Sunday of Easter.

skeptic to be merely opium. And there is an incongruent humor in performing badly against an aspiration that is so exalted, exalted even beyond our expectations. The delight of mankind arises because its "comedy" is played out against the divine.

The sense of our unworthiness is most poignantly set against our call to the joy of the vision of God. Samuel Johnson wrote on Easter Day, 1777, most soberly:

> I am to renew the great covenant with my Maker and my Judge. I humbly hope to perform it better. I hope for more efficacy of resolution, and more diligence of endeavor. When I survey my past life, I discover nothing but a barren waste of time, with some disorders of body, and disturbances of the mind very near to madness, which I hope he that made me, will suffer to extenuate many faults, and excuse many deficiencies.[9]

This is a remarkable passage from a man so full of humor— the discovery of the barren waste of time, on Easter, the sense of desolation and dryness that is conscious of life as no mere dream, the realization that it can therefore be wasted. Johnson was closer to Gregory the Great than to Luther, it seems.

In his "Rules for Discerning Spirits", Ignatius of Loyola paid a good deal of attention to desolation, almost using some of the words Johnson was to use later on. Ignatius was aware that desolation could be the result of our own faults as well as the result of a divine freedom which we do not control. Prayer, then, is not a relationship based on "rights". Rather it is something much closer to drama, just as each human life is not a repetition of what went

---

[9] *Samuel Johnson: Rasselas, Poems and Selected Prose*, ed. B. Bronson (New York: Holt, 1958) 38–39.

before but something quite new, quite unique. George MacDonald said:

> There is no forgetting of ourselves but in the finding of our deeper, our true self—God's idea of us when he devised us— the Christ in us. Nothing but that self can displace the false, greedy, whining self, of which most of us are so fond and proud. And that self no man can find for himself. . . .[10]

The laughter of creation is precisely the fact that our aspiration, God's idea of each of us, suffuses all the things we do with an incompleteness, a performance that hardly begins. "It is the heart that is not yet sure of God that is afraid to laugh in his presence."[11] The most poignant thing about our performances is that even at their best, when we really do what we ought, when we delight in it, as Aristotle said that we should, we know we are only being introduced to something so much more lovely and happy.

Happiness, thus, is not something we "pursue", in spite of the famous Declaration to the contrary. "For each, God has a different response. With every man he has a secret —the secret of a new name. In every man there is a loneliness, an inner chamber of peculiar life into which God only can enter. I say not it is the *innermost chamber*."[12] And what is wonderful about such a passage in MacDonald is its awareness of corresponding reality in the divine freedom and being. For God too has a similar chamber which only each separate person can enter. Out of this chamber, "man has to bring revelation and strength to his brethren. This is that for which he was made—to reveal the secret things of the Father."[13]

[10] C. S. Lewis, op. cit., no. 320.   [11] Ibid., no. 319.
[12] Ibid., no. 17.   [13] Ibid., no. 18.

And this is certainly why too there is often dryness in our lives. "The true man does not feel, does not even always desire," MacDonald said of dryness.[14] For this is God's way of bringing out what is in him in us, of never allowing a creature to confuse us with him for long, even though we are to lead others to him.

We believe we live in no ordinary world, but in a redeemed one. Eric Mascall remarked: "If we are living in the grace of God, heaven is the destination to which our journey is leading us. It is therefore the merest folly for us to behave as if our whole destiny were contained within the limits of the present life."[15] But our contemporaries will no doubt laugh at us for the incongruity of our performances and *their* expectations and aspirations. There really is a temptation in our time to identify the two. God does not continually light our countenances such that our neighbors are going about muttering "See how they love one another", as our ancestors were once said to have caused the pagans to remark. Our dryness is real enough. Our desolation is no mere pretending.

Karl Rahner wrote:

> We human beings are of such a kind that we are always beyond and above ourselves. It is our burden and our dignity. We are free and responsible for ourselves, we are those who hope. We are already beyond and above what can be mentioned, designated and specified. We live the tangible on the basis of the intangible.[16]

[14] Ibid., no. 136.
[15] Eric Mascall, *Grace and Glory* (Denville, N.J.: Dimension Books, 1961) 11.
[16] Karl Rahner, "Grace in the Abyss of Man", *Everyday Faith* (New York: Herder and Herder, 1968) 38.

We know, with Waugh, that often enough no one sees the divine chamber in which we were created. We know we see it not ourselves. The Crucifixion has always symbolized that redemption which men effected knowing not what they did.

George MacDonald said of our lovely world:

> Let me, if I may, be ever welcomed in my room in winter by a glowing hearth, in summer by a vase of flowers; if I may not, let me think how nice they would be, and bury myself in my work. I do not think that the road to contentment lies in despising what we have not got. Let us acknowledge all good, all delight that the world holds, and be content without it.[17]

This is, I suppose, the real Christian picture of the world we do live in, one wherein we can be desolate and dry amidst incredible delights, simply because of the "holy laughter", as MacDonald called it, that stands behind all creation reminding us that our performances yield ultimately, if we be willing, to aspirations we are not even capable of imagining.

Did God never withdraw, then, were we never dry and desolate, we should be, indeed, like the good pagan tempted to be content merely with the hearth and the pleasant vase of flowers. Christianity gives the hearth and the flowers so that we do not doubt that there be some joy. But we soon enough find the loveliness of the world contents us not, even while contenting us. We are empty, barren, dry, desolate even amidst these pleasant meadows about our homes. Indeed, let us with George MacDonald, "acknowledge all good, all delight that the world holds, and be content without it."

17 C. S. Lewis, op. cit., no. 274.

At last, dryness shades into possession and possession into what we do not possess, into what is revealed to us. "You are redeemed", the most minimal of religious promises, cannot be seen—otherwise it would not be a promise. "He that is made in the image of God must know him or be desolate."[18] God too is free to move his arm. We live the tangible on the basis of the intangible. By our interiority we exceed the whole universe of things. Hearts feeding in the green pastures of Eternity—the last words from George MacDonald: "He who has God, has all things, after the fashion in which he who made them has them."[19]

[18] Ibid., no. 87.   [19] Ibid., no. 68.

XVI

ON THINGS THAT CANNOT BE FORGIVEN

"The remedy against the irreversibility and unpredictability of the process started by action," Hannah Arendt wrote in *The Human Condition*,

> does not arise out of another and possibly higher faculty, but is one of the potentialities of action itself. The possible redemption for the predicament of irreversibility—of being unable to undo what one has done though one did not and could not have known what he was doing—is the faculty of forgiveness.[1]

Christianity claims for one of its most distinctive characteristics the need and, with revelation, the power of forgiveness. This has turned out also to be a solution for one of the gravest problems of the public order, of how to stop justice from carrying out its logical conclusions on and on throughout time.

Chesterton once remarked that we can be sorry for our sins but not for spilling gravy on our ties at a formal banquet. And in the *Ethics*, Aristotle suggested that we ought to forgive some actions even "when one does what he ought not under pressure which overstrains human nature, and which no one could withstand" (1110a25). A soldier who cracks under tortures, for example, or a lover who kills out of jealousy, these can be excusable, but require something more to be set totally aright. Obviously,

[1] See Hannah Arendt, *The Human Condition* (New York: Doubleday Anchor, 1959). See the section on Forgiveness.

247

the "voluntary" in such cases is reduced or eliminated. Nonetheless, Aristotle felt that specific pardon was needed to restore balance. Or, take the case of a man who injures another person in an automobile incident, one clearly not the driver's fault. In a real sense, however, he still needs "forgiveness" from the injured and from society, a forgiveness he cannot "demand". Too, Scripture recalls the sin against the Holy Spirit, which will not be forgiven. Thus, some things evidently cannot be forgiven, while others need forgiveness even though they are inculpable.

Another kind of forgiveness seems yet in order. On most university campuses, for instance, at any one time there will be one or two students hobbling about on crutches. When we pass them on the walks, we naturally assume they have broken their legs playing football or skiing, or perhaps in a road mishap. We ask, on casually meeting them, "And what happened to you?" They respond, recounting their particular story of how they slipped on the ice or tripped on the soccer field. Most people, we know, like to narrate their ills. We mostly like to listen. We assume the break will shortly mend.

Walking out the door of a university building, through a double series of glass door mechanisms on a cold winter day not too long ago, I was carrying some books, not paying much attention to anything. Several people were trying to get through the doors at the same time. Between the double sets of doors, out of the side of my eye, I noticed a young student on crutches catching up with me. So I politely blocked the door open so she could get through more easily. I really did not get a good look at her, but I asked pleasantly, the usual "What happened to you?"

In return, to my surprise, I got the most poignant and unforgettable look I have ever seen in anyone's eyes. I was puzzled for a moment, until the girl swung away quickly down the street with no audible answer to my initial question except a kind of groan or cry. Then, taken aback, I realized suddenly she simply had no second leg. She was born without it or had lost it through accident or disease. Indeed, I then recalled vaguely that I had seen her once before on campus, but did not recognize who it was. To my light-hearted pleasantry in that circumstance, no answer existed, none except the structure of the universe itself.

Needless to say, I felt terrible, with the kind of depressing sensation that no real way existed to repair immediately such embarrassments. Somehow, I judged that running after her apologizing would have only made it worse. In such things, we are not allowed even one mistake. This was not like a sin or spilling gravy on the tie, though probably closer to the latter.

A fellow professor from the history department happened along just then on the way to class with me. I recounted to her my gaffe. She told me sympathetically that everyone does much the same now and then. This was true, I knew, and seemed a kind of forgiveness in the name of the human condition, that in which we all find ourselves locked together. Still, the feeling remained that the girl's forgiveness was needed too, even though such incidents probably happen to her rather often. We are more bound by our neighbor's sensibilities than by our mutual faults at times.

Inadvertently, then, I had asked something that could not be forgiven, a kind of total unawareness in not noticing what ought to be noticed. Moreover, on reflection, the girl herself—to account for the feeling—would first, in her own spirituality, already have had to forgive the structure of reality that gave her only one leg in a world of the normal two. In a way, her own sense of self-possession and religious depth would decide her attitude to the normal curiosity that fails to notice. She could not forgive me unless first she forgave her own situation. And it would not matter whether someone else was culpably responsible for her loss or whether it was some genetic or household accident.

We all complain, to be sure, about our sundry ills and deficiencies, until we meet someone in worse condition than we are. And there will always be such, if we have but eyes to see. Indeed, even the blind find others worse off than they are. Christian literature has ever told us to be content with our own crosses and talents lest we end up with those which are not ours. Aquinas said that without some defects and lacks, even sins, many another virtue would not be able to exist in fact. And the very possibility of disorder has to do in part with the intrinsic nature of rational order and freedom. The spiritual problem of the young woman with the one leg may not in fact be nearly as acute as that of the "normal" abortionist, for example, who thinks no deformed babies should live in the first place. The spiritual lives of people with serious physical or mental handicaps are, in a very profound way, the judgment on the belief of our time that only the perfect *should* exist. We know that such a belief is not the way of God. Physical defects are not moral vices, even though Shakespeare recalled in his deformed King that such defects can occasion them, just as they can occasion saintliness. No human being, whatever his condition, is exempt from moral choice about his own condition. This is the only really solid meaning of human "equality".

The young woman's forgiving the universe is, then, a real part of her character, even though the more astonishing thing is that she exists at all. Furthermore, the Psalmist often wondered, "Why do the unjust prosper?" Yet not only must we wonder why they prosper, but why there is injustice in the first place. Professor Frederick Sontag once suggested, in his *God, Why Did You Do That?*, that we even have to forgive God. This seems a rather strange, if not blasphemous, paradox. Nonetheless, of these two perennial questions—Why is there something rather than nothing? Why does evil exist in the world?—the latter surely remains the more difficult for most since we moderns, at least, have the implicit suspicion that evil does not *have* to exist. Even the first pages of the *Book of Wisdom* suggest that death "is not God's doing." Thus, in the case of physical evil—the missing leg—we feel that an explanation is due, a forgiveness is required. Neither evil, death, nor the missing leg needs be. Christianity would say that if they are, they are somehow signs of a greater love, a love whose reality lies also in what might otherwise seem fitting and due.

The alternatives open to account for the fact that such evils are operative in our world seem to imply that we must either a) rebel against a God who willed or allowed it all in the first place, or b) deny the evil to make it only an illusion, as the Stoics once did, or else c) forgive it. Indeed, Aristotle seemed even to have attributed to man a natural tendency to rebel against his very condition as the least of the spiritual beings in the universe, the one who had a struggle within his very being itself, his own heart. Owen Francis Dudley or Robert Hugh Benson, I forget which, once wrote a book called, *Will Men Be Like Gods?* The Christian answer seems to be, paradoxically, "No, man is better off as he is." Were men like gods, then God would perhaps have to turn around and wonder about creating creatures "like men". And once he did this, we would be back at the original problem. Modern thought, no doubt, has tried to turn the tables on God, to replace him with the atheist-humanist proposition, a kind of collective divinization of ourselves. Ancient religion looked to God to forgive us. Modern culture, insofar as it does not reject him altogether, thinks we need to forgive him and, thereby, allow him to exist, a creature like unto ourselves in all things. Man judged God and found him wanting. Therefore, he must be forgiven.

In his *Autobiography*, Chesterton recalled a statement of his father, that he would still have thanked God for his existence even were he eventually damned. Countless pious readers have been scandalized by this. And in the Gospels we have the Lord's charge that it would have been better for some not to have been born, while the last myth of Plato's *Republic* concludes that if we do not live rightly in this life, we would not live correctly in any life, no matter how many chances might be given to us. For we are who we are indeed, ourselves and none other. Not only does all this serve to emphasize and ground the utter importance of each human life, its intrinsic seriousness, but also its adventure, its sense of a goal to be achieved even amidst its failures and deficiencies, especially the great adventure that our kind is given personally, individually, not collectively, that of the vision of God, one which no doubt is creative of the only ultimate and real community in existence.

Hannah Arendt remarked that the most powerful political action Jesus set loose in the world was the power of forgiveness. This power alone was able to stop the cycles of justice from destroying us all. What this means, of course, is that the intrinsic imperfections of justice, its essential harshness and unclear proportions—the blindfold and the scales and the sword of classical symbol—will beget other injustices endlessly unless something transcending justice itself stops its cycles. Societies without forgiveness are, quite literally, doomed. What cannot be personally and even "corporately" forgiven cannot cease down the ages, amidst the nations. This is why the remembrance of past atrocities is not wholly a healthy thing. Vendetta and vengeance are strictly speaking immoral unless they are stopped. And justice will never be enough to accomplish this feat.

One of the most crucial and least understood aspects of Christianity is that it naturally accepts all God's creation, but that man's own powers and concepts—and of these, justice is most central in this world—are not enough, even in this world, as it turns out. The life of God, what was traditionally called grace when given to us by God, incited us to transcend what we know to be merely "right". There was a sense in which generosity and sacrifice—Jesus said not "love your neighbor as yourself", but "love one another as I have loved you"—appeared "unjust". In this sense, the poor, the maimed and the crippled became a kind of striking symbol of what the love of God was about. And God, for the normal, needed "forgiveness" for sharing his astonishing life, because it made what was in fact "ordinary" seem like not enough.

Ironically, this goes back to the Aristotelian problem of man's natural tendency to rebel against his own condition. And now we also have an inclination to rebel against our condition as recipients of the life of God. C. S. Lewis in *Out of the Silent Planet* projected a fully rational life for a creature not offered a higher destiny than that "due" to it. But our race of mankind is not in this neutral position. In our on-going relationship with our kind, the life of grace is included as an intrinsic possibility because of God's gift. Our life would thus be "simpler" without God's trinitarian life offered to mankind.[2]

To return to the one-legged girl, in conclusion, her existence, her story, is, in Christian terms, only hers. Only then does it also become ours. She is called into existence as a person unique in the universe. She has a spiritual life which includes the "lack" of what "ought" to be there, ought to be hers, an "ought" judged by comparison to the general run of our kind to whom God gave two legs. This means that she has an active, probing intelligence that can forgive or blame the very structure of the universe. Analogous to Chesterton's father, she can thank God even if she has no leg. Life is good even if we abuse it. So it is good even if we do not possess everything "due" to us. Faith asks the young lady to believe that her loss is not only our but also her gain, that she too, in the end, would not want to be anyone else, or in any other universe, since her existence is not only hers, but ours too, because we all, each, are not of ourselves. She is the one who makes us realize that not all broken legs will be repaired, because all things are redeemed in the Lord, even the lack of one leg.

That young girls lack legs is not just. Yet, because of this, we can worry about what is more than justice, as it was out of more than justice that the universe was evidently made.

[2] See Chapter 7 of the present work.

We can feel sorry for what is not our own, nor perhaps anyone's, fault. And the existence of these things that cannot be "forgiven" leads us to the other side of God's essential teaching about us—that we never have here all we "ought" because our lot is precisely to receive what is more than anyone "ought" to be given.

John Paul II has said:

> We are all in some way aware in this passing world that it is not possible to realize the measure of justice. . . . Justice is, in a certain way, greater than man, than the dimensions of his earthly life. Every man lives and dies with a certain sense of insatiability for justice, because the world is not capable of satisfying fully a being created in the image of God.[3]

In this sense, then, God is "unjust" with us because justice is not his inner life. And this inner life is what is given to us. The girl on the crutches remains in a way our symbol. We do, indeed, lack what will make us ultimately the completed beings "created in the image of God", what will in fact make us whole. But Christianity—and this is what is unique about it—says that *we* lack, of our own power. It does not say that nothing can be given to us. And Christianity recognizes clearly that for a spiritual being, it is far more difficult to receive than to give, to accept than to make for oneself.[4]

[3] General Audience, November 8, 1978. See also John Paul II's encyclical *Dives in Misericordia*, 1981.

[4] See "Of God's Jokes, Toys and Christmas Trees" in the author's *The Praise of 'Sons of Bitches': On the Worship of God by Fallen Man* (Slough, England: St. Paul Publications, 1978).

XVII

ON SPIRITUAL AND PHYSICAL EXERCISES

Sport and Contemplation

The ancient Greeks used to hold that athletics were more than just pastimes. Paul of Tarsus knew about races and getting prizes for the winners.[1] Not a little of our lives is devoted to playing or watching people play. There has been a tendency to look upon such activity as merely "physical", or at least as something to do merely while passing time or loafing. I think that there is more to athletics than that, and I want to suggest that there is a Christian way to look upon our exercises and games, a way that in fact flows out of the distinctiveness of Christianity. To do this, I am going to suggest two ways in which our exercises might in fact be more than just that.

Even though, and this will be my first suggestion—the second will deal with "jogging and walking"—Departments of Physical Education exist in most universities, often merely by sufferance, rarely are athletics taken to be an exercise worthy of serious intellectual attention. Indeed, there is a kind of academic mind that looks upon competition, itself at the heart of most sport, as beneath human worth, and some even presume to attribute to sport the cause of war—on the playing fields of Eton, as it were. Such are the oddities of the mind of the don. Moreover, all athletics are presumed to hire student participants who

[1] See the author's *Play On: From Games to Celebrations* (Philadelphia: Fortress, 1971); *Far Too Easily Pleased: A Theology of Play, Contemplation, and Festivity* (Los Angeles: Benziger-Macmillan, 1976).

become in effect "public employees"—as indeed they are in many countries not to be mentioned here—or else athletes "on the take", as it is put quaintly, without which they never would have appeared in the ivy-covered halls in the first place.

The cynic wit will thus maintain that the whole Southwest Conference, for example, exists to give Texans something to do with their oil money on Saturday afternoons. The implication is, dubiously, that anyone with all that money cannot be smart, hence such a person watches sports. Athletics, consequently, are generally looked upon with a good deal of pity, something in great need of some secular redeemer, like, say, Ralph Nader or Jane Fonda.

Curiously, classic political philosophy was rather of a different mind. Everyone, of course, knows of the Discus Thrower, the Marathon, and the original Olympics, the Greek love for the perfect human form. But beyond this, athletics had a certain intrinsic quality that seemed to form the basis of a more profound reflection. Plato suggested in *The Laws* that sport might well be the proper analogy for understanding our relation to the divinity, while Aristotle felt that athletics were very near to pure contemplation. Usually, when Plato and Aristotle take something seriously, it is a wise man or woman who follows in their paths. And Jesuit theologian Hugo Rahner suggested that some of the Church Fathers thought the best way to explain the nature of creation and redemption was after the example of playing.[2]

Moreover, if we look at what the ordinary men and women in most countries of the world do persist in doing in this regard, we find that they continue to be fascinated by

[2] Hugo Rahner, *Men at Play* (New York: Herder and Herder, 1963).

an athletic event. The effete philosopher has been inclined to write this off under the category of "bread and circuses", as merely "entertainment", to give a more pejorative meaning to a most valuable word. Yet, we cannot explain the phenomenon of athletics by its abuses, ancient or modern —a principle, incidently, of wider application than just the ball field.

In recent years, I think, something has been happening to athletics on the participation side. Stress is placed on athletics as a cause of health. But anyone who plays games for the sake of health undoubtedly misses what sport is about. The jogging movement that has developed into the country's newest traffic hazard has changed the face, as it were, of participants in traditional sports. In any case, the Long Distance Runner is no longer lonely.

Here, however, I do not want to speak so much about the participant in sports. The new Georgetown Student Athletic Center was even built without facilities for spectators. This is a pity, I think, if it was a philosophical and not a financial decision, because the intellectual relation between "watching" and "playing" is very delicate and profound. In any case academic people are forever heard saying that college athletic programs ought to be designed to get all the kiddies out onto the fields of Harrow or Rugby. This is a disease particularly acute among college administrators talking to alumni. And I have no doubt that participation in sport is one of the key experiences in human life, not the only one, to be sure, not the highest necessarily, but one of the key ones still.

Yet, I am going to maintain, decidedly a minority opinion, no doubt, that watching a game as a spectator is probably even more important than playing, at least if we prescind from the metaphysical problem that we cannot have watchers without players.

Anyone who has ever seriously asked himself why so many actual human beings do turn out to watch a fine basketball game, or what fills the Oakland Coliseum to watch the Raiders, or why a few thousand odd fans persist in watching baseball teams at the bottom of the league, anyone, in short, who wonders about such questions will be hard pressed to explain it all in terms of self-interest, or boredom, or betting (itself one of the more profound games), or any other motive except the wonder of the game itself.

The experience of watching a true game, one being played before the world—the spectator is the world in the game—according to arbitrary yet absolute rules, to win or lose, to unfold the drama of the contest, the game must end like all life, watching how an event unknown and unknowable in advance is *turning out*—a most profound phrase—this is the main experience by which the normal person begins to suspect that something beyond him is utterly fascinating, worthy of being merely beheld. This is why, at a truly well-played game, from lacrosse to Wimbledon to horseshoes to Indianapolis to the Redskins, the spectator ceases eating, drinking (especially drinking), even thinking other thoughts, simply to watch something unfold. This is why Aristotle said that athletics is the nearest thing to pure contemplation, of less ultimate import, to be sure, but still something "for its own sake". The only thing that needs to be added to this is Chesterton's notion that if a thing is worth doing it is worth doing badly. This applies to our playing as to our watching. There are no good games without lousy ones—this is the first law.

Contrary to many current opinions, the university ultimately exists so that the student may once in his life at least realize that there is something worthwhile in itself, something not touched first by utility or pleasure, something that is merely fascinating. The common man, I suspect, learns this more from athletics than from theology or philosophy or, even yet, from government departments. But universities exist that we may reflect on what is true beyond ourselves. In this context, then, I would suggest that the lowly Departments of Physical Education, often apart from even their own theories, may lay claim to upholding that experience that the great Greeks said came closest to metaphysics, to contemplation.

Yet, even this department teaches us merely how to play. Ultimately, we must learn to watch by ourselves. To learn this is to begin to learn at all. Watching, like grace, is something we first receive.

Walking and Jogging

Walking and jogging are, perhaps, less formal kinds of sport, but they too bear insights well worth our Christian reflection. In the *Rambler* for April 3, 1750, Samuel Johnson wrote: "A French author has advanced the seeming paradox, that 'very few men know how to take a walk'; and, indeed, it is true, that few know how to take a walk with the prospect of any other pleasure than the same company would have afforded them at home."

The day before the Feast of the Ascension one year was called "Sun-Day" in Washington, even though it was in fact a Wednesday. As there was to be a concert with several large exhibits on solar power over by the Washington Monument, I decided to walk over from Georgetown to see what exactly was "new under the Sun", so to speak. This same Sun had been often deified by religions in the past, beginning with the Egyptians at least. And I am not at all sure there is not a touch of idolatry in this new solar enthusiasm. Too, I often wonder if we might be more "advanced" if we had remained classical sun-worshippers, except that the very idea of the use of nature through science and technology probably depends on the Judaeo-Christian belief that de-divinizes the sun and material creation, that distinct truth that founds so many others.

Anyhow, it was a glorious May day, so I headed down the C & O Canal Path to the bicycle trail along Rock Creek leading to the edge of the Potomac, beneath the famous Watergate, which does look from the riverside so Italian in a way. The path then went along below the Kennedy Center. I stopped at the rail to watch some small fish in the river. Two men were on a grassy bank, beating slowly two marvelously sounding African drums, a scene, a sound that seemed both odd and fit, as I looked back, against the Georgetown Towers above the river bend, I strolled on to the Lincoln Memorial, to the Reflecting Pool, and on to the Washington Monument.

As I went onto the lawn before the Monument, a couple with a little girl on her father's shoulders, all with fine southern accents, wanted to know if I was from Washington. Then, the lady remarked that she had never seen so many joggers in one place before. And it had been true all along my own walk. Everyplace, there were joggers of various ages, male and female, in their variegated colors and togs from great and small schools, universities, and clubs. There was even to be a "Solar Race" that afternoon. Running was the new fashion, no doubt, and I would doubt if it is correct to classify it mainly as a "health fad". I do not think it ought to be looked upon as merely "exercise" either, so it is worth some spiritual reflection.

I think the human person is so basically one unity that using the word "spiritual" exercise was not properly meant to set it off from physical exercise, but rather to suggest the fullness of the human experience, including both. I do not want to argue a "Yogi" or Eastern position here, especially since I think Christian thought makes much more sense of exercise than any other view. I want merely to suggest that running for its own sake, for its own enjoyment, is rather close to prayer and contemplation. I am very much of the belief that today, perhaps, the best way to understand what the Christian religion is about is to approach it through the phenomena of play and games.[3]

Jogging, walking, ritual, dancing are, of course, very closely related ways we move on this earth, ways we bless it finally. I remember the beautiful scene at the end of the Brazilian film *Black Orpheus*, when the three children danced the sun up in the morning. The sun and the run— the new symbols of cosmic and human energy, so it is well to wonder what it does all mean, as we begin to run 'neath the sun. Old soldiers are used to being turned out early in the morning for calisthenics, and there is something frightening in the massed Chinese populace doing their exercises in unison. So the kind of jogging and walking that is most spiritually important is precisely the kind we do because we do not "have to". Hardly anything of the spirit really counts unless we choose to accept or do it—this is the first law, and the last, too.

Not so long ago, I had occasion to fly to Kansas City for

---

[3] See Chapter 2 in the present work.

a conference, a flight I almost missed because I first went to the wrong Washington airport. Had it not been for an on-time, speedy bus, I should have missed my plane. Neither walking nor jogging from Dulles to National Airport would have saved me. Once, with some relief, on the plane, I found sitting next to me a middle-aged, thin, scholarly gentleman, who turned out to be the head of the Eye Surgery Department at a medical college in Albany, New York.

During the course of the subsequent conversation, the doctor told me he had just competed in the Boston Marathon, which may be the largest single participation sporting event in the world. He related to me how a competitor entered the marathon, the feeling, the details, how it all looked to the runner. He had only recently taken up running, in fact, so his enthusiasm was not the revival of youthful accomplishments. Jogging had changed his life in a very tangible way, he thought. People who run, whom one meets running at various marathons, are a special kind of people, a kind he could not have met otherwise, or perhaps even imagined.

"Also, it has changed my attitude toward travel," he admitted. As he did travel a lot in his profession, it was getting boring, but now he made it a point to run eight or ten miles a day in whatever city he happened to be in, including his own. In this way, almost any city can be more thoroughly and enjoyably seen, in a way no mere tour could imitate. And he also observed that something special happens, a kind of feeling, something maybe like a "religious experience", while one is trotting some place early in the morning. The literature of jogging, an ever-growing business, also often speaks this way.

Though I am not a jogger myself—I used to run the

shorter dashes in high school and college track—I am a persistent walker. Long ago, I discovered this was the only way really to see a city. I tend to think of walking as more contemplative than jogging somehow, less easily confused with caring for our health, which is fine, but not exactly where the "physical" and the "spiritual" fuse. I once read an article in the *New Yorker* about a couple who spent their recreational lives walking city streets throughout the world, never repeating any, trying to be on each street at least one time.

I have done this too, though many walks and streets I love to repeat. So I have walked in San Francisco, Paris, San Jose, Frankfurt, Pau, Freiburg, London, Dublin, Tokyo, Cairo, Bari, Addis Ababa, Boston, many lesser towns like Stevens Point, Wisconsin; Wernersville, Pennsylvania; Rocca di Papa above Rome; beaches all over, and a hundred other small and large towns and their countrysides.

When I study, I usually am at my desk, in a room, a familiar place to me. But it is astonishing how often the ideas and clarities one finally arrives at occur while walking. If we read Plato, we often find Socrates taking little walks, though he never seems to have gone too far, while Aristotle's followers were actually called the Peripatetics —those who learned by walking and conversing in the Lycaeum. Jesus and Paul certainly walked a lot. Jesus' parables are obviously walking parables often, images that arose in the normal course of seeing things in fields and towns and lakes and hillsides. Recently, too, I saw a fine short film on a Walk for Hunger in Los Angeles, a film that marvelously made the point that most people in the world, even today, have their feet as their primary mode of transportation.

Yet, for me, walking is not primarily conceived as "a means of transportation"—though it is that, and often the cheapest and best. I try never to go any place unless I walk—not an absolute principle, yet a freeing one in many ways. The trouble with being inside a car or bus is just that, you are inside. I am not antimachine or antitechnology; cars and buses have made many a good walk possible. Yet I do believe walking and jogging give us a sense of needed independence, a proof that we can get about on this earth if we want to. Further, Ignatius of Loyola used to talk of being "contemplatives in action", and I have always felt this meant in part, that walking was itself a kind of contemplation; at least it has been so for me. The world is filled with myriads of little places and incidents, wonders and sorrows too, that have their own patterns and poignancies. We need to see these too, to get out of our own minds, as it were, to be refreshed by the reality that is not already a part of us.

So how is it possible for walking to be contemplative? Walking can, of course, be a trek with many, with another, alone—all are valuable. Chesterton once said there was more difference between two and three than between three and three million. And undoubtedly there is the same kind of distance between walking by oneself and walking with another; and at times, we should do both. Walking by ourselves, however, is one of those essential signs of innerness, of a spirit within us that connects us to God somehow and to no one else, however much we be connected with others and the world.

And walking, our spirit in its place, also connects us with this particular, concrete world. We walk at a certain time of day—it should not always be the same time—in a definite season, place. Our angles are no one else's, our eyes see in a way no one else's will ever quite see. No foot quite walks as ours does. Thus, there is no walk we take that can be quite repeated. It is ourselves, our experience, that spiritualizes what we walk by, on, what we see. And memory, where we have been, is part of the walking. Augustine was not wrong to place our memory at the heart of our internal selves.

"Finishing schools" are designed to teach young ladies how to walk "properly". And ritual is in many ways simply how to walk, to go about, around an altar. Yet I do not want to be too much concerned with the technicalities of walking, though they are not unimportant. But I do think the idea of a man or a woman covering this earth on foot, jogging or walking, is related to Genesis, to our way of putting not just the sign of man on this earth, but our own small, personal sign, our footprint. Each person is unique, a mystery with a capacity, as Aquinas said, of knowing "all being", all the earth and cosmos. These are what are given to us. And we always begin with the particular place and time in which we are. When we walk, being open to what we see, we begin to behold.

The planet Earth is both large and small. We can cover rather much of it in a lifetime, should we choose, much even if we do not. Yet we can never fully appreciate even one square mile of it, running or walking, or even working on it or studying it. We touch it at dawn or at midday or at dusk, and it remains while we go away. Often our awareness is so low.

John Cage, in his touching *Silence*, recounts this incident:

> Morris Graves introduced Xenia and me to a miniature island in Puget Sound at Deception Pass. To get there we traveled from Seattle about seventy-five miles north and west

to Anacortes Island, then south to the Pass, where we parked. We walked along a rocky beach and then across a sandy stretch that was passable only at low tide to another island, continuing through some luxuriant woods up a hill where now and then we had views of the surrounding waters and distant islands, until finally we came to a small footbridge that led to our destination—an island no larger than, say, a modest home.

This island was carpeted with flowers and was so situated that all of Deception Pass was visible from it, just as though we were in the best seats of an intimate theatre. While we were lying there on that bed of flowers, some other people came across the footbridge. One of them said to another, "You come all this way and then when you get here, there's nothing to see."[4]

My sister once took me to Deception Pass when she lived in Seattle. I still remember the ice-cold water, the awesome rush of water, the majestic beauty.

So as John Cage rightly hinted, what we see depends mostly on us. I have often remarked that our "knowledge" of anything does not change it. The very nature of our mind seems to be such as to give us the world while yet allowing us to keep the world as it is. And this is our relation to the earth. It remains when we walk on it. I once heard of an Indian chief who apologized to the grass for walking on it. Though this is somewhat extreme—to be walked on may well be part of what grass is for—I still think we should walk with some openness to what is not ours. We are indeed to "become" what is not ourselves, as the old philosophers used to say.

If there is any basic Christian attitude to what is about us, I think it is that all is gift. After we finish our interminable disputes about mine and thine, about who is responsible for

    [4] John Cage, *Silence* (Boston, Mass.: MIT Press, 1961) 56.

what, about "justice", we still really have only barely begun to sense what Christianity is about. As Frederick Wilhelmsen has recently written, "For us Christians, Being is a gift, and our response to such a dazzling inheritance of Being is to bend the knee in thanksgiving, thus saying to God through his world: Amen."[5] What I want to suggest here is that there is more than one classical "position" for prayer—kneeling, to be sure, standing, sitting, yes, but also running and walking. One of the places we are most likely to be alone with God is walking through his world by ourselves, the crowded Via Frattina in Rome, or charming Clement Street in San Francisco, or in Quincy Market in Boston on the Fourth of July, to be there, but still alone.

For me, the best "walking" essay in our language is William Hazlitt's "On Going a Journey". Written in the early part of the last century, this still remains the classic reflection of seeing our own home, what we have been given. "One of the pleasantest things in the world is going a journey; but I like to go by myself . . ." so Hazlitt began. And his sentence—"Give me the clear blue sky over my head, and the green turf beneath my feet, and three hours' march to dinner—and then to thinking"—this is the best introduction I can think of to the nature of walking and running as contemplation. When Samuel Johnson cited the Frenchman to the effect that very few men know how to take a walk, he was right, I think. And the reason is that our walking is a manifestation of our spirit, of our ultimate spiritual independence, of our capacity to accept our world as a gift of God, something we did not make.

[5] Frederick Wilhelmsen, "The Christian Understanding of Being", *Intercollegiate Review* (Winter-Spring 1978) 93.

Yet if walking by ourselves is a kind of solitary meditation, a kind of sign that we really exist in ourselves, that we also stand outside of nothingness, that the whole world, beautiful as it often is, is not our ultimate home, still walking with another, with our friends, is also a way of deep discovery. The word "adventure" has become somewhat trite, yet it is a great word, an undertaking involving risk, unforseeable danger or an unexpected excitement. I like to think that walking with another always involves this sense of adventure. Our lives are intrinsically, and theologically, dramatic. This is what the very meaning of our personhood involves.

The world God gave us is itself a risk—on God's part especially, I think. To me, this is one of the most fascinating things about God as we can know him, that he accepted the risk, the obvious danger, and the excitement of creating this world. Genesis, I believe, even said he walked in the cool of the evening with our kind. The Christian God, the trinitarian God, is the only concept of God that allows us to walk together ultimately, allows us to discover real worlds and real persons, allows us to wonder about them, to reflect that if they exist beyond our wildest imaginations, of what must be the Creator? And they are probably not wrong who want to connect resurrection with the actual cosmos, that we may have indeed a destiny that includes, as is said in Genesis, walking in the cool of the evening in the mansions and gardens of God.

And so I delight to see the joggers and walkers. There is something spiritual here, or can be—for we too, all of us, can stroll or trot by Deception Pass and see nothing there. We are fully capable of looking on the most marvelous thing in creation and allowing ourselves to be deflected, deceived. Spiritual life, spiritual exercise exists that we might not miss the gift that is about us. We walk alone and together, ultimate symbols of our destiny. So if we are dull, it is largely because we choose to be so, because we neglect physical and spiritual exercise. The world is there, and it is a gift. We are given time, I think, that we might come to appreciate this givenness, this "giftness", in every hour and angle and corner of the world, in every friend we have. This world need not have existed. Ultimately, what it is composed of is nothing so narrow as justice and obligation. I think we should walk enough to begin to realize this, that our friend is indeed, as John said, "grace upon grace", someone also walking with us in a world that need not have been.

XVIII

LETTERS AND THE SPIRITUAL LIFE

In the year 53 B.C., Marcus Tullius Cicero, perhaps one of the greatest letter writers of history, wrote these lines to his friend, Gaius Scribonius Curio:

> As you know very well, there are many sorts of letter. But there is one unmistakable sort, which actually caused letter writing to be initiated in the first place, namely, the sort intended to give people in other places any information for our or their sakes they ought to know. . . . There are two other sorts of letter, which I like very much, one intimate and humorous, the other serious and profound.

Cicero himself went on to write volumes of letters, many of which have fortunately survived.

That so many basic documents of Christianity were fashioned as letters has always struck me as more than odd. It is indeed very distinctive and significant. How much of our faith we should miss were we to lack those marvelous introductions and warm salutations that Paul addressed to his friends in Rome, Corinth, or Philippi, not to mention his writings to Titus and Timothy. How little we would catch of the personalities of these men and women were Christianity presented first in heavy tomes instead of letters.

Msgr. Ronald Knox said somewhere, speaking of inspiration, that Paul's request to Timothy to pick up the cloak he left with Carpus at Troas could not be considered to contain anything fundamental to the central message of the revealed religion, the central object of inspiration. Moreover, when Paul admonished Evodia and Synthyche to "agree in the Lord", he seems to have brought up unnecessary feminine bickerings, a spat better left uninspired. Yet the very meaning, the very format of a letter is such that we can chatter of such small, trifling things, and this even within revelation and providence. The letter touches what human lives are mostly about. To neglect the ordinary, insignificant, to have a Scripture chock-full only of doctrine and proclamation and solemnity, no matter how important these be, would obscure the kind of redemption given to us.

In this light, I have been more than usually consoled when I read, for example, John Henry Newman's blunt remarks written to his sister Harriet on June 4, 1823: "Pusey took orders Sunday last, and is to be married next week. His book has been out about ten days. It is sadly deformed with Germanisms: he is wantonly obscure and foreign—he invents words."[1] Newman, of course, liked Pusey and his book, but were he not writing to his sister familiarly, we should not know so well his reaction, or even that a Newman could so react to Germanisms and obscurity and the invention of words.

And how delightful it is to come across this letter Teresa of Avila wrote to Father Gracián in Madrid on April 26, 1578:

> Jesus be with your Paternity, you who are both my father and my superior as you say, which causes me no little laughter and pleasure. In fact, whenever I recall your words I am amused at the solemn manner in which you declared that I must not judge my superior. Oh, my Father! How little need

[1] *Letters and Correspondence of John Henry Newman During His Life in the English Church* (London: Longmans, 1911) 163.

there was for you to swear, even like a saint, much less like a muleteer, for I thoroughly realize that fact.[2]

Probably nuns do not write like that any more, but it is nice to know Teresa of Jesus knew how a muleteer might swear and cuss. The very thought of the most famous sixteenth-century Spanish contemplative with a twinkle in her eye on being advised solemnly not to judge her male superior puts some perspective on the abidingness of the human condition.

The "letter" somehow transcends our formality, however necessary this latter be, transcends it to reach that "correspondence" between two persons in their very particularity, in that inner place where they most are. That Christianity is a "word" faith is no accident, so we should be attentive to those words that pass between us when we are apart. The letter presupposes, however, both intimacy and distance—even though we can also write quite nasty little notes to our next door neighbors. People who are actually living together, seeing one another daily, do not for the most part, as Iris Murdoch observed, write letters. Soldiers away at war write endlessly, but suddenly become almost illiterate when they return to their loved ones. And this is as it should be. In a real sense, we do not desire what we already have. Sometimes, too, we may have to write "official" letters of record or receipt, and these may also be personal. But usually "real" letters are not "official", nor are they handed to the person we are directly looking at or talking to.

Letters, consequently, depend on a certain apartness. They are the stuff of the metaphysics of distance. And

[2] *The Letters of Saint Teresa* (London: Baker, 1922) III, 82.

letters also presuppose and require a privacy that has a kind of sacredness about it. There is something absolute in not opening a letter addressed to someone else. Mail systems that cannot assure either security or some regularity attack the very roots of our culture. It is probably all right to read the letters of persons already dead, even though some delicacy is required even here. This is why archives usually insist we wait fifty or seventy-five years before using the correspondence of famous figures. Yet how deprived should we be had we no private letters of other men and women from all ages of our past! Nevertheless, we should never have had such letters at all were the correspondents not secure in the belief that the letter sent would arrive unopened and be treated as something quite confidential by its recipient. Thus, it is no accident that we call the state totalitarian that opens our mail, for this strikes at the very basis of our personal lives, as such states intend it to do.

Mutual consent, I suppose, would justify publication of letters. Often, we can cite wise or witty remarks from our letters that cannot betray confidence or authorship. Too, some letters are designed to be "circulated", encyclical as the papal usage is, writings to be passed around. The eighteenth century was, to our delight, full of such letters in circulation, letters which are now part of our literature. Yet I am sure that great letter writer of antiquity, Marcus Tullius Cicero, was quite correct in the indignation he showed to Anthony in his *Second Philippic*:

> Who with the slightest knowledge of decent people's habits could conceivably produce letters sent him by a friend and read them in public, merely because some quarrel has arisen between him and the other? Such conduct strikes at the roots of human relations; it means that absent friends are excluded from

communicating with each other. For men fill their letters with flippancies which appear tasteless if they are published—and with serious matters which are quite unsuitable for wide circulation.

Letters, consequently, can contain our flippancies along with our faults, ponderings, distorted notions, and vanities, things we can bear and even delight in at times, but things which are not, in fact, our "public" selves.

Christianity, I think, was the revolutionary religion it was because it held our "private" selves were not to be identified with our public reputation and estimation before the world. God alone scrutinized the heart. We could not know by the looking who were the saints, who the sinners. There was a private reality to each person that, to some degree, might be revealed to our friends, yet over which we must retain our own control. To be sure, we do not even know for certain how we stand before God, except that we know that we are all sinners. But without the literal sanctity of this privacy, there can be no authentic spiritual life and, consequently, no public life either. When Aristotle delineated in the *Politics* the nature of the absolute tyrant, he saw his essential evil in his destroying all private communication and friendship, something all subsequent totalitarian regimes to this day have tried to imitate.

At various periods in my life, I have had friends living in Eastern Europe. Invariably, with complete earnestness, as if I somehow could not be expected to understand, they told me to remember that every line I wrote to them would be read by state censors. So we corresponded about the weather and scenery, items to which, of course, I have no intrinsic objection, but still not the normal stuff of human communication. And too, I tried to figure out what I might possibly know or say that could be dangerous. But that was the point, the uncertainty, the destruction of confidence in private correspondence. So letters in such circumstances became rather signs of existence, nothing more. I have a Chinese friend who has many brothers and sisters in China. Correspondence between them ceased several years ago because the simple fact of receiving letters could put the family in a hazardous position.

Most religious orders and seminaries, I suppose, have had some form of censorship over correspondence—"voluntary", to be sure, still a reality that reduced letter writing from an art form and mirror of personality to a mechanical reporting designed to reveal nothing but the edifying. I hope most of these unpleasant customs have now disappeared so that the sanctity of the personal letter can be rigidly presumed and respected. Letters can be dangerous, unsettling, wastes of time, no doubt. Yet I think they are so important to spiritual life and general sanity that their peculiar import needs more specific recognition.

I must confess first, though, that I am mostly an antitelephone person, even though my brother works for Pacific Tel. and Tel. Neither do I hesitate much to chat on this particular auricular medium which rings inadvertently when it wants, and demands my immediate attention. Next to cigarettes and housebound pets, the telephone is perhaps the most "impolite" of our technological inventions in that it feels itself justified to interrupt our reveries, conversations, thoughts, prayers, and studies at any hour of the day or night. The letter, on the other hand, is the most civilized of our ways to reach one another when we are not already mutually present. This has something to do with the fact that, as Aristotle said, man is that being in the universe with a hand and a brain, so that our hand—both the physical organ and our script—touches, reveals almost immediately who and what we are. Thus, at the end of Second Thessalonians, Paul added: "This greeting is in my own hand—Paul's the signature in every letter of mine. This is my handwriting."

The letter comes unexpectedly some morning or afternoon in the post. It bears that element of surprise, which is almost the deepest of our spiritual concepts. We can read a letter, read it again, set it aside, answer it in a week or a month or, sometimes, not at all. And even though we can now tape phone calls, and ultimately, I suppose, phono-vision calls—God forbid!—nobody really thinks of relistening to a phone conversation just as we reread a letter. There is a profound reason for this, I think. For the phone makes us "present" in a way, while the letter reaches rather our privacy, our aloneness. And this is where we are most ourselves, most protected from the blare and glare of the world that tempts our vanity and engulfs our meek, halfhearted efforts to be good.

When we write to someone, we necessarily imagine that the person receives our letter when he is most alone. I am not arguing here, of course, that ideally we should be partitioned off so that we can be most ourselves in some cell, though that approach has often been tried, not always unsuccessfully. We need the world, the privacy of friends —even enemies. But there are times to write and to be written to. "Prayer", Iris Murdoch wrote, "is properly not petition, but simply an attention to God which is a form of love. With it goes the idea of grace, of a supernatural assistance to human endeavor which overcomes empirical limits of personality."[3]

And the letters of Paul, I think, showed this expression of attention to God to be mostly occasioned by attention to someone else to whom we write.

> Paul, an apostle of Christ by command of God our saviour and of Christ Jesus our hope, to Timothy, my true child in the faith: Grace, mercy, and peace from God the Father and Christ Jesus our Lord. As I urged you when I was going to Macedonia, remain at Ephesus that you may charge certain persons not to teach any different doctrine . . . (1 Tim 1:1–3).

This is solemn, to be sure, and affectionate, and hard-hitting too. In it, there is place, time, personality, along with the Father, grace, mercy, and peace. A letter can do this.

Yet letters are usually off-handed, familiar, funny, even when serious. The letter remains the closest reflection of how we see ourselves because it pays direct attention to someone who is outside us, hopefully someone for whom we are concerned just because he exists and is who he is. The limits of our own personality are most clear to us in apartness, through absence. The letter seeks to transcend this separation, to "keep in touch", as the almost literally accurate phrase goes. In this sense too, our letters will reveal to us soon enough the very boundaries of our happinesses. Christianity believes that God transcends our happiness precisely in the happy experience we do have. The letter reveals how we want to be with and before others with whom we do not want to lose "contact". Cicero began his Third Book of De Officiis with the famous

[3] Iris Murdoch, *The Sovereignty of the Good* (New York: Schocken Books, 1971) 55.

line: "[Scipio] was never less idle than when he had nothing
to do, and never less lonely than when he was by himself."
Letters arise out of this context, I think. Thus, the letter is a
kind of a defiance of space and time, even in space and time,
a defiance of loneliness when we are lonely. This is why
somehow, I think, letter writing lies close to the Divinity,
to Incarnation, to Word.

Ignatius of Antioch was killed in A.D. 107 under the
Emperor Trajan. Before he died, he wrote a famous letter
to the Romans, a letter which revealed how the early
Christians looked at this new faith of his:

> I am writing to all the Churches to let it be known that I will
> gladly die for God if only you do not stand in my way. I plead
> with you, show me no untimely kindness. . . . No earthly
> pleasures, no kingdoms of this world can benefit me in any
> way. I prefer death in Christ Jesus to power over the farthest
> limits of the earth. He who died in place of us is the one object
> of my quest. He who rose for our sakes is my one desire. . . .

Suddenly here, we have a revelation of the private life and
belief of an early second-century man, his values, his beliefs, his charm really. We know that our "calling" may not
be exactly his, though there are martyrs in our time too.
Still our faith is only so inasmuch as we think about
kingdoms and resurrection in the same way, that we also
are to be concerned when we find other doctrine being
taught.

On April 29, 1605, on the other hand, Robert Bellarmine
wrote to a Jesuit Provincial about the then upcoming papal
election. Belloc once remarked that as we get older, we
begin to have doubts about the human side of the supernatural faith. Bellarmine seems to have also had such worries
in his time. And thus when we now read his letter, we will

realize that even saints do worry about the Church, while our own age is not so unique after all.

> Here we are, then, once more preparing to enter the conclave, and we need prayers more than ever because I do not see in the whole sacred college one who possesses the [proper] qualifications. . . . What is worse, the election made no effort to find such a person. It seems to me a very serious thing that, when the Vicar of God is to be chosen, they should cast their votes, not for one who knows the will of God, one versed in Sacred Scriptures, but rather for one who knows the will of Justinian, and is versed in the authorities of the law. They look for a good temporal ruler, not for a holy bishop who would really occupy himself with the salvation of souls. I, for my part, will do my best to give my vote to the worthiest man. The rest is in the hands of providence, for, after all, the care of the Church is more the business of God than man.[4]

We have access to private letters, of course, because somebody kept them. I doubt if Robert Bellarmine went around the conclave telling all his fellow cardinals that none was worthy. Only a letter to someone could have recorded for us how he really felt. And because of this, we know something of how to look on the human side of the Church.

Letters are, it strikes me, a fundamental part of spiritual lives—to write them, to receive them, to read them. I do not wish here to restrict the spiritual life to so-called spiritual topics. Often our best letters cannot be called, strictly, "spiritual". Yet all letters are expressions of our spirit. They are an effort to share what we are, to hope for a correspondent, a word back, a sign that the words we throw into the world are received and come back from another. I know, to be sure, that letters can be bitter and

---

[4] In *Letters from the Saints* (New York: Hawthorne, 1967) 171–72.

unfortunate and even senseless. This too expresses something about our condition. We are to know what goes on in the human heart even though it be not always perfect virtue.

Somewhere about the turn of this century, Robert Hugh Benson wrote these curious bits of advice to one of his penitents. I cite them both for their quaint charm and their delightful advice:

> I am really sorry for writing as I did about my life here [probably Rome]. I hadn't at all realized what yours was like; and the dreariness of it, externally. I wish I could say something; but what can I say except what would be threadbare by now—if that were possible—of the marks of the Cross? And with nerves it must be nearly intolerable.
>
> Personally, I believe that *the* cure for nerves is an attempt at contemplation. I hope this does not sound absurd. But it seems to me that the one thing that does cure the maddening soreness of spirit that we call nerves is to *sit still*, in body, mind, and soul, and exclude every thought but that of God as he is in himself. But it is foolish to say all this   5

This is a cure for nerves we do not come across too often any more, I must say. I am not at all sure it would not work, even though Benson himself worried that it might be foolish and absurd, something he could easily do in a letter.

Yet whatever we might say for this as a cure for *nerves*, there is no doubt that Benson's advice is at the heart of Christianity—the need at times to sit still in mind, body, and soul, to exclude every thought but that of God as he is in himself. Such advice, it seems to me anyhow, is the more effective because it was in a casual letter, never really

5 Robert Hugh Benson, *Spiritual Letters* (London: Longmans, 1915) 95.

intended for our eyes. I do not think spiritual life cannot exist without letter writing and letter receiving, of course. This too would be "foolish", as Benson might also say. Yet to write a letter, we must also sit mostly still, we must be "attentive". And we must read a letter in the same way. Letters should be written and read in silence, in privacy, I think, for they stand close to what we are to ourselves and to each other. Like prayer, letters should cause us to retire behind closed doors for a spell.

Christianity insists that we are but pilgrims and strangers on this earth. This is not, I think, such a popular doctrine today, when so much social spirituality evidently strives to convince us that we really ought to make our home here. Scripture does not talk this way. So for me, the writing or receiving of letters is a continual reminder of our essential homelessness in this world. Nevertheless, the very fact that letters are attentive to someone, from someone, reminds us of our destiny. The very fact that creation and redemption are conceived to be "word" convinces us that the inadequacy of our correspondence, its very root in absence, is itself a promise. This all may strike us as foolish, I have no doubt. Yet our foolishness too is a basic Christian theme, and we should not be surprised if it occurs in our letters.

John Henry Newman wrote to his mother from Falmouth on December 5, 1832, after a night-stage journey through Devonshire and Cornwall, a trip I have even taken a couple of times, though by train, as I have a cousin with a home near St. Ives. "The night was enlivened," the young cleric wrote,

> by what Herodotus calls a night engagement with a man, called by courtesy a gentleman, on the box. The first act ended

by his calling me a damn fool. The second by his insisting on two most hearty shakes of the hand, with the protest that he certainly did think me very injudicious and ill-timed. I had opened by telling him he was talking great nonsense to a silly goose of a maid-servant stuck atop the coach; so I had no reason to complain of his choosing to give me the retort uncourteous. . . .

He assured me he revered my cloth. . . . It is so odd, he thought I had attacked him under personal feelings. I am quite ashamed of this scrawl, yet since I have a few minutes to spare, I do not want to be otherwise employed than in writing.[6]

It is no small consolation to know that the future author of the *Essay on the Development on Doctrine* and the *Apologia Pro Vita Sua* was once called a damned fool for sticking up for a silly goose of a girl, against a man called by courtesy a gentleman on a night-stage in Devonshire. And too, for those of us whose handwriting leaves something to be desired, to learn that a complete *Apologia Pro Vita Sua* has to include even our handwriting, restores some semblance of justice into the world. Our own scrawl, we vainly think, always contains gold.

Letters, to recall Cicero, give information; they can be humorous and intimate, serious and profound. They attend to others in their uniqueness. They are how God in his own uniqueness was in large part revealed to us. A letter, preferably "writ by hand", as Al Capp used to have his characters say, reveals that there is spirit in the world, that deep within our friends lies a spiritual life that we glimpse, if we are lucky. Yet letters exist only because of distance and absence. They are the symbols of our ultimate earthly

6 Newman, ibid., 249–50.

status as wayfarers and pilgrims, reflections of what we see, what is in us as we pass by.

"The mail must go through" was once the motto of our postal system in the United States, through all kinds of weather and hardship, a service first. I have often thought, however, that the phrase seemed more than just the duty and efficiency of the postal system, which has lost much of its luster, now that it seems more like an employment agency. A postal system is, however, near to the heart of civilized life. The mail must go through because our letters almost more than anything else reveal how we are when we are alone, in our privacy. The function of the public service is to protect, make possible, guarantee the private. And it is in our private selves that we respond to each other. Precisely in our privacy are we most open to God, where we sit still, body, soul, and mind, to account both for the fact that we all are damned fools and that God is as he is.

Chesterton once observed that the posting of a letter is almost the most romantic thing we can do, for it is an absolute act that cannot be recalled. In this, it reveals how we are to someone else. And in so revealing, it enables us to know ourselves. Aquinas was not wrong in insisting that we know ourselves only by first observing and knowing something, someone else. And how we are before our friends and before the Lord, how we "co-respond" in our letters, is, ultimately, what the adventure of human life is about in the first place.

So in our spiritual lives, let us be flippant, sit still for our nerves, denounce Germanisms, and cuss like muleteers. Let us do this, because we are never less alone than when we are idle, when we finally write because someone half-way across the world or around the corner, someone not present is recalled, is realized to be absent. And we attend to our friends in that chaotic, amazing order of our lives, alone in our cells and our privacy, when we write to others. And thereby, astonishingly, we discover ourselves, where we are from and where we are going. The letter is indeed at the heart of our civilization and of our spiritual lives.

XIX

PATHS THAT LEAD TO ROME

And so in our letters and walks, in our contemplations and conversations, we can, perhaps, best end these reflections back at Rome, on a "path" to Rome, with a walk Hilaire Belloc once took from France to Italy. We can thus look back on where we have been to see where we might be going.

The only temptation to the faith really worth worrying about is the one that suspects, in spite of all the passing fame to be gained by doubting it, that the Christian faith might just be quite literally true. *Credo in unum Deum.* . . . And this is not Pascal's wager, a playing of the odds, but rather something that can be called a "grace", were our age not so pitiably enamoured with justice, the harshest, most "inhuman" of all the virtues.

In spite of all our vanities, then, we remain first of all a chosen people, hence, we are, in principle, free from the "Unended Quest" of a Karl Popper whose "deserved" happiness results from the struggle with his own intellectual "Third World", with ideas and constructs which "originate with us".[1]

Credo in unum Deum. . . . *Credo ut intelligam.* . . . *Credo quia intelligo.* . . . (I believe in one God. . . . I believe in order that I may understand. . . . I believe because I understand. . . .) I believe that what originates with us

[1] Karl Popper, *The Unended Quest* (London: Fontana, 1976) 196.

also leads one to God. I believe not merely *in order to* understand, but *because* I understand. I believe because I understand that the faith does indeed teach that we are finite beings *given* nothing less than everything, nothing less than the one God, who is Trinity. This is, at last, why we are restless, as Augustine taught.

"It is hard to accept mysteries, and to be humble", Belloc wrote in *The Path to Rome*.

> We are tost as the great schoolmen were tost, and we dare not neglect the duty of that wrestling. But the hardest thing of all is that it leads us away, as by a command, from all that banquet of the intellect than which there is no keener joy known to man. I went slowly up the village place in the dusk, thinking of this deplorable weakness in men that faith is too great for them. . . .[2]

The wrestling, the command, no keener joy, the deplorable weakness the restlessness goes on, along the paths that lead to Rome.

Revelation is itself designed to make us, rather to incite us to, think about what does not originate within us. The very last discovery I ever want to make in this universe of Karl Popper's First, Second and Third Worlds is the discovery that I have created what there is. That, I think, would be the ultimate despair.

And so, rather, I believe in newness, in an infinity which does not originate within myself. Popper, in his own way, also caught some of this: "We may gain more knowledge from our children or from our theories than we ever

[2] Hilaire Belloc, *The Path to Rome* (New York: G. P. Putnam's Sons, 1915).

imparted to them." Indeed, we receive more than we give, mostly. This is why, again, the only temptation worth worrying about is the one that would allow us to live only in our own world, closed off, perhaps forever, from a newness of which we are not the origin, but only the pale, yet sparkling, images.

"The Italian lakes have that in them", I quote from Belloc again, "and their air which removes them from common living. Their beauty is not the beauty which each of us sees for himself in the world; it is rather the beauty of a special creation, the expression of some mind."

Recently, unexpectedly, I received a letter inviting me to a Conference at Lake Nemi above Rome, that tiny, gem-like volcanic pool, about which the delightful minia-ture strawberries are grown.

How paradoxical, I thought, that after I had "gone back" to Rome so many times during the more than a decade I taught there, that I would be invited to return just after reading again *The Path to Rome* at mid-semester break, while walking slowly on the windy, lonely, wide Jersey beaches at Avalon and Stone Harbor. How odd suddenly to think of going back!

In a way, as I left Rome for what I assumed was the last time in the Summer of 1977 (see Chapter 1), admitting a heavy portion of nostalgia in my character, I have not thought so much about the Eternal City. And, when asked, I always have answered, "No, I do not miss it, though I loved my time there—but, yes, there is one thing, the *spaghetti*, that I do miss." And I am mostly serious. We cannot spend our lives "missing" things, however much we do miss them in fact. We miss people mainly, some-times people we do not even know. Places are people;

people, places. Paths are what connect them. There is a veil about our lives, I think, that hides the real map of where we are. Thus, our paths, even to Rome, even on the straight line Belloc walked from Toul to get there, are often uncharted, at least to ourselves.

Yet it is true about the spaghetti. . . . When Belloc first made it into Italy, he reflected on the Church.

> Have you ever noticed that all the Catholic Church does is thought beautiful and loveable until she comes out into the open, then she is suddenly found by her enemies to be hateful and grinding. . . . She lays her foundations in something other, which something other our moderns hate.

This brought Belloc to a little trattoria where he had to show the waiter what he wanted by gestures:

> I first pulled up the macaroni out of the dish, and said "Fromagio", "Pommodoro", by which I meant cheese-tomato. He then said he knew what I meant, and brought me that spaghetti so treated, which is a dish for a king, a cosmopolitan traitor, an oppressor of the poor, a usurer, or any other rich man, but there is no spaghetti in the place to which such men go, whereas these peasants will continue to enjoy it in heaven

My friends, who do not believe in Resurrection, cannot understand how much such lines comfort me. So this, too, is part of the faith—no spaghetti in the world we create for ourselves, while the simplest peasants will be enjoying this food of the gods in the everlasting. Quests are ended when the spaghetti is served. My old Roman friends, Bob Taft, Ernie Martinez, John Navone understood this, the truth about the being with sadness in his eyes who knew that joy was not an illusion because the spaghetti was served.

John J. Mulloy, who edited the collection of Christopher

Dawson on *The Dynamics of World History*, which I used in class this semester, and which Sherwood Sudgen, bless him, reissued recently, saw a review of mine on Professor McCarthy's new book—*Edwardian Radical*—on Belloc. There are still Belloc lovers in this cruel world. God be praised. Perhaps there are those of us who sense the sadness in the joy. For there was a sadness about Belloc, in his delight.

"All you that feel youth slipping past you and that you are desolate at the approach of age, be merry; it is not what it looks like from the outside.

"And let us especially pray that the revival of the faith may do something for our poor old universities." It didn't, of course.

Mr. Mulloy was kind enough to send me a copy of Sir Arnold Lunn's "Memories of Hilaire Belloc", an essay I had never seen before. (In *And Yet so New*, 1958.) Lunn had corresponded with Belloc about his light verse in about 1910. "Either before or after this exchange of letters", Lunn reflected, "I had read and been fascinated by *The Path to Rome*, which remains to this day my favourite book."

Lunn, I think, is not alone here.

Another friend over in Maryland, who also had seen my review, wrote in the very style of Belloc's book:

"But in 1957, I read *The Path to Rome*, and toward the end, I will confess to you, that I knelt down to receive his blessing.

Lector: Why on earth would you do a thing like that?

Auctor (Auctoress, Auctora? What do you do to the feminine 3rd declension? [I suggested later *Auctrix* without looking it up.]): It just seemed the natural, spontaneous thing to do. When you have spent a volume of ideas and delights with an author, via the mysterious scribbling on paper called words, there is an 'oughtness' (as some philosophers would put it) about kneeling. Besides, it does tend to settle the crowding and jostling of the ideas.

Lector: You are carrying your romanticism too far. It is one thing to enjoy a good book, or a bottle of wine or whatever, without being religious about it.

Auctor: I think not. There is a certain grace that flows from God through some men and some writings, that brings with it a heavenly kind of happiness, and, for ordinary readers, this must be acknowledged in humility to be bearable. The response must compliment the gift, or try to.

Lector: You are taking it all too seriously. But I suppose women are like that.

Auctor: When heart hears heart—it is on the knees the sound is best.

Lector: Have the last word."

Belloc would have liked such a fine tribute, I think. And it does read like his playful controversies with himself, *Lector* and *Auctor*.

Indeed, Belloc was genuinely concerned about those who would chance to read this book beyond his time. *The Path to Rome*, thus, began with this Dedication: "To every honest reader that may purchase, hire, or receive this book, and to the reviewers also (to whom it is of triple profit), greeting—and whatever else can be had for nothing." Need I recall, that in the Christian tradition, "what can be had for nothing" is precisely the best thing, indeed, the only thing ultimately worth having.

He recounted immediately after this Dedication the incident upon which the whole theoretic structure of the book was based. He had returned to his native town—we should not forget that, in Christian tradition, our lives are most properly described, somehow, as precisely a "homecoming"—where he greeted all. With the grocer, he argued politics; and "all but made the carpenter a Christian by the force of rhetoric"—*credo quia intelligo.*

Then, "after so many years", he went into his own town church in France, "a church that I love more than Mother Church herself . . . for this place is the shell of our soul, and one's church is the kernel of that nut." Upon this, he vowed a pilgrimage to Rome, but not to discover a Church he knew not at home. Rome is already at home—this is the faith of Europe.

Belloc somehow expected his book to be read in 1910, in 1957 with my friend in Maryland, even in about 1968 when I re-read it a second time in Florence, and again in 1980, on the Jersey Shores when I read it a third time. For this is how he addressed his readers:

> And now all you people whatsoever that are presently reading, may have read, or shall in the future read, this many-sided but now-ending book; all you also that in the mysterious disposition of Providence may not be fated to read it for some very long time to come. . . .

The wait, dear friends, is still worth it, the Path is still there to be taken, "after so many years."

Thus, *The Path to Rome* can still be read, with its temptation, and the sadness of it. How often have I quoted these lines, mostly to myself, lines near the end:

> The leaves fall, and they are renewed; the sun sets on the Vixen hills, but he rises again over the woods of Marly. Human

companionship, once broken, can never be restored and you and I shall not meet or understand each other again. It is so of all the poor limits whereby we try to bridge the impassable gap between soul and soul.

"How sad!" another friend said, when first reading such lines. Yet, there is the spaghetti and the hope of the vow, the vow, the vow in which all is broken but its essence:

> The essence of a vow is its literal meaning. The spirit and intention are for the major morality, and concern natural religion; but when a man talks to you of the Spirit and Intention, look at him askance. He is not far removed from Heresy.

Indeed, our times are more full of such heresy than even Belloc's, of people, monks, nuns and philosophers who have torn down the structures of rite and dogma that uphold the essence of faith, because they concerned themselves with heart and sympathy, with spirit and intention. They thereby ended up doubting because the essence of faith, as the essence of the vow, is not dependent upon our subjective selves, of what we make. Relying on spirit and intention, ours, not God's, we give the people the faith God would have revealed if he had been us. We have forgotten the newness, the vow, the revelation of what is not us.

And so there is advice about drinking: "Never drink what has been made and sold since the Reformation. . . . Drink red wine and white, good beer and mead. . . . " And do not forget the three phrases that

> keep a man steady. . . . I mean the words (1) "After all, it is not my business", (2) "Tut! Tut! You don't say so", and (3) "Credo in Unum Deum, Patrem Omnipotentem, Factorem omnium visibilium et invisibilium. . . ."

The Path to Rome, no doubt, I shall read again, on some shore, on some walk, in some city of this world, for perhaps more than Rome itself, the end of the pilgrimage, it reminds me of the faith, of the final temptation against which we each must struggle, the one that arises when we finally do realize that the doctrine is indeed the truth, in our own small churches, in our walks and in our paths, we discover that we are sad enough, to be sure, yet infinite too.

"We laughers", as Belloc called us—without the sadness, the Cross and the doctrine, we cannot laugh in heaven forever, and probably not here either.

"To what emotion shall I compare this astonishment? So, in first love, one finds that *this* can belong to *me*."

This vow of God shall not be destroyed by our spirit and our intention. This ultimate first love, as Augustine said, is God himself. And the essence of the faith is "that *this* can belong to *me*". This we call a *grace*, if we be Christians who walk to Rome.

The only temptation, the one still so prevalent in "our poor old universities" which did not accept the faith, is that this is true. How awful to make ourselves and our world—except after we know that we are made, that we are blessed, that we are hearing "on our knees, where the sound is best".

 Auctor: Drinking when I had a mind to,
    Singing when I felt inclined to;
    Nor ever turned my face to home,
    Till I had slaked my heart at Rome. . . .

CONCLUSION

In a recent essay, Karl Rahner recalled Simone Weil's remark that of two men who have never really experienced God, the one who denies him may be closer than the one who affirms him merely as a social cliché. The denier of God may have a real yearning and suffering for what he lacks, may feel that something *is* to be denied. Rahner went on to say of this, in words of rather monumental complexity, but ones worth citing still:

> The man who places his trust in the fact that the incomprehensible, into which no exact formula shows the way, communicates itself, saving and forgiving, in incomprehensible immediacy, cannot be characterized as a "theist". This man has already experienced the "personal" God when he correctly understands this "formula" and does not conceive "God" as another "good" man.[1]

So this God must be "personal" yet not merely a "good" man. But he must not be less than man either. Rahner continued:

> This, however, means that God can be no less than man with personality [freedom and love] and that the mystery is saving grace and not "objective order", which one can authorize but not guard against. This man, by virtue of his experience, has also received insight and basically accepted that which the Christian world calls divine grace. The original event of

[1] Karl Rahner, "The Understanding of God and the Word of God Today: Aspects of Theology", *Universitas* 21, no. 1 (1979) 38.

Christianity has returned to the innermost part of existence: the immediacy of God, to men in the Holy Spirit.[2]

This personal spiritual experience, subsequently, needs to be identified with and related to the appearance of Jesus Christ in what he established, in what and who he was. Christianity is distinctive because it does not identify the deepest and most essential human experiences with the care and construction of the world. Only when the world is seen as less than ultimate can it really be seen and cared for at all. The doctrines, traditions, institutions, and spiritualities of Christendom are all of a whole.

If anything is characteristic of Christianity, it is its enormous fertility, creativity. The Christian creeds intimate that the source of this is the inner trinitarian life of God himself. In this sense, Christian spiritual life is nothing less than the "newness" of the persons and situations that occur to the redeemed men who are still men, as Tolkien put it.

Lest I err, then, I think the most difficult thing of our era is for Christians to discover, and more especially to retain, what is uniquely theirs. And the nature of Christian faith is such that it does not partake of the narrow economics that would suggest that what we each are given must likewise be a deprivation for someone else. Grace upon grace, the words of John's prologue, are still the great charter of Christianity.

From a Distinctive Tradition, With a Distinctive Opposition, For Distinctive Doctrines, By Distinctive Institutions, and For a Distinctive Spirituality—such is Christianity, a Christianity, I think, that is worth keeping, for it has indeed been given to us. And in Christianity, the loss of

2 Ibid., 38–39.

what we have been given, ultimately, must include the loss of what we are and might be.

Paul told the Galatians: "Let me tell you that if even we ourselves or an angel from heaven should proclaim to you a Gospel other than we have proclaimed, let him be accursed" (1:8). The truth of Christianity is not for angels from heaven, even though they might belong to ultimately the same city. And its truth is also a sword, as Christ intimated.

The risk of God remains the risk of man—Christianity exists, in the end, that the risks be taken in the innermost part of human and divine existence. The God of Christianity is not just another "good" man. "It is not true at all," Dorothy Sayers wrote,

> that dogma is "hopelessly irrelevant" to the life and thought of the average man. What is true is that ministers of the Christian religion often assert that it is, present it for consideration as though it were, and, in fact, by their faulty exposition of it make it so. The central dogma of the Incarnation is that by which relevance stands or falls. If Christ was only man, then he is entirely irrelevant to any thought about God; if he is only God, then he is entirely irrelevant to any experience of human life. It is, in the strictest sense, *necessary* to the salvation of relevance that a man should believe *rightly* the Incarnation of Our Lord Jesus Christ. Unless he believes rightly, there is not the faintest reason why he should believe at all.[3]

So there is, in my view, reason to believe. God has revealed himself not as an "objective order", but as a saving grace manifested in Jesus Christ, about whom our Creed and

[3] Dorothy Sayers, "Creed or Chaos", *Christian Letters to a Post-Christian World* (Grand Rapids, Mich.: Eerdmans, 1969) 34.

Scripture have spoken. For Christianity, we are a people who not only must believe and know, but believe and know rightly, *distinctively*. No other gospel preached to us, and there are many, is nearly so full of risk. Unless we believe *rightly*, there is indeed not the faintest reason why we should believe at all.